D0205524

Eugène Ionesco Revisited

Twayne's World Authors Series

French Literature

David O'Connell, Editor

Georgia State University

TWAS 863

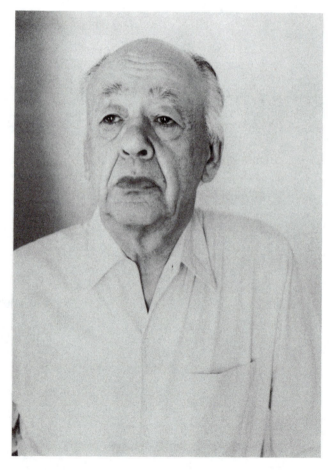

EUGÈNE IONESCO
© *Jerry Bauer*

Eugène Ionesco Revisited

Deborah B. Gaensbauer

Regis University

Twayne Publishers
An Imprint of Simon & Schuster Macmillan
New York

Prentice Hall International
London • Mexico City • New Delhi • Singapore • Sydney • Toronto

Twayne's World Authors Series No. 863

Eugène Ionesco Revisited
Deborah B. Gaensbauer

Excepts from *Théâtre complet d'Eugène Ionesco,* edited by Emmanuel Jacquart.
Copyright © 1991 by Éditions Gallimard.
Reprinted in English by permission of Éditions Gallimard.

Twayne Publishers
An Imprint of Simon & Schuster Macmillan
1633 Broadway
New York, NY 10019

Library of Congress Cataloging-in-Publication Data

Gaensbauer, Deborah B.
    Eugène Ionesco revisited / Deborah B. Gaensbauer.
        p.   cm.—(Twayne's world authors series ; TWAS 863)
    Includes bibliographical references and index.
    ISBN 0-8057-4304-9
    1. Ionesco, Eugène—Criticism and interpretation. I. Title.
II. Series.
    PQ2617.06Z69 1996
    842'.914—dc20   96-33242
                                                                     CIP

The paper used in this publication meets the minimum requirements of American
National Standard for Information Sciences—Permanence of Paper for Printed Library
Materials, ANSI Z39.48-1984. ∞ ™

10 9 8 7 6 5 4 3 2 1 (hc)

10 9 8 7 6 5 4 3 2 1 (pb)

Printed in the United States of America.

Contents

Preface

Eugène Ionesco is among the few absurdist playwrights recognized by nearly everyone. The humorously confounding verbal frenzy of *The Bald Soprano* and *The Lesson*, and the incarnation of fascist herd instincts as rhinoceroses in the play that made him world-famous, have etched themselves in memory and have found a place among the classics. Along with Samuel Beckett's *Waiting for Godot*, Ionesco's early plays became hallmarks of the irreverent, revolutionary theater now widely known as "theater of the absurd." When *Godot* became an unlikely success, the shy Beckett resisted the limelight and refused to explicate his work. Ionesco was not disposed to silence or mystery about his theatrical endeavors. In essays and interviews that began to proliferate like the dislocated language and incongruous stage properties in his plays, he became one of the principal spokespersons for this new theater. Much as his Romanian compatriot Tristan Tzara had done for the dada movement some 30 years earlier, Ionesco contributed to the success of theater of the absurd both as an exciting playwright, in whose works many of the revolutionary literary experiments of the first half of the twentieth century converge, and as its chief impresario.

That he became the absurdist "man of the hour" during the early phase of his dramatic career was in some respects an aberration. For the public, it was a fortunate occurrence. His descriptions of what he preferred to call "antitheater" or "theater of derision" remain among its most lucid and challenging assessments. For Ionesco, however, it created a long-lasting conflict. From the beginning of his career, he manifested a deep-rooted antipathy to ideology and authority, whether literary, political, or familial. He also suffered from what he would later portray as spiritual "hunger and thirst." The brooding, "metaphysical" Ionesco had been perceptible in the early plays but was not pronounced. When he began to break the absurdist "mold," which accommodated only limited aspects of his dramatic imagination and personal aspirations, many of his initial admirers were disappointed. Critics were often unwilling to explore the origin or the full implications of the shift in his theater from verbal anarchy to phantasmagoric visions increasingly centered on autobiographical and metaphysical themes. They accused Ionesco of becoming distressingly unrevolutionary and solipsistic and claimed that he had betrayed his best and most spontaneous theatrical instincts.

Nostalgia for the laughter and anarchistic verve of the early Ionesco is easy to understand. However, much of what seemed "new"—and to some unwelcome—as Ionesco's dramatic career evolved in more serious and personal directions was in fact "old." A comprehensive scrutiny of his long career as a writer, which continued until his death in 1994, reveals that an obsessive thematic coherency binds his work from beginning to end. This study "revisits" Ionesco's diaries, theater, fiction, and combative essays—and, briefly, his painting—in the context of a biographical "frame tale" that sheds light on the direction and purpose of his linguistic, existential, and spiritual prospecting as well as on his remarkable stage imagery. It is in this context that Ionesco can best be understood both as a playwright and as a person determined to remain fully human, even when his particular definition of the terms "playwright" and "human" conflicted with the literary, political, and philosophical vogues of the moment.

Certainly not all negative critical reactions were unjustified. For a playwright as prolific and polemical as Ionesco, unevenness in literary quality was inevitable. He sometimes lost what Hélène Cixous has described as a crucial "outsider's" distance from language—"the most important thing is that you never become too familiar and you never come to the point when you can hear it speak to you and you think you speak it."[1] His fall from critical "grace" during the 1960s and 1970s (as was true, paradoxically, for his "rehabilitation" in the 1980s and 1990s) had much to do, however, with the fact that in his plays and other writing he took the risk of revealing in a very personal way the unpredictable combinations of unsavoriness and occasional grandeur that make human beings so complicated.

Ionesco was fundamentally a creature of paradox, "afraid to be and not to be" in a world that is "both marvelous and atrocious, a miracle and Hell."[2] The human species' most valuable endeavor, he once claimed, has been the attempt to explain itself in the midst of the inexplicable (A, 222). That is exactly what he spent the major portion of a long career attempting to do by "travelling back though History within myself, or by inventing characters who are variations of myself or like other people who resemble me" (A, 222).[3] He was persuaded that his anguish and concerns were not his alone, but exemplary of human existence: "It is even only what is most personal to me that truly interests everyone; what is most intimate is the most universal" (A, 298).

Having witnessed very young in fascist Romania the devastating effect of the herd mentality, he consistently refused to buckle to external pressures or definitions, adamant that "to write is to discover."[4] The titles *Découvertes (Discoveries)*, and *Un homme en question (A Man in Question)* given to personal journals published in 1969 and 1987, could be broadly applied to all his work. Few of his questions or discoveries led to either the existential or the spiritual sustenance he was seeking. Thus he returned to them obsessively again and again. *Ionesco Revisited* is to a great extent an account of Ionesco himself in the process of a constant "revisiting": language, places, ideas, relationships, and symbolic dreams.

This look back at Ionesco is indebted to Emmanuel Jacquart's extensive documentation in the 1991 Pléiade edition of Ionesco's theater, the increasing availability of French and English translations of his Romanian writing, and significant recent critical studies incorporating interviews with the playwright and personal recollections.[5] Ionesco's published journals and polemical essays have also been essential guides. These works, which are examined at some length in the first part of this study, are too often treated as subsidiary material. They have been frequently quoted as sources of biographical data or to bolster an interpretation of his theater, but not sufficiently valued as autonomous texts. The memoirs, essays, and Romanian texts, which, like his theater, are humorous, plaintive, and sharply polemical, provide an important counterbalance to some of the myths and masks created by critics for Ionesco's playwright persona, often much to his distress. Now that it is possible to survey his entire career, it becomes very evident that all the literary genres he experimented with, as well as his painting, constitute significant elements of an oeuvre that is essentially a long autobiography, or a "subterranean biography," as Ionesco called his last play.

Acknowledgments

I thank Éditions Gallimard for consent to quote from works by Ionesco; Grove-Atlantic for permission to quote from Grove Press translations of his work, and Riverrun Press for authorization to quote from *Journeys among the Dead,* by Eugène Ionesco, originally published as *Voyages chez les morts,* copyright © 1981 by Éditions Gallimard, Paris. This translation copyright © 1985 by Calder Publications, London/Riverrun Press, New York. Reprinted by permission of Riverrun Press. Portions of Chapter Ten appeared in altered form in *Modern Drama* (28:3). I thank the editors for permission to reprint.

A Faculty Summer Research Grant from Regis University helped subsidize research for this study. I wish to express my gratitude to my colleagues at Regis for their support and to Dominique Akoka for her generous hospitality in Paris. In particular, my friend and colleague Eleanor Swanson provided invaluable guidance and insights and much-appreciated encouragement. Finally, I am much indebted to David O'Connell, editor for Twayne's World Authors Series, for his meticulous reading and helpful comments; and to Ann Kiefer and Susan Gamer at Twayne Publishers for their careful and supportive editorial assistance.

Chronology

1958 London controversy.

1959 Premiere of *The Killer*. World premiere of *Rhinocéros* in Düsseldorf, Germany.

1960 French premiere of *Rhinocéros*.

1961 Broadway production of *Rhinocéros*.

1962 Premiere of *Exit the King*. Publication of *Notes and Counter Notes* and *The Colonel's Photograph*. World premiere of *A Stroll in the Air* in Düsseldorf. Premiere of *Frenzy for Two or More*.

1963 French premiere of *A Stroll in the Air* at the Odéon.

1964 World premiere of *Hunger and Thirst* in Düsseldorf. *Rhinocéros* performed in Bucharest.

1966 French premiere of *Hunger and Thirst* at the Comédie Française. Premiere of *French Lessons for Americans*. Premiere of *The Gap*.

1967 Publication of *Fragments of a Journal*.

1968 Publication of *Present Past Past Present*.

1969 Publication of *Découvertes*. Receives Grand Prix National du Théâtre.

1970 Elected to Académie Française. World premiere of *The Killing Game* in Düsseldorf in January. French premiere in September.

1972 Premiere of *Macbett*.

1973 Publication of *The Hermit*. Premiere of *A Hell of a Mess*. Receives the Jerusalem Prize.

1975 Premiere of *The Man with the Luggage*.

1977 Publication of *Antidotes*.

1978 "Decade Ionesco" at Cérisy-la-Salle.

1979 Jorge Lavelli directs *Exit the King* at the Odéon. Publication of *Un homme en question*.

1980 Previews of *Journeys among the Dead* at the Guggenheim Museum in New York.

1981 Publication of *Le Blanc et le noir*.

1982 Publication of French translation of *Hugoliad*. French radio broadcast of *Journeys among the Dead*. *Scène* performed at Avignon Festival.

1983   Roger Planchon creates *Spectacle Ionesco.*

1984   Exhibits paintings and lithographs in Germany, Switzerland, Italy, and France.

1986   *Nu* translated into French.

1987   Thirtieth anniversary of *The Bald Soprano* and *The Lesson* at the Théâtre de la Huchette. Receives medal from city of Paris.

1988   Publication of *La Quête intermittente.* Premiere of opera, *Maximilian Kolbe.* Exhibition of lithographs at Centre Pompidou.

1991   Gallimard publishes *Théâtre complet* in the Pléiade edition.

1994   Ionesco dies in Paris.

Part 1. The Frame Tale

Chapter One
Biography

At a colloquium organized in his honor in 1978, Ionesco declared, "I have been devoured by literary ambition, by literary passion, from my earliest years."[1] It was a passion nourished by an early understanding of the powerful role that artistic creation could play in a quest for a meaningful identity. With his first school composition, writing became the means of staging his existence, offering the promise of rediscovering himself as "the mirror of the world, a self that was suddenly not a monstrous scandal" (D, 91). Throughout his life, he remained eager to interpret himself to his public in published personal journals, numerous essays, readily granted interviews, prose fictions, film scenarios, and, most important, his theater, which he described as "my own drama . . . usually a confession."[2] His depictions of significant autobiographical events are not always consistent, varying with the mood and sometimes the political climate of the moment. He readily acknowledged and prized this inconsistency as essential to his artistic and intellectual honesty: "If I write a new play, my point of view may be profoundly modified. I may be obliged to contradict myself and I may no longer know whether I still think what I think" (NCN, 39).

The availability of so much autobiographical material can obscure an important fact: What makes Ionesco's writing compelling is that it is fundamentally about the difficulty of comprehending anyone, not least oneself, given an existence which, the more we learn about it physically, becomes more problematic metaphysically. His most autobiographical plays, the early Victimes du devoir (Victims of Duty) and the two he wrote at the end of his dramatic career, L'Homme aux valises (The Man with the Luggage) and Voyages chez les morts (Journeys to the Land of the Dead), serve as reminders that he "stages" personal material because the puzzle of his self-portrait inevitably remains incomplete. At the end of his life he was still asking: "Am I a liar, a puppet, an actor, or am I genuine?"[3] The dilemma is compounded by the insufficiencies of memory and language. It is the "light of memory or rather the light that memory lends to things" that is the palest of all (PP, 190). As for language, not only is it subject to abuse and distortion, but "authentic anguish has no language."[4] A significant factor contributing to Ionesco's anguish was his intense awareness of contradictions. He billed himself as "Everyman" but at the same time was "furious at feeling lost in the formless paste of the multitude," a friction perhaps made inevitable by the complicated circumstances of his life.[5]

Eugen Ionescu was born in Slatina, Romania, a provincial town not far from Bucharest, on 16 November 1909.[6] His mother, Thérèse Ipcar, was French, the daughter of a civil engineer employed by the Romanian railroad company. His father, for whom he was named, was a municipal government official. There were two younger siblings; a sister, Marilina, born in 1911, and a brother, Mircea, born in 1912 or 1913, who died of meningitis at 18 months. This tragedy—about which, curiously, Ionesco has said almost nothing—may well have precipitated his early and enduring obsession with death. The family moved to Paris when Ionesco was 2 years old, where his father pursued a law degree. It was a quarrelsome household, sometimes violently so, further destabilized by frequent moves. Ionesco, who was extremely attached to his mother as a child, returns in both his published journals and his theater to a childhood memory of a parental quarrel that culminated in his mother's attempt to take poison. He cites the incident as the source of his conviction that happiness is impossible. It also gave rise to the conflicted sense of anxious betrayal and the misogyny that play out again and again like an exorcism in his theater: "My pity for my mother goes back to this day. I must have been absolutely astonished to perceive that she was only a poor, helpless child, a puppet in my father's hands, and the object of his persecution. Ever since I have pitied all women, rightly or wrongly. I have taken my father's guilt upon myself. Being afraid of making women suffer, of persecuting them, I have allowed myself to be persecuted by them. It is they who have made me suffer. I have made women suffer. Because everybody makes everybody else suffer" (*PP,* 20–21).

Ionesco's marriage in 1936 to Rodica Burileanu, who had been a fellow student at the University of Bucharest, seems not to have eased the conflict. He tells on various occasions of an unspoken rite, one which he imagined had been somehow mysteriously communicated through the ages, in which a brief mutual gaze exchanged by his mother and his future bride accomplished "a sort of handing over of powers."[7] His marvel at the instinctive ritual is complicated by melancholy. The burden of culpability was intensified by the proximity of the marriage and his mother's death, which took place 3 months later. Memories of his mother in his journals and autobiographical plays remain connected to a conviction that he had abandoned her. The many wife-mother figures in his plays tend to be reflective less of a mysterious bond than of a guilty confusion. There are important exceptions, but the majority of Ionesco's female characters are perfidious seductresses, drearily practical wife-mother figures, and vulgar concierge types whose dominance reduces the male characters to ineffectual bumblers and dreamers.

Ionesco described his obsessional struggle with the "unacceptable" inevitability of death as also being rooted in his complex ties to his mother. It was she who informed him that everyone must die: "At age four, I learned of death. I howled in despair. Then I grew afraid for my mother, knowing that I was going to lose her, that it could not happen, and I pressed against her to attach myself to her non-immortal presence, and I clutched her and drew her toward me as if to snatch her from duration" (*D*, 58). As he became increasingly haunted by his own mortality, writing to "cry out my fear of death and my humiliation at the thought of dying," death became the defining theme of his work (*NCN*, 227). Writing, and later painting, were his means of "snatching from time." One becomes a writer "in order to vanquish death . . . not to die entirely" (*A*, 333).

In Ionesco's accounts of his childhood years, his father appears mostly as a tall, frequently angry figure in a dark coat, with a forgotten face. When Germany declared war on Romania in 1916 he returned alone to Bucharest, severing contact with his family. Assuming that he had been killed in the war and struggling to support her children, Madame Ionesco found work in a factory. Ionesco, at age 7, was obliged to spend several lonely months in a dreary children's home outside Paris. In fact, Ionesco's father was not dead, but his son did not see him again until he was 13. In Ionesco's dreams and theater, his father is frequently reincarnated as a detective or a bizarrely metamorphic man named "Schaffer" (given varied spellings), a recurrent menacing figure.

From an early age, Ionesco was disposed to experience his existence as a cruelly imbalanced pendulum swinging between euphoria and despair, evanescence and heaviness, lightness and darkness. Many of his childhood recollections take shape as though on a darkened stage: evocations of dim streets and trains in tunnels, the gray light of autumn and winter evenings, the oppressive darkness of the Seine; and dank apartments where he lived with his mother, sister, and maternal grandparents. The troubled affect of these memories, only partially attributable to the blackouts and fuel shortages of wartime, did not fade in his adult years:

"Really, that *is* the world: a desert of fading shadows" (*NCN,* 154). Among his recorded early memories, there are also, however, vignettes of almost mystical discoveries illuminated by an intense projection of light. Significantly, one of the first memories evoked in *Present Past Past Present* is the flashing of a magic lantern image on a screen. A brilliant light dominates his recollections of the one period of sustained happiness in his young existence, a sojourn from 1917 to 1919 on an old farm known as "Le Moulin" in La Chapelle-Anthenaise, a rural village near Laval.

There he was removed from the grayness of wartime Paris and his mother's material difficulties, and sustained by the rhythms and rituals of the seasons, the Church, and a country school where he became the star pupil and first experienced his flair for written dialogue. He responded to the colors and light of the rural setting with a rare, unconflicted, youthful euphoria. The transcendent power of these luminous memories became his measure of paradise. When La Chapelle-Anthenaise faded into a lost paradise, the image dimmed by age and habit, the loss became a defining theme of his work. "It is true," he wrote around 1940, "that a person who has not completely lost the measure of paradise . . . will suffer endlessly. . . . What revolutionaries think they are bringing about is the ideal society, leaving economics and History behind. They do not dare let themselves be aware that it is really paradise they are looking for" (*PP,* 150).

The experience of a transforming luminosity was briefly repeated when he was in his late teens. Walking in summer sunshine in a white-washed provincial village under an intense blue sky, he was profoundly altered by the light: "Suddenly I felt as if I had received a blow right in the heart, in the center of my being. A stupefaction surged into being, exploded, burst its boundaries, dissolving the limits of things. . . . Even the pleasure of flight would have been less great than the pleasure I felt at this moment at simply touching my forehead and my chin. And above all neither flight nor anything else could give me greater euphoria than that of becoming aware that I was, once and for all, and that this was an irreversible thing, an eternal miracle" (*PP,* 154–56). The state of grace did not long endure. A journal entry from the 1940s notes, "I live in a grayness that for such a long time, for as long a time as I can remember, has been interrupted only rarely by the negative lucidities of the night or by a dream that reveals my desperate thirst for the light . . . , for the plenitude that reveals our separation" (*PP,* 153). Nevertheless, the early experience of luminous evanescence continued to play a determining role in Ionesco's literary and metaphysical quests, whether in the form of the modern alchemy of stage technology or as an elusive spiritual illumination. "There is no state of consciousness or unconsciousness," he proposed, "but two different consciousness states which serve sometimes to mask, sometimes to illuminate" (*A*, 264).

At age 13, Ionesco experienced the ordeal of exile. In Romania, his father had secretly divorced his mother (on the pretext that she had abandoned him) and remarried. He was able to influence the Romanian courts to grant him custody of his children in 1922. Thus the difficult transitions of adolescence were intensified for Eugène Ionesco by abrupt separation from his mother, the need to learn a new language, and being uprooted to a country succumbing to fascism. These experiences provided an early and indelible experience of the kind of grotesque metamorphoses that figure prominently in Ionesco's plays. His recollection that he was a very handsome child until age 13 and then became ugly had significance beyond the normal vicissitudes of adolescence.[8] His sister, quickly evicted by her stepmother, was able to live with their mother, who had returned to Bucharest. Ionesco remained in his father's household, which was a bizarre one, until he was 17, when he fled and supported himself by giving French lessons. He disliked his stepmother and her omnipresent familial entourage. He also quarreled constantly with his strong-willed, choleric father, whom he despised for being as unfaithful to his second wife as his first and for his shameless political maneuvering.

Ionesco's father switched from being chief of police in a government collaborating with the Germans in 1918 to a soldier in a resistance movement when Germany began to lose the war. He embraced the Iron Guards and fascism during the Second World War and then the Communist regime when it came to power. In *Present Past Past Present*, drawing a portrait of his father as the prototype for the chameleon-like paternal tyrants, professors, policemen, detectives, judges, and petty bureaucrats who are so abundant in his plays, he explains that "everything that I have done was done more or less against him." He was not an intellectual, according to Ionesco, although he "reacted" . . . like an orthodox rightist or leftist intellectual," not an opportunist either, but "an instinctive Hegelian: the truth for him . . . could only be the state . . . the truth of the official journal, or else, if it was not the state . . . the most massive and most general power" (*PP*, 17, 130). His father was determined to have his son become "a bourgeois, a magistrate, a soldier, a chemical engineer"; Ionesco immersed himself instead in literature

and wrote poetry, his rebelliousness nourished by the discovery of the
French surrealists and the poetry of his fellow Romanian, Tristan Tzara
(1896–1963), a founder of the dada movement (*PP,* 16–17).

In 1928, Ionesco began studying French literature at the University
of Bucharest. At the same time he established connections to Romanian
literary circles as a poet and critic. His career as a poet was brief, ending
in 1931 with the publication of *Elegii pentru fiinte mici (Elegies for Minuscule Creatures).* Evocations of a naive, childish universe influenced by the
symbolist movement, these poems present early evidence of his preoccupation with death and spiritual malaise. Ionesco later emphatically dismissed them as juvenile beginnings, "a strange mixture of Maeterlinck
and Francis Jammes, with a few surrealist touches" (*NCN,* 120).[9] His
career as a critic, spanning a period of more than a decade, fit better
with his defiant pursuit of fame and resentment of authority. He sparred
ostentatiously, and often one-sidedly, with distinguished literary figures
in Bucharest. In a provocative book entitled *Nu (No),* he attacked well-
known Romanian writers and critics only to later reverse his opinions in
order to prove that all literary criticism, at least in Romania, was subjective, contradictory and gratuitous. His contemptuous dismissal of the
Romanian literary establishment for believing that Romanian culture
could be taken seriously reflected how firmly his allegiance and identity
remained rooted in France during these years. Only after a long series of
fascist and communist Romanian dictatorships ended in 1989 could he
finally say, "I have 'unloved' Romania for such a long time, but now I
feel I am again their brother."[10]

In addition to Tzara, only a few Romanian writers escaped Ionesco's
derogation. One of them was Urmuz, the pen name of Demetre Deme-
tresco-Bouzau (1883–1923). An apparently unremarkable magistrate,
he was revealed after his suicide in a public garden to be the author of
wildly nonsensical, antisocial short fictions described by Ionesco as
"dadaist before dada and . . . surrealist before surrealism."[11] Urmuz,
according to Ionesco, who translated his fictions into French during the
1940s, rejected the weight of all constraints to liberty and unmasked
the void hidden beneath "the juridico-moralo-logic of the 'reality' in
which we think we live, in which we suffocate."[12] The spirit of Urmuz's
writing permeates Ionesco's early theater. The acid humor of Ion Luca
Caragiale (1852–1912), a self-exiled dramatist and short story writer,
offered another early absurdist model. Ionesco, who described his work
as "a criticism of society unequaled in its ferocity," was adapting one of
Caragiale's short stories for the stage at the time he was launching his

own dramatic career with *The Bald Soprano* and *The Lesson* (*NCN,* 140–41).[13]

Ionesco claimed indifference to the classic French dramatists, Corneille, Racine, and Molière. He maintained that dramatic works other than Caragiale's and Shakespeare's held little interest for him during his formative years as a writer, noting a preference for novelists, poets, and philosophers.[14] As did many of the young writers in Europe who were his contemporaries, he fell under the spell of the monumental quest through time and memory by Marcel Proust (1871–1922) in *À la Recherche du temps perdu* (*Remembrance of Things Past*) and the obsession with individual authenticity in the writings of André Gide (1869–1951). It was Gide's journals that Ionesco admired, however, not his novels. Only two writers were readily acknowledged by Ionesco as actual literary influences: Gustave Flaubert (1821–80) and Franz Kafka (1883–1924).[15]

Flaubert described the ideal novelist as someone who would mirror in his fiction the real universe created by an inscrutable God, the effect of which should be dumbfounding: "one should feel crushed without knowing why."[16] This model is reflected in *Un coeur simple* (*A Simple Heart*), the story which Ionesco, who discovered it at age 12, credited with teaching him how to write. Ionesco was one of many absurdist playwrights who acknowledged a debt to Flaubert's *Bouvard and Pecuchet* and *Dictionary of Accepted Ideas,* masterpieces of irony constructed from the banal bombast of a middle class ascending to self-importance during the industrial revolution in France. Kafka's influence also pervades absurdist theater. It was Kafka's depiction of irrational guilt and the revelation that "monstrousness has countless faces, collective or otherwise, striking or less striking, obvious or less obvious" that initially captured Ionesco (Bonnefoy, 1971, 39–40). As Ionesco's literary quest focused increasingly on a "second set of wonder . . . grafted on the first. A bewildered act of judgement, a realization of evil, or simply of something gone wrong," he drew from Kafka's spiritual interrogations the lesson that "when man is cut off from his religious or metaphysical roots, he is lost, all his struggles become senseless, futile and oppressive" (*NCN,* 257).

Well before his discovery of Kafka, however, Ionesco's uncomfortable suspension between the cerebral and the mystical had drawn him to less fashionable sources: the Neoplatonist philosopher Plotinus, St. Augustine, early Christian and orthodox mystics, and, most enduringly, St. John of the Cross. It is one of many contradictions in Ionesco's existence that for so many his name became exclusively associated with the fundamentally profane theater of the absurd. His most sustained search, obscured by his flamboyant early literary persona, was a spiritual one. The all-too-brief experiences of light and euphoria in childhood and adolescence evolved into a long quest for a state of grace.[17] Ionesco's early interest in mystical writings expanded under the guidance of his compatriot Mircea Eliade (1907–86), an internationally recognized scholar of myth and religion, to eastern religions and Hasidic texts. In Ionesco's later theater and his one novel, this background blended with his explorations of Freudian and Jungian psychology into a unique combination of myth, mysticism, and oneiricism.

From 1936 to 1938, Ionesco taught French in secondary schools. Barraged with a mounting wave of fascism, he watched in horror as colleagues, friends, and former professors succumbed. In 1938 a grant from the French Institute of Bucharest to complete a thesis on the themes of sin and death in French poetry after Baudelaire allowed him to return to Paris for the first time since 1922. He did not write the thesis. The sojourn was a time of literary renewal and nostalgia, reflected in a series called "Letters from Paris" published in Romania. In the spring of 1939, he returned to La Chapelle-Anthenaise, making rounds in the company of a woman named Marie who had taken him under her wing as a child. Differences in memories kept their reconstructions of these years from coinciding. Many years later, Ionesco published his journal from this visit, calling it "Printemps 1939. Les Débris du souvenir. Pages du journal" ("Spring 1939"). The subtitle "Remnants of Memory," which was not retained for the English translation, is key to this moving document of a Proustian quest for lost time that foreshadows the nostalgic anguish of the many autobiographical protagonists in his theater.

In Paris he became involved with the group attached to the review *L'Esprit,* founded by Emmanuel Mounier (1905–1950), a leader of the movement known as *"personnalisme."* Its adherents shared the anticapitalist views of the Marxists and existentialists but from a distinctly antimaterialist perspective. Their concern with individual spiritual vitality is reflected in one of the "Letters from Paris," in which Ionesco concludes that the principal problem facing the world at present is "to chose between spirituality and liberty on the one hand and barbarianism and slavery on the other."[18] The theme would echo through his writing until the end of his career, by which time unsympathetic French ideologues had replaced fascist "barbarians" as the objects of denigration. Ionesco also took an interest in the Paris theater. After the 1939 premiere of *Ondine*, by Jean Giraudoux (1882–1944), he applauded the French theater's break from naturalism. In terms predictive of his future plays, he called for a new kind of "truth" in the theater: "Essential realities can only be found in the fantastic world that one carries within oneself, in the most intimate and cherished reality, in metaphysics. . . . Does a play seem realistic? then it is a bad play. . . . As is true for all the arts, the theater's mission is knowledge. Knowledge does not come from imitation but from diving into, disassociating, purifying realities" (G. Ionescu, 1989, 160–61).

The outbreak of war in Romania put an end to the Paris sojourn. Ionesco was mobilized upon his return but stayed in Budapest as a lycée professor, good fortune he attributed to a general's fear that Romania would again lose its young intellectuals as it had during World War I (*TC*, lxxviii). For the next 2 years, isolated by their antifascism and physically threatened, Ionesco and his wife attempted to obtain exit visas for France. When they were finally allowed to leave in 1942, France was a defeated country. They stayed in Marseille until the end of the war, living in impoverished circumstances and essentially in hiding, fearing the consequences of their foreign name (Lamont, 1993, 37). Their only child, a daughter named Marie-France, was born in 1944. The first years in postwar Paris, where they were finally able to establish themselves in 1945, were nearly as difficult. Ionesco found work as a proofreader for a publisher of medical and legal books, which faced him day after day with the kind of jargon that would find its way into his absurdist plays.

In 1948, Ionesco began to work on a sketch parodying an English language manual he had been studying. It started out in Romanian as *Englezeste fara profesor (Learning English without a Professor)* and finally became *La Cantatrice chauve (The Bald Soprano)*. In 1950, the year Ionesco became naturalized as a French citizen, Nicolas Bataille, a talented, novice director without a theater of his own, scraped together the resources to stage it. The initial reception of *The Bald Soprano* was unpromising; the surrealists and a very few open-minded critics were among the few to appreciate it. It was not long, however, before Ionesco's name, along with those of the Russian émigré Arthur Adamov (1908–1970) and the Irish playwright Samuel Beckett (1906–1989), became synonymous with the "new French theater" of the 1950s.[19] Because Ionesco was essentially unknown in Paris until the staging of *The Bald Soprano,* an appealing story came into existence that a fortuitous encounter with nonsensical phrases and situations in the English-language manual had suddenly uncovered an unsuspected dramatic talent powerful enough to revolutionize the theater. Enjoying the role of such an astounding persona, Ionesco fostered the legend, claiming that he did not want to write for the theater and that "it was because I failed to learn English that I became a playwright" (*NCN,* 175). He later acknowledged that this was not the case. Reviewing the early days of his career in a 1979 letter to the woman who first showed the manuscript to Bataille, he emphasized that he was not a novice at the time but armed with a substantial literary preparation: "dozens and dozens of articles published in Romanian periodicals, a small collection of poems that were not good, and, above all, a book, *Nu,* where I attempted to explode literary criticism. I wanted to repeat a similar experience by blowing up the theater. . . . I knew very well what I was doing, which was, if not a play, then an anti-play" (*HQ,* 178).

The *Bald Soprano* was the beginning of a prolific dramatic career. Ionesco wrote *The Lesson* and *Jack, or the Submission* in 1950. The following year he completed *The Future Is in Eggs* and *The Chairs,* still considered by many to be his finest play. During the first performances of *The Chairs* in 1952, the theater seats were nearly as empty as the symbolic chairs on the stage. In 1956, however, when Jacques Mauclair staged a revival with Tsilla Chelton, a remarkable actress who subsequently played many roles in Ionesco's theater, *The Chairs* was hailed by the well-established playwright Jean Anouilh (1910–1987) as a "classic." In an enthusiastic article which appeared on the first page of a major daily newspaper, Anouilh wrote, "I think that it is better than Strindberg because it is dark in the fashion of Molière, sometimes madly funny, it's frightful and ridiculous, poignant and always true."[20] Already, by 1954, Ionesco's theater was being published by the distinguished Gallimard press. By this time too, with ready access to literary reviews and newspapers, he was sparring with critics in lively articles defending the underlying seriousness of the "new theater" and earning himself a position as its principal spokesperson. A revival of *The Bald Soprano* and *The Lesson* in 1957 at the Théâtre de la Huchette in the Latin Quarter was successful enough to become a permanent fixture.

By the early 1960s, Ionesco's plays, which he continued to write at a steady pace, were being performed around the world. The 1960s were the most successful years of his career. Three of his plays were produced at the prestigious Odéon-Théâtre de France in the 1960s: *Rhinoceros* in 1960, *A Stroll in the Air* in 1963, and *Frenzy for Two or More* in 1966. Bearing out Anouilh's earlier prediction, Ionesco became an "official"

French classic playwright in 1966, with the production of *Hunger and Thirst* at the Comédie Française. His dramatic style and subject matter had undergone significant transformations by this time. The humorously derisive antics of his early "antitheater" had given way to longer, more somber, and increasingly autobiographical material, and also to more overtly political themes. During the late 1960s his dramatic production slowed, replaced to some extent by work on a novel and a film and an interest in painting, but also due to an increasing number of polemical distractions.

In 1970 Ionesco was elected to the Académie Française, a "royally constituted" body generally as conservative as it is distinguished. From unknown author of *The Bald Soprano* to "académicien" in just two decades was an astounding leap. For many of his first admirers it was also a disappointing one. Long before 1970, however, a political rift had separated Ionesco from his early champions. The rift began in France in the mid-1950s, when the theater avant-garde switched its loyalties to Berthold Brecht (1898–1956), whose Berliner Ensemble performed *Mother Courage* at a theater festival in Paris in 1954. In 1958 the quarrel became international with what came to be known as the "London controversy." This began as a debate pitting Ionesco against the British drama critic Kenneth Tynan, initially an enthusiastic supporter who had introduced Ionesco's theater to the London public. After a London performance of *The Chairs,* Tynan, whose political sympathies were to the left, objected to Ionesco's dismissal of words as "useless and fraudulent." He compared Ionesco's theater to "a funfair ride on a ghost train, all skulls and hooting waxworks, from which we emerge into the far more intimidating clamor of diurnal reality," concluding that it is "pungent and exciting, but . . . remains a diversion. It is not on the main road: and we do him no good, nor the drama at large to pretend that it is" (*NCN,* 88–89).

In the long run, it was claims like Tynan's that were not good for Ionesco. The cold war atmosphere seemed to require that intellectuals choose between the east, in spite of Russia's political excesses, and the perceived hegemony of the United States. A significant number of French intellectuals and critics opted for the former and became devotees of Brecht. Ionesco experienced this phenomenon as a revival of the fascist scenarios of his years in Romania. Indignant, he made it abundantly clear that "rhinoceritis" was a diagnosis that now fit the left in France. By refusing to remain where others expected or wanted him to be, he found himself cast once more as a pariah in an all-too-familiar irrational discourse. As he has a cynical character remark in *The Killer,* "It's heroism to think against your times, but madness to say so" (*K,* 83). Ionesco initially took on Tynan and a broadening circle of critics with relish, arguing that "a work of art has nothing to do with doctrine" and criticizing Tynan for acknowledging "only one plane of reality . . . the 'social' plane . . . the most external and superficial" aspect of the the-ater (*NCN,* 90–91). He then launched the first of his many attacks on Jean-Paul Sartre (1905–1980) and on Brecht, accusing them, along with the playwrights John Osborne (1929–) and Arthur Miller (1915–), of being "representatives of a left-wing conformism which is just as lamentable as the right-wing sort" (*NCN,* 91). The polemic degenerated into abuse of persons and prose on both sides. Ionesco railed against leftist ideologues, accusing them of stifling individual voices and duping a vast public with hypocritical notions of revolutions and history. He objected repeatedly to the harm caused by those who stifle imagination and thus "truth" by reducing language to jargon. Lan-guage, he kept reminding his readers, is our means to discovery.

By the 1960s, the political essays and published excerpts from his personal journals were becoming inflexibly partisan and short of saving humor. He defended the change with a rueful paradox: "I have not got a partisan mind. If there is one thing I detest it is the partisan spirit: often to such an extent that in detesting hatred I become full of hatred myself" (*NCN,* 160). Estranged from former supporters, Ionesco found himself regarded by many of them during the 1960s and the 1970s as a once-revolutionary playwright who (although he was also blamed for taking himself too seriously) had never been as profound as Beckett, nor a true rebel like Jean Genet (1910–1986). He dismissed the new wave of criticism as another example of the double standard that unsympa-thetic critics had been applying to his theater since the debate with Tynan, noting that those who once accused him of "not believing in lan-guage, destroying it, disarticulating it, refusing communication, writing badly, leading to silence" were now accusing him of writing *"too well,* believing in language and being eloquent" (*A,* 283). He resented as well the director-driven, experimental theater that had come into vogue in the late 1960s, with its Artaudian emphasis on spontaneous, collective experimentation and its deemphasis on or even elimination of the author. Ionesco insisted adamantly that his stage directions be treated as an integral part of the play. Expressing opposition to the liberties taken with classic texts by the new wave of experimental directors, he com-pared the practice to putting mustaches on the "Mona Lisa" and saying

"Look, we have demystified her; she always had mustaches that had been hidden from you."[21]

The new "avant-garde" had not ignored the earlier absurdist generation. The happening-like "panic theater" of Fernando Arrabal (1932–) fit their interests very well as did Jean Genet's revolutionary approach to political theater.[22] Beckett's plays remained very much in vogue. The contrast of the latter's fate with his own particularly vexed Ionesco, provoking him to expressions of jealousy and occasional denigrations. In fact, to compare Ionesco's work with Beckett's after the 1950s made less and less sense. Their goals had never been analogous, but the differences had been masked in the 1950s by their similar determination to revolutionize theater language and their refusal to cater to the conventions of realism. In the 1970s, Beckett's increasingly tight and abstract dramas matched the minimalist mind-set and the depersonalization of the postmodern literary world. Ionesco's sprawling political-Jungian-Christian theories were incompatible with the new wave of theater born of the political-sexual-moral revolution that crystallized in France during the student revolts and general strikes of May 1968. It was not a sympathetic time for Ionesco's conservatism or for his metaphysical quests. He noted bitterly in his opening address at the 1972 Salzburg Festival that "the notions of love and contemplation are not even ridiculous notions anymore, they are completely abandoned. The very idea of metaphysics provokes snickering when it doesn't arouse anger" (*HQ,* 72).

Ionesco's focus during the 1970s shifted inward. As ill health made the menace of death more concrete, he became increasingly drawn to his dreams and spiritual crises as a dramatic source. He approached his metaphysical discomfort not as an intellectually formulated longing for meaning in an inscrutable universe, but as a need for a very real God. The religious sentiments fostered during his stay at La Chapelle-Anthenaise had remained an integral part of his makeup: "I have been waiting for grace for a long time, what a lot of patience" (*HQ,* 95). Ionesco remained characteristically confrontational, announcing, for example, that since critics were either reproachful or derisive when he spoke of metaphysics, he would "use on purpose and as often as possible the words: metaphysics, soul, unknowable, essence, nirvana," or remarking that "only journalists, literati, ideologues, and philosophers of the tenth order" treat God lightly (*A,* 219). Even his very short and political *Scène,* written in 1982 in honor of Vaclav Havel (1936–), turns a political discussion between two imprisoned dissidents into a religious statement. After Vanek, an idealistic young prisoner who has been arguing for imaginative and spiritual freedom, is led off in handcuffs to be tortured, the disenchanted Béranger, an old-guard proponent of social conditioning, envies him his faith in God. Ionesco's last major plays, created from recorded dreams and familial conflicts, were defiantly out of synchrony with a theater vogue that was moving away from fixed authorial anchoring to focus on epic events and collective creative experiments. These plays have rarely been staged.

Ionesco was embittered by his dismissal from the avant-garde: "Now that I know what it means to have written, to have been understood, to have been misunderstood, to have been detested, I finally understand that it was not worth it to have done what I have done, it was for nothing" (*HQ,* 11). He remained nevertheless a central and admired figure in the arena of world theater during the 1970s. His plays were regularly performed in France and abroad and he was much sought after as a lecturer. Among the many significant honors he received were the Austrian Grand Prize for European Literature in 1970; the Jerusalem Prize in 1973, a medal at the Salzburg Festival in 1976, and a prestigious Cérisy Colloquium organized around his work in 1978.

Ionesco also turned in new creative directions. In 1971 he made a film, *La Vase (The Slough),* in which he played the principal role.[23] His novel, *Le Solitaire (The Hermit)*, appeared in 1973. During the last two decades of his life he was more active as an artist and an art critic than as a playwright. His water colors and lithographs were exhibited primarily in Switzerland, where he had a studio in Saint Gall, but also in Germany, Italy, and Paris, including an exhibition at the Centre Pompidou. Early in his career, he had wondered with anguish, "How . . . can I express everything that words hide? How can I express what is inexpressible?" (*PP,* 168). Painting supplied a partial answer and became a palliative against physical ills, boredom, and a host of obsessions and resentments. Words, he stated, had lost their meaning and value, whereas colors had remained alive, still able to provide him with what words had lost: "If I stopped painting, I would be in utter despair" (*QI,* 13). He came to fear nonetheless that his pleasure in color would also wear out. This apprehension, expressed in 1986 at a time when he was in seriously ill health, may well have reflected his physical state more than the vicissitudes of his career.

In 1979 a magnificent production of *Exit the King* staged at the Odéon by Jorge Lavelli, one of the most creative avant-garde directors in Europe at the time, heralded a significant resurgence of interest in Ionesco's work during the 1980s. In 1984, six of his plays were performed in Paris theaters: *Rhinoceros, Exit the King, The Chairs,* Roger Planchon's *Spectacle Ionesco,* and, in permanent repertory at the Théâtre de la Huchette, *The Bald Soprano* and *The Lesson.* French translations of his youthful *Hugoliad* and *Nu* were published in 1982 and 1986 respectively. Illustrated editions of his *Stories for Children under Three Years of Age* appeared from 1983 to 1986. *La Quête intermittente* was published in 1987. Major critical studies of his work were also in preparation in France and the United States, and in 1987 he was the subject of a lengthy documentary film produced for German television. That same year, on the occasion of the thirtieth anniversary of uninterrupted production of *The Bald Soprano* and *The Lesson* at the Théâtre de la Huchette, he received the medal of the city of Paris. The opera *Maximilien Kolbe,* with music by Dominique Probst, for which he had written a libretto about the actions of the heroic Polish priest in a Nazi concentration camp, premiered in 1988 at the Rimini Festival.[24] A 1989 production of *The Chairs* won the Molière Prize. In 1991 a complete edition of Ionesco's theatre was published in Gallimard's deluxe, painstakingly annotated Pléiade series, an event as momentous as election to the French Academy.

As the cold war ended in the 1980s, many of Ionesco's political claims were vindicated and he was accorded the status of a kind of modern Tiresias, shunted aside for seeing uncomfortable truths. It was an appropriate Ionescan role. "Born for literature," as he notes in *Découvertes,* his "truths" had taken many forms: defiant hyperbole in *Nu,* an irreverent social mirror in his absurdist dramas, cataclysmic insights in his politicized theater and satirical essays, obsessive archetypal landscapes in his dream theater, and finally the religious mysticism in his later years (*D,* 65). "From the beginning," he wrote in *La Quête intermittente,* "I have insisted on being beyond boundaries" (101). It was the limit imposed by human mortality which he was most desperate to transgress, but he attacked a multitude of more remediable obstacles in his writing and painting as well. He illustrated again and again the difficult necessity for the individual to look for questions, not answers; to struggle against the herd, and to clear space for authenticity and the wonderment of childhood: "always question, above all question" (*A,* 333). Ionesco's interrogation ended on 28 March 1994, when he died in Paris. On the evening of his death, *The Bald Soprano* and *The Lesson* were performed at the Théâtre de la Huchette for the 11,944th time since 1957. The theater director announced that there would be no other homage that night because "to pay tribute to a playwright is to perform his work."[25]

Chapter Two

Writing in Romania:
An Antiestablishment Debut

As a university student and a young professor, Ionesco led a bohemian existence in Bucharest. Literary activity, with the exception of theater, flourished there during the 1920s and 1930s, animated by poets, novelists, and critics, and by numerous periodicals representing diverse artistic and political credos.[1] Ionesco's first "theater" was created in the pages of literary reviews, where he cast the intellectual coteries of Bucharest in murky satirical farces. The primary lesson he drew from his literary debut in Romania was an "iron firm belief in the supreme buffoonery of the serious."[2] Ionesco's negativity distinguished itself from customary youthful impatience with the cultural establishment by its exceptional abrasiveness and absence of nuance. During his years in Romania he remained closely attached to France, emotionally through ties to his mother and childhood, intellectually through his study and teaching of French language and literature. He described with amusement being denigrated by a professor as a "decadent pawn" of French influence (G. Ionescu, 1989, 246). The francophilia strengthened his resistance to ideological and nationalistic contagion, just as later, in France, he remained sufficiently marked by his Romanian experience to respond to reigning postwar ideologies from a critical distance. At the same time, his estrangement from Romanian culture exacerbated an already pronounced nostalgia for both roots and individual meaning. Attempting to come to terms with these conflicts, he assiduously cultivated nonconformity and succès de scandale.

Nu (No)

In 1934, the 25-year-old Ionesco earned the nickname of "literary Brutus" with the publication of a book entitled *Nu,* a hybrid collection of critical essays, confessions, meditations, short satirical fictions, and excerpts from his personal journal, the only literary genre, he believed at the time, that permitted honest self-expression (G. Ionescu, 1989, 186).

Ionesco says "no" in these pages to a gamut of bêtes noires that carried over into his theater: trivialized and inflated language, authoritarian literary posturing, and the uncritical herd mentality that encourages them. He also attempts to negate the specter of death: "no, there is nothing, truly nothing in me which consents to accepting death" (*N*, 99). Writing the Foreword to the French translation nearly half a century later, he acknowledged the "sometimes unjust violence and excessive paradoxes" of "the work of an angry adolescent," but insisted that in its "most profound, most spiritual affirmations" it expresses what he continued to say throughout his life (*N*, 7). In 1934, however, Ionesco flaunted less lofty aspirations: "I am tortured—tor-tur-ed by every vanity, every ambition" (*N*, 98). Thus *Nu* was not perceived at the time as "profound" or "spiritual," but was greeted with varying degrees of amusement, admiration, or outrage in proportions largely determined by the reader's prior sympathies for either Ionesco or his targets. It made him enemies and was dismissed as the work of a jealous arriviste. It also won a Royal Foundations Editions prize.

"Part One" of *Nu*, which is both acrimonious and humorous, is largely devoted to denying the aesthetic and intellectual merits of Romania's most reputed writers and critics. In spite of distortions and inconsistencies (which do not preclude critical insight), *Nu* is captivating as an introduction to several writers whose work is not widely known outside Romania. Ionesco's 1986 Preface to the French translation even describes it as a "rehabilitation" of a period that had come to seem incredibly free compared to Romania in the 1980s. Tudor Arghezi (1880–1967), then widely considered to be Romania's most outstanding poet, is the first prey.[3] Arghezi, whose influence on Ionesco's *Elegies for Minuscule Creatures* was recognized by their contemporaries, had facilitated Ionesco's early career as a writer by publishing the young writer's poetry in his review *Bilete de Papagal*. Nonetheless, with comically derisive venom, in what is often a line-by-line, even word-by-word, analysis of his work, Ionesco turns him into an "antipoet," a prototype for the wordmongers that proliferate in his theater. Ridiculing Arghezi's "syllogistico-sentimental edifice," he singles out the kinds of mechanical, bloated rhetoric that will become the primary matter of *The Bald Soprano*, *The Lesson*, and *Jack, or the Submission:* clichés, imitations, banality, facile psychologism, and exaggerations of "that galloping heresy of image for image's sake" (*N*, 57).

Frustrated ambition, youthful impatience with a style of poetry Ionesco wanted to consider outmoded, rebellion against a paternal figure, and the desire to be noticed all played a role in this overdetermined reaction, which he prefaced by a searing attack on any critic so insecure or sycophantic as to have admired Arghezi's poetry. A very probable additional explanation is that Ionesco recognized that he was as tempted as Arghezi by grandiloquence, although he generally masked his rhetorical bent with a constant play of irony. Catching himself, for example, toward the end of *Nu,* in a florid discussion of the omnipresence of death, he expresses embarrassment at being pathetic and sentimental, then slips into a posturing rhetoric that he can pointedly deflate: "With your legendary sagacity you will have naturally understood that this beautiful piece of eloquence, cut clean through by the knife of irony, was carefully conceived and arranged with the unique goal of obtaining a handsome stylistic effect. You are thus invited to appreciate it as such" (*N,* 275). Ionesco insists that "cries, true ones, are brief and say everything" (*N,* 233). This sober measure is elusive in the nearly 300 pages of literary, psychological, and metaphysical ruminations in *Nu,* as it will be in some of his later plays. Reversing his negative opinion of Arghezi in the next essay, he claims that "it is a spirit of contradiction that makes me write. . . . The word 'true' isn't in the dictionary of my conscience" (*N,* 83–84).

After Arghezi, still with the intent, as he freely admits, of provoking a scandal, Ionesco takes on Ion Barbu (1895–1961), a mathematician, a respected poet, and an editorial staff colleague. In the Arghezi essay, Ionesco had singled out Barbu as a lucid critic and exemplary poet. In the Barbu essay, flaunting his "spirit of contradiction," he claims that Barbu's poetry has been contaminated by Arghezi's "picturesqueness and verbosity" (*N,* 83–84). Ionesco's principal concern, however, is to denigrate Romanian culture, particularly as represented by its poets and critics whom he holds up for negative comparison with French writers (*N,* 96). Reflecting on the apparent gratuity of his evaluations of both Arghezi and Barbu, he blames it on the humiliation inherent in any literary activity for a writer in Romania. The country, he claims, is so unremarkable that Aldous Huxley had dismissed it as "a place somewhere between the Latvians and the Laplanders" (*N,* 85). Given the fundamental insignificance of Romanian literature, according to Ionesco, any critical assessment of it becomes equally meaningless. Cautioning young writers to be systematically distrustful of Romanian values, he briefly abandons his ironic stance to salute his youthful fellow critics, who share the goal of "the most severe and implacable reappraisal of established values . . . with no compromises" (*N,* 72).

Nu turns next to Camil Petrescu (1894–1957), a prominent novelist, poet, dramatist, and literary theorist who had asked Ionesco to review his *Patul lui Procust (Procrustian Bed)*, a novel about Bucharest society. Before Ionesco's critical response, which he justifies as a necessary bit of "literary hygiene," the two were on friendly terms (*N*, 110). Ionesco's essay lambastes first the critics who had praised Petrescu and then the novelist. Charging him with an inept copying of Proust, he dismisses his novels as "practically worthless . . . a clear literary fraud" (*N*, 107).[4] Ionesco is saved from appearing simply mean-spirited and insolent in these pages only by the warranted nature of his condemnation of the political machinations operative in Romanian literary society and by his spirited, dramatic style.

In a long appendix to the essay, Ionesco "stages" himself as a literary "nobody" in an absurd skirmish with the grand Petrescu. As the scenario shifts from the streets of Bucharest, to Petrescu's study, to numerous editorial offices, he plays for his readers the role of a Chaplinesque hero bent but not broken by the literary powers that be. Invited to Petrescu's home, he gives a timorous reading of the critique that appears in *Nu*. The novelist responds by threatening to destroy the young critic's reputation. Regretting that his "little joke" (his definition of any act of literary criticism) would end the friendship, Ionesco tears up his lengthy manuscript page by page, restoring Petrescu to his habitual gregariousness. The following day brings a change of heart. Sneaking back to Petrescu's study, he retrieves the scraps of his essay and laboriously pieces them together. He then sets out to find a publisher, hoping that the jealousy afflicting Bucharest's literati will prompt someone with editorial clout to prefer rendering the novelist apoplectic to fawning. Buttonholing one spineless editor after another, at last he finds a willing editorial accomplice. With only a third of his essay in print, however, the review folds for lack of funds. The farcical confrontation with Petrescu degenerates into an "interminable little scandal in the wings such that my left hand punch landed on sturdy solar plexuses and I didn't have a knock out to my credit" (*N*, 157). Many of the characters in Ionesco's plays will joust in similarly lopsided combats.

Reflecting on the miserable evening in Petrescu's study, when, with all the linguistic devices and turns of phrase available to him, he could find "nothing that worked, nothing true, nothing that did not turn into literature," Ionesco concludes that "every true relationship is difficult, impossible really, among writers because language, a means of communication for others, separates them" (*N*, 138). "To express myself is to become uniform," he laments later in *Nu,* "to become like the others. . . . Expression . . . suffocates me under cadavers of law, tradition, convention. How can I distinguish myself?" (*N,* 251). The Bergsonian recognition that the mechanical quality of language spills over into interpersonal relations is one that he will exploit for all its humorous and tragic effects in his theater. *Nu* was described by a member of the jury that awarded it a prize as a "tragic farce" (G. Ionescu, 1989, 250). The label, which Ionesco adopted as a subtitle for *The Chairs,* was an uncanny forecast of his leap from an unhappy, dilettantish literary critic to a remarkable absurdist playwright. Part of the fascination of *Nu* is that beyond the hubris and the bitterness engendered by personal frustration emerge the kinds of apocalyptic comic forces that will make a mockery of rational man in Ionesco's theater.

The second part of *Nu* is entitled "False Critical Itinerary." Ionesco's approach in some of the liveliest entries resembles the creation by Beaumarchais (1732–1799) of the partially autobiographical Figaro to ridicule French society in the final years of the Old Regime. In "You Will Be a Great Writer," Ionesco outlines for young writers a Figaro-like itinerary for "becoming as famous as possible in a minimum of time" (*N,* 235). Claiming Petrescu as his model, he proposes assiduous flattery and acquiescence to the reigning literary ethic in a lesson that then rapidly shifts into a travesty of *Everyman.* His aspiring writer, "terrorized by the thought of the thousands of obstacles awaiting him, lives in a veritable Hell" and must be taught to be "calm, patient, humble and obedient" (*N,* 239). In contrast to the medieval figure who must abandon flattery, false friends, and worldly rewards on his way to salvation, Ionesco's aspirant to the Elysium of Romanian letters requires an arsenal of sycophantic stratagems. Promising that his method guarantees a place among the local literary and philosophical celebrities and in the schoolbooks, Ionesco also makes clear that it guarantees increasing receptivity to the kind of ready-made moral, scientific, and aesthetic values that were being imposed by fascism.

A similar point is made in "Intermezzo," which precedes the writer's lesson. Pedants of diverse nationalities—early models for Ionesco's *L'Impromptu d'Alma (Improvisation, or the Shepherd's Chameleon)*—wage a ferocious statistical battle to prove, depending on the national origins of the research, that the ratio of four-leaf clovers to three-leaf clovers is either 3 to 97, 2 to 98, or 6 to 94. A Polish scholar, unable to find any four-leaf clovers at all, complicates the quarrel with "irrefutable" evidence that they do not exist. Temporarily united in opposition to the

Pole, the others fight back with a weighty volume demonstrating that "the reality of clover is irrational, illogical, or more exactly a-logical, thus logical criteria cannot be applied to it" (*N*, 232). Partisan camps form; tempers flare. When a Chinese scholar has the temerity to oppose the wisdom of the West by theorizing that "fifty per cent of clovers are four-leaf clovers, and thus, after minute further calculations, that three-leaf clovers constitute the other fifty per cent," the fury unleashed surpasses the diplomatic capacities of the League of Nations, leaving the world on the verge of global war. Peace is finally restored when the inconclusive results of clover-gathering expeditions innocently undertaken by five children, "a Japanese, a Bengal, a Dutch child, a South American and an anti-semite," persuade the readily manipulated general public that science proves nothing (*N*, 234). The world is made "safe" by hounding the scientists into hiding and limiting them to strictly theoretical research in a place where there are no clovers. Ionesco was never averse to parodying the scientific world. There is not much laughter, however, when he ends his tale with an abrupt comment and a disheartening question: "This story has no end. How could it?" (*N*, 234). A few pages later he observes darkly, "If we were sincerely persuaded of being only equal to others, we would promptly commit suicide. Life is only bearable to the extent that we scorn our fellow creatures and overestimate ourselves" (*N*, 237).

In one of the last essays, referring by name to the successful Romanian writers and intellectuals of his day whom he considers to be particularly mediocre, Ionesco lashes out at his compatriots who have mindlessly lionized them: "I hold you responsible . . . you and the historical circumstances which are your own (it is not the times which govern man, but rather man who governs these miserable times) for all the inadequacies of my intelligence, my culture, my intellectual life, my genius. [Had I been] French, perhaps I would have been a brilliant poet" (*N*, 268). Ionesco recognized that the political movements threatening Europe made it naive to nurse illusions about a magically salutary escape from Romania. His complaint in the earlier Barbu essay that he will die "without having played even a minimal role on the European stage" is blunted with the pessimistic premonition that this Europe, "which will do without him," will also, ultimately, "founder in the void" (*N*, 84). He adds a "serious parenthesis": "Its subject: death is there, lurking about us" (*N*, 99).

Among the mortifications that plague the young writer as he evaluates the limits on his freedom, happiness, and authenticity is his unsatisfactory spiritual state. It is described, with the self-irony characteristic of *Nu*, as being "as disastrous as possible tra-la-la" (*N*, 217). When Ionesco notes, however, that the state of his soul is in conflict with his desire to blunt the fear of death with the hope of attaining a little corner of paradise, he is introducing a variant of his most enduring theme (*N*, 217, 220). In contrast to his later metaphysical struggles, he thrives at the beginning of his career on the very paradoxes that cause his suffering, proposing that "what finally saves our joy is precisely its lack of authenticity thanks to which it is colored with sadness. A lack of authenticity thanks to which sadness is colored with joy" (*N*, 258).

Hugoliade (Hugoliad, or the Grotesque and Tragic Life of Victor Hugo)

Ionesco undertook one other long work in the 1930s, an "epic" lampoon of Victor Hugo (1802–1885). A preliminary version of *Hugoliad* appeared in installments in a Romanian literary review in 1935 and 1936, but the work remained unfinished.[5] When Ionesco left for France, he lost track of it altogether. By the time this "ironic biography," as he called it, was recovered and translated into French and then into English in the early 1980s, Ionesco's circumstances added an additional layer of irony. Himself a member of the French Academy, he had reached a point in his career where he was being criticized, not always with any more fairness than he had shown to Hugo, for some of the same excesses.

Hugo's life and writing provided abundant material for further exploration of the "buffoonery of the serious" begun in *Nu*. A poet, playwright, and novelist, and the most famous figure of French romanticism, Hugo was literally worshiped during his lifetime. He was buried with great ceremony in the Panthéon after a state funeral worthy of Napoléon Bonaparte. Ionesco, revolted by any manifestation of a herd mentality, relates with disgust the admission by another romantic poet, Théophile Gautier (1811–1872), that "he fainted with emotion at the sight of Hugo and the host of people groveling at his feet."[6] By the turn of the century, however, Hugo was denigrated by avant-garde poets who were debunking the myth of inspired genius and seeking their models in the works of Baudelaire, Verlaine, Rimbaud, and Mallarmé. "When I wrote this book decades ago," Ionesco recalls in his 1982 Preface, "eloquence was out of style and Verlaine's precept was observed: 'Take eloquence and wring its neck' " (*HU*, 7). Increasingly persuaded that "poetry resides not in opulent expression but in the naked word,"

Ionesco objected to Hugo's unrestrained sentimentality and verbosity, which he dismissed in one of his milder critical moments as "platitudes in color" (*HU*, 28). *Hugoliad* echoes the observation in *Nu* that "rhetoric negates the imagination and intuition and suffocates the lyrical intuition" (*N*, 45). As he indicts Hugo, Ionesco promotes his own definition of true poetry as "outcry, not discourse . . . a spiritualized biology" (*HU*, 20).

The epic feats suggested by the title are created from material culled selectively from biographies, diaries, historical documents, and some of Hugo's most preposterous lines. Ionesco "stages" Hugo in incident after incident as a logorrheic, egotistical buffoon operating behind a screen of fine sentiments and indiscriminating admirers: "The very mountains, which had not come to Mohammed, gathered round him. . . . The cosmos was so charged with Hugoism that if one touched a flower, it made a rhyme; if one touched a tree its bark said in a thin, shrill voice (bark's usual tone): 'Hugo . . . Hugo . . . the dreamer . . .'; while the leaves, lacking the critical spirit, recited his verse" (*HU*, 33–34). *Hugoliad* turns into theater, with detailed indications for stage properties, costumes, and poses. Chapters entitled "Mise en scène" and "Dramas and Illuminations" read like hybrids of vaudeville and *drame bourgeois*. Whether making grandiose poetic declarations until not only his mistress but Nature herself begs for silence, or creating a dramatic tableau with his children on his lap for the benefit of visitors, Ionesco's Hugo is always acting.

Portrayed as a shameless self-promoter, swimming "in pure, guileless, unabridged vanity," womanizing, turning even family tragedy to personal gain in carefully crafted poetic grief, Hugo becomes one of many in a long line of despicably opportunistic father figures in Ionesco's writing. He is "a royalist . . . at the fall of Napoléon. A Republican at the fall of Charles X. An Orléanist during the reign of Louis Philippe. . . . But each revolution brings in a little something: a pension . . . the Legion of Honor . . . the peerage" (*HU*, 22, 29). In light of Ionesco's statement that "it is always myself that I place at the heart of my interests and my preoccupations," the pillorying of Hugo, like that of Arghezi, also suggests an element of counterphobia (*N*, 88). The dual Hugolian role of virtuoso author and philosopher king tempted Ionesco as well. "All glory is the prize of spiritual deficiency," he claims apropos of Hugo (*HU*, 15). But in *Nu*, with tongue in cheek yet not without foundation, he states, "I suffer like a beast at not being the greatest poet in Europe, the greatest critic in the world, the strongest man in Europe, and, at least, a prince. I cannot bear that it doesn't happen, that it will never happen" (*N*, 98).

Hugoliad introduces a second antihero: François-Auguste Biard, a popular cartoonist and unsuccessful painter who is also the unhappy husband of one of Hugo's mistresses. Biard's presence affords Ionesco such pleasures as setting up a scene where the "poet-Member-of-the-French-Academy-Peer-of-France" is caught by Biard and the local police in his long johns "in flagrante delicto," in other words, holding forth on "sparkling clouds of silver, the zenith, the constellations, starry hydras, the effluvia of the abysses, diamond celestial bodies," for the benefit of the naked Madame Biard. His primary role, however, is to provide a vehicle for expressing frustration with his literary career in Romania (*HU*, 77). Biard, a model for a recurrent character type in Ionesco's theater—comical, irreverent, ineffectual, and sad—is portrayed as "an interesting and laudable figure . . . who in his travels to every latitude of the entire globe . . . found nothing sublime and everything perfectly ridiculous, grotesque, coarse . . . in other words, human" (*HU*, 63). His dilemma mirrors that of Ionesco after *Nu* earned him the reputation of a critical gadfly. Referring to the caricaturist's attempts to do serious painting which his public refused to take seriously, Ionesco observes, "Yes, the world forges you a personality that in the long run ties you down, suffocates you, strangles you. . . . In this life everything depends on the first step you take. . . . You are not allowed to retrace your steps and set out on a different course, the world needs to confine you once and for all within the bounds of a simple definition, brief and final" (*HU*, 65–66). Some 30 years later, Ionesco would be frustrated by similar "typecasting" when a public finally accustomed to his "antiplays" would not forgive him for turning to more personal and serious themes in his theater.

In the Preface to the French translation, written when he too had experienced the mercurial nature of literary fame, Ionesco excuses *Hugoliad* as a youthful "exercise in mischief" (*HU*, 8). Nonetheless, this "antihagiographic monument" as the French translator calls it, conveys, as do many passages in *Nu*, genuine outrage at intellectual pettiness enlivened by a sense of the absurd, both linguistic and social, and by Ionesco's singular capacity for rendering incongruous human behavior in dialogue form. Not yet masterpieces of Ionescan "antiart," *Nu* and *Hugoliad* offer appealing evidence of Ionesco's potential as an absurdist *moraliste* with a remarkably fine eye for the fuzzy border dividing the ridiculous from the tragic.

Chapter Three
Memoirs and Personal Journals

In *Fragments of a Journal* Ionesco offers this justification of literature: "One cannot get to know anyone through conversation, nor even by taking his hand, nor even by walking close beside him. It is only through another's writing, that's to say his confession . . . that communion can be achieved" (*F,* 87). This is the guiding spirit of his published journals. Like Gide's journals, they were not meant to be "supplemental documents." Ionesco had a reader very much in mind as he wrote and arranged these pages where fragments of memories, self-portraits, confessions, polemics, short pieces of fiction, literary criticism, and spiritual reflections mingle kaleidoscopically.[1] He was 10 when he made his first attempt at keeping a diary, a project abandoned after 2 or 3 days. Taken up again in his adolescence, it became a lifelong enterprise. As an aspiring writer in Romania, inspired by Gide and *The Confessions of St. Augustine,* Ionesco vaunted the superiority of the journal to the novel, to drama, and to poetry because it allowed a "true story" to be told with "a thousand and one beginnings that stay beginnings, adventures barely underway, undertakings cut short, aborted tragedies, groundless anguish . . . an accumulation of episodes free of all coherence, not presenting themselves as the bases for a grandiose esthetico-logical edifice" (*N,* 262–63).

"Printemps 1939: Les Débris du souvenir. Pages du journal" ("Spring 1939")

In the spring of 1939, Ionesco was in France. He was supported by a fellowship for completion of his doctoral thesis but was far more concerned with current events in Paris than with the nineteenth-century French poets he had proposed to study. Europe was suspended in an unpromising hiatus that held neither realistic hope for peace nor the political will for all-out war, in spite of the German invasion of Czechoslovakia in March. Ionesco was deeply affected: "As the ship goes down I live through my own fears multiplied. . . . this universal death is my own death."[2] About to turn 30, he was also halted in what seemed an unpromising interval between a dilettantish existence as a critic in Romania and a hoped-for mature literary vocation that remained without focus. His prospects for a serious career as a writer began to seem more and more elusive, as France and Romania were being radically affected by the sweep of fascism and the threat of war.

Visiting France for the first time since his departure at age 13, he was "tormented by nameless longings for things I have lost for ever, which I have never had, never seen; I have never even known what they were" (*CP,* 131). Hoping to salvage meaningful remnants of his childhood, he returned to La Chapelle-Anthenaise. "Spring 1939," which was not published until 1962—when it was included in a collection of his short stories—is a record of that return. It is also a blueprint for his future writing. His principal themes, many of them already broached in the essays in *Nu,* begin to take a definite shape here: preoccupation with the limits of language and memory, nostalgia for the timelessness of childhood, fear of aging, obsession with death, reflections on war and violence, and longing for some kind of salvation, at this point still a more literary than metaphysical pursuit.

At the time of his return to La Chapelle-Anthenaise, Ionesco was considering writing an autobiographical novel. "Spring 1939," in which fragments of memories are recast as a barrier against time, suggests that the novel would have been a Proustian one. Beginning with the farm gate that opens to Ionesco's memories like the tinkling garden gate at Combray that signals to the narrator of *À la Recherche du temps perdu (Remembrance of Things Past)* that time and memory can be recovered through literature, there is much that is evocative of Proust in Ionesco's highly visual account of "memories, mingled with present impressions . . . fragmentary and haphazard" (*CP,* 127). As the gate opens to Le Moulin and recollections of the broad grid of country roads, paths, rivers, and streams that gave a safely circumscribed world a magical boundlessness, Ionesco reconstructs his childhood in a series of *tableaux vivants.* He brings to life a whole cast of village characters: farmers, fellow boarders, schoolmates, railroad workers, poachers, the village priest, the schoolteacher, the local count, and the "red" blacksmith. Although he claims to be daunted by the challenge of putting into words the light of childhood, he succeeds remarkably in recapturing the magical textures of the light and colors of rural France. Ionesco has noted that his taste for violent and aggressive colors was acquired at La Chapelle-Anthenaise. The blue and gold of his Sunday suit, the intense blue of the summer skies, golden fields, and poppies as brilliantly red as the burst of fireworks at a village celebration dazzle in these pages against the strong white of a church steeple lit by the sun, a first communion dress, or the blossoms of a hedge. Factual memories have inevitably faded in the 20-year interval—"There's nothing left but the kindness without the people, like Lewis Carroll's grin without a cat"—but the luminosity of these years seems undimmed in these pages. Landscapes and portraits are rendered with a clarity of affect and image belying Ionesco's discouraged characterization of himself as an archeologist digging through the ruins of ruins. In the final pages he acknowledges that perhaps these lost treasures are not entirely lost: "the sign that these things are alive is this distress, this cherished and unendurable anguish" (*CP,* 146).

Journal en miettes: Images d'enfance en mille morceaux (*Fragments of a Journal*)

Ionesco had turned 50, "bearing the heavy weight of time, like an ass's burden," when he began writing the pages that make up *Fragments of a Journal.* An "exploration in the tangled impenetrable forest in search of myself," *Fragments,* like "Spring 1939," reflects nostalgia for a paradise outside the mortal confines of time (*F,* 116). Both journals open with evocations of La Chapelle-Anthenaise. In contrast to the image of a bridge and an open gate at the beginning of "Spring 1939," however, the first paragraph of *Fragments* introduces limits, a village never visited, autumn with the old roof of the mill lost in fog. Ionesco portrays himself as a writer "cut off from myself, my deeper self no longer supplying sustenance to my mind" (*F,* 63).

In *Fragments,* as in *Nu,* he aggressively stakes out his position as an outsider. His darkest "political" plays, *Jeux de massacre* (*Killing Game*), *Macbett,* and *Ce formidable bordel* (*A Hell of a Mess*), were still a few years away, but the events that inspired them—the conflicts in Algeria, Vietnam, and the middle east, and the Soviet repressions in eastern Europe—were very much on his mind. His political assessments were angry. They were also alienating. French liberals are categorically dismissed in *Fragments*: "spouting justice and charity they practice a shocking, petty-bourgeois, Leftist meanness," whereas the right wing, according to Ionesco, "had the courage of its hates, did not profess any absolute moral claims" (*F,* 146). *Fragments* also reflects an intensifying struggle with the issue of salvation. Ionesco, who had avidly consulted an array of spiritual texts that included *The Tibetan Book of the Dead,* Eastern mystics, Hasidic writings, and, again and again, *The Confessions of St. Augustine,* poses the question: "Are we unique beings, that's to say immortal, since that which *is* only once *is* for all time, or are we merely the receptacle for anonymous forces which combine and join within us and then are severed and dispersed?" (*F,* 70–71). Fundamentally averse to the notion of anonymity, he rejects the materialist hypotheses that accept it. Only Judaism and Christianity, he proposes, "have the audacity to be personalist" (*F,* 71). Neither, however, offered a fully satisfactory solution to someone unable to "detach myself from this world or from the other . . . afraid of making a wrong choice . . . I choose neither religion nor politics" (*F,* 28). In *Fragments* he chooses instead a psychoanalytic approach, exploring his dreams as the key to the mysteries of the human psyche. "I incline to think," he writes, "that the language of dreams . . . contains an unquestionable, living truth" (*F,* 34). Although passages in *Fragments* reflect a surprisingly reverent application of Freudian imagery and theory, Ionesco ultimately preferred Jung to Freud because "Jung does not ban religion" (*F,* 60).

Fragments of his dreams compose a significant portion of this journal, some analyzed by Ionesco, others by his analyst, some simply recorded, but all tendered as a means to self-understanding and proof that, given the archetypal nature of dream imagery, Ionesco's "case" has universal significance. Elements of these dreams reappear in many of his plays, particularly the colorful sensations of euphoria and lightness, images of damp, sinking houses and unscalable walls and mountains; family conflicts; and the unsavory father figure Ionesco calls Shaffer or Schaeffer. The dream at the source of *L'Homme aux valises (The Man with the Luggage)* is presented in detail. Compared to the plays there is little "life" in these recorded dreams. Flat and obsessional in the context of the journal, they underscore the extent to which Ionesco's themes were enriched by the physical resources of the stage.

When *Fragments* was published in 1967, although he was still refusing to acknowledge the theater as his "real work" or his "true vocation," Ionesco was already a world-renowned playwright (*F,* 24). *La Soif et la faim (Hunger and Thirst)* was in rehearsal for a production at the Comédie Française as he was writing the last entries to be included in the journal. The play's title captures the thrust of *Fragments.* At the pinnacle of his career, the persistent questioning of his role in the larger human comedy and his morose sense of the accelerating degradation of body and mind had only become more pressing. "I am at the age when you grow ten years older in one year, when an hour is only a few minutes long. . . . yet I still run after life in the hope of catching it at the last minute" (*F,* 21). *Fragments* is a compelling, if sometimes disconcerting, canvas of a complex literary temperament—nostalgic, polemical, and metaphysical—a kind of twentieth-century Don Quixote tilting obstinately at existential windmills. Ionesco describes having been overwhelmed for the last 15 years by an "enormous weariness." Although no doctor had been able to diagnose its cause, he attributes it to "that perennial doubt, that 'What's the use?' that seems to have been rooted in my mind all my life and that I cannot get rid of" (*F,* 24). This journal courageously reveals a man who is not always admirable but who dares to make "What's the use?" a genuine question and not a signal for capitulation.

Présent passé passé présent (Present Past Past Present)

In 1967, Ionesco recovered a diary that he had kept from 1940 to 1942, his last years in Romania. *Present Past* juxtaposes passages from the early journal, written when he was feeling like "the last man in the monstrous island . . . an anomaly, a monster," with the observations of the 58-year-old writer, whose state of mind in the late 1960s was alarmingly similar to that of his younger self (*PP,* 113, 26).

In the 1940s, trapped in Romania for lack of a visa, Ionesco turned in his diary to his childhood years in France. *Present Past* contains some of his most poignant early recollections of his family, including outings with his father, whose physical characteristics he can scarcely remember and whose face he says he has forgotten, as well as portraits of his more clearly registered mother, remembered as occasionally laughing, but more often anxious and despairing. In these vignettes—Sunday excursions, late nights at the cinema, a children's home where he stayed during a particularly difficult time—and especially in the descriptions of the varied light of Paris and its suburbs, many of the key elements in Ionesco's theater can be identified. By recreating the light effects of a scene barely remembered otherwise, perhaps half-imagined, Ionesco conveys the quality of childhood memories that are indelible yet blurred.

Moments of "lost" childhood come forward and recede, flashing like the magic lantern show remembered in the opening pages. Like the small boy who cries out "Again!" when the projected image is taken off the screen, he grasps at the images he fears losing to darkness: "Childhood is over the moment that things are no longer astonishing. You keep the memory, the nostalgia of a present, of a presence, of a plenitude that you try to rediscover by every possible means. Rediscover it or the compensation" (*PP,* 174). One of his compensations was to transform existence with words, making his words, as usually only children can, into astonishing worlds.

Four humorous, very short stories—later collected as *Contes pour enfants de moins de trois ans (Stories for Children under Three Years of Age)*— were written in the 1960s and interspersed among the generally anguished memories and reflections in *Present Past.* These stories recapture, if only fleetingly, that capacity for wonder.[3] Ionesco's use of the word "compensations" is important. Even these flights of fancy where words, like surreal trampolines, seem so easily to launch the little heroine and her father beyond constrictive realities can make only partial poetic restitution. The humorous use of the fantastic in these tales is close in spirit to Ionesco's early absurdist theater. A destructive adult irony bores into the childlike verbal magic. Each tale involves a caricatured, Freudian family triangle modeled with affectionate irony on Ionesco's own. A free-spirited fabulist who is also a weary daddy with Rabelaisian appetites for food and drink and his 33-month-old daughter, Josette, an eager little "Electra," subvert the protective conventionality of the mama and her prosaic surrogate, the maid Jacqueline, by escaping into phantasmagoric word worlds. The omniscient narrator's matter-of-fact account mimics the narrative style of classic fairy tales, but his comic mania for minute detail and unblinking presentation of the preposterous strongly suggest the presence of Ionesco.

In the first tale Josette is delivered by the maid, along with the morning paper, the mail, and an exaggeratedly copious English breakfast, to her weary parents, who are suffering the consequences of an evening that took them to a restaurant, the theater, back to the restaurant, to a puppet show, and again to the restaurant. Unable to get rid of her, Daddy sweeps Josette into a world that has taken its cue from the proliferating Bobby Watsons of all ages and sexes in *The Bald Soprano* and the families of Roberts and Jacks in *Jack, or the Submission.* He tells a story about a little girl who is named Jacqueline, as is everyone and everything else in her surroundings: mother, father, cousins, aunts and uncles, and friends of both sexes, as well as wooden horses, lead soldiers, and dolls. Daddy goes back to sleep; Josette stays in her new world. Meeting a little girl named Jacqueline while shopping with the maid Jacqueline, she states categorically, as the other shoppers stare in wide-eyed alarm, "I know. Your daddy's name is Jacqueline, your mama's name is Jacqueline, your brother's name is Jacqueline, your doll's name is Jacqueline, your grandpa's name is Jacqueline, your wooden horse is named Jacqueline, the house is called Jacqueline, your little potty is called Jacqueline" (*PP,* 34). To reassure the other shoppers, the maid Jacqueline explains, "it's the stupid stories her father tells her" (*PP,* 34). Josette, who is as much an alter ego for Ionesco as her daddy is, must parry the "reasonable" world that lurks, fearful and disdainful of fantasy, ever ready to impose the safety net of a rational explanation.

The humor in the second tale is more sadistic and oedipally layered. Mama and Jacqueline are both away. Able to woo her daddy undisturbed, Josette pesters him to open the door to the bathroom, where he is dressing. Suffering once again from overindulgence, Daddy dispatches his daughter, not with a fairy tale but by persuading her that he is no longer there. During a game of hide-and-seek in which Josette appears to be less an accomplice than a victim of her father's conjurations, she runs frantically from room to room, searching under tables, behind bookcases, in cupboards, in pots and pans, under the mattress, and in Daddy's pants pockets. Finally, fully dressed, he emerges like a surprise from a magician's hat ready to embrace his worthy little offspring, for whom the imaginary is not a separate reality.

The third tale is a variation on the theme developed in *Le Piéton de l'air* (*A Stroll in the Air*). From the warmth of his bed, where he is recovering as usual from nocturnal excesses, Daddy invents a fantastic Sunday outing that lofts father and daughter beyond the practical caveats issuing mechanically from Mama, Jacqueline, and the concierge. Flying over the zoo and La Chapelle-Anthenaise, they reach the moon, which tastes like melon. Josette adds sugar, but Daddy cannot because he has diabetes. When they reach the sun, the plane melts, simultaneously with Mama's arriving to tell them to get out of bed and chastising her husband for ruining Josette's mind with his "silly little stories." Briefly, however, the magical words have taken Josette beyond the contagious fear that if she soars, she must fall.

In the fourth tale, a world symbolized by the intrusiveness of the telephone is recreated in Magritte-like fashion by renaming its contents, starting with the "telephone," which is declared to be a "cheese." As Daddy teaches Josette the "right meaning of words," the "cheese" becomes a "music box," the "rug" a "lamp," the "ceiling" a "floor." Only one term remains absurdly sacrosanct, perhaps because Ionesco was already hard at work on his illustrations for *Découvertes.* "Pictures" are still called "pictures." However, as he explains, sounding much like the Professor in *The Lesson* expounding upon the comparative philology of the indistinguishable neo-Spanish languages, "You mustn't say 'pictures,' you must say 'pictures' " (*PP,* 137).

With the world satisfactorily rearranged, the last of the *Stories for Children* ends on a conciliatory note. Mama, who had gone out early in the morning, stylishly dressed in her "pretty dress with flowers . . . her pretty coat with flowers . . . her pretty stockings with flowers" and "with a beautiful bouquet of flowers in her hand," returns at the end of the story, "her eyes like a flower, her mouth like a flower" (*PP,* 136, 138). She is not assigned her usual deflationary role. Asked about her outing by her husband, whose "aside" in the second tale suggests that he has some reason to wonder about her absences, she answers: "picking flowers," to which Josette responds, "Mama, you opened the wall" (*PP,* 138).

There is a similarity here to the ending of Ionesco's only novel, *The Hermit,* where the flower-patterned walls of the narrator's confining bedroom melt away, revealing a promising vision of a luminous, flower-covered meadow and a suspended silver ladder. Rarely, however, do the many walls that appear in Ionesco's dreams and writing open up. Only the imaginative innocence of children, a state so dimly remembered in adulthood as to be almost impossible to recapture, can open the walls that haunt Ionesco. What is true of many fairy tales is also true of Ionesco's. Although childish wonder can open the wall, which is a recurring symbol of death in his dreams and theater, an adult world encroaches upon the enchanted gardens.

Much of *Present Past,* like much of *Fragments,* focuses on political antipathies and metaphysical concerns. In 1940 Ionesco had written, "Ideologies are mad, everybody is an ideologue, everybody is passionately, fanatically ideological. . . . Ideologies are crises" (*PP,* 43). The 1967 commentary reprises this theme, denouncing the leftist "isms" of the day, particularly Marxism, existentialism, and structuralism, as abstractions and hypocritical tyranny. Ionesco's venom can be attributed in part to personal rivalry and some bitterness provoked by fear that his dramatic career had peaked. It was also motivated by political concerns. Attacking slogans and intellectualized justifications for fascist conversions in the 1940s, he made distinctions that remained fundamental to his perspective. "Humanity does not exist," he insisted. "There are men. Society does not exist. There are friends" (*PP,* 79). The metaphor of the rhinoceros, made famous by the play *Rhinoceros,* is first developed in the journal pages from the 1940s where the "new master of the city" is described as a rhinoceros for whom "the concrete person is a phantom."

He "uses the same words as you and yet it is not the same language" (*PP,* 67, 79). In 1967, faced, he believes, with a similar situation, Ionesco writes, referring to the language of his political foes, "It is not a new sort of thought, not a new language, but a clever manipulation of terms so as to create confusion in the minds of their adversaries, or to get those who are undecided on their side" (*PP,* 67–68). He returns again and again to the Arab-Israeli conflict, which troubled him to the point where he was unable to create. Defending Israel's cause, he denounces the use of doublespeak to promote a new wave of intellectually justified antisemitism among those who claimed to uphold Israel's right to exist but sided with the Arab states out of solidarity with their socialist programs and Russian ally.

Early in his career, Ionesco had turned his writing into a forum for the defense of the individual. The more complex question of how to define and sustain the notion of the individual is a dominant theme in *Present Past.* Enraged in the 1940s at "feeling lost in the formless paste of the multitude" but confronted at the same time with the loss of all that he has valued, Ionesco examines the need for an "essential unity" binding individuals and civilizations (*PP,* 122). "To be oneself does not prevent one from being universal," he proposes, negatively contrasting Otto Spengler's philosophy of culture, which denies the possibility of a universal history with the "universalist" French mentality (*PP,* 105). In 1967, he is still struggling with this issue. He recasts it in the light of his confrontation with the "intellectuals," as he dismissively labels a gamut of leftist thinkers that includes Sartre, Claude Lévi-Strauss, Lucien Goldmann, Roland Barthes, Michel Foucault, and the theater critic Bernard Dort. Ionesco insists that the depersonalizing collectivism promoted by contemporary literary, sociological, and political theories is the legacy of "both Communist totalitarianism and the totalitarianism of certain forms of Nazism" (*PP,* 115).

Découvertes (Discoveries)

Published in 1969, *Découvertes* might best be described as polemical memoirs. It is also a moving description of Ionesco's stake in his literary career as a protection against the "paradoxically heavy void" of existence (*D,* 93). Unique among his personal essays, *Découvertes* was illustrated by Ionesco with a series of childlike black and white lithographs. Primitive to the point of seeming almost scribbled, they convey a compelling dramatic intensity. Many of these illustrations are self-portraits in which he appears as a jester king wearing an outsized crown. One of the most striking images is a stark drawing in which a large female figure with blackened eyes like burned-out suns bends powerfully over a small, male figure. His round, wide, startled eyes, like those of the woman his only facial feature, stare out in another direction. He may be looking for the kind of image depicted below a cometlike, astonished eye in another drawing, a phantasmagoric black suggestion of a foundering ship vaguely "crossed out" as though meant to yield to the gentler image of the rocking shape beneath it. "A faculty for astonishment which allows me to get out of this whirlwind and reinstate myself in my true place, in immobility" is the caption accompanying the eye (D, 75).

Among the discoveries referred to in the title are an infantile apprehension of the world and language and the finding of his vocation. Literature was a means of redemption from the calamitous discovery of human mortality and difference. At age 7, looking in a mirror, he "relived the original sin": "I saw that I was naked . . . that I was not the others, that I was not like the others" (D, 84). All the others, he imagined, were comfortably alike; he alone was of "an entirely different species . . . isolated in his non-resemblance" (D, 84). The revelation of his vocation, according to a focal and very appealing anecdote, came as early as the assignment of his first schoolboy composition—written, astoundingly, in the form of a dialogue. The momentous event is remembered as a source of some anxiety but primarily as an extraordinary empowerment and freedom. The tools of his imagination would no longer come from the outside world, but would "spring forth" from within: "it was I who was going to reveal myself . . . appear in the world, place myself there" (D, 90–91). Writing was also associated with lightness. He compares himself about to write this first composition to a parachutist ready to throw himself into dazzling space, a sensation later ascribed to several of his alter egos in his theater, although none of these characters finds the mystical sustenance that seemed promised to the excited schoolboy.

Découvertes expresses outrage at contemporary "scientific" critics, whose "methods of prospection" include "depth psychology, sociology, political systems, linguistics, structuralist or not," and who presume to know more about creative processes than the artist knows (D, 9). There was a time Ionesco recalls when poets were believed to be inspired by voices from on high. At present, he claims, those voices are assumed to issue "from down below, from the cave crawling with all sorts of instincts or insects, toads, or from obscure passions, inhibited tendencies

. . . that only the projector of the new criticism can illuminate" (*D*, 10). He is particularly repelled by the notion, widely accepted among contemporary linguists, that thought is entwined with language and can neither precede nor avoid it.[4] Instinctively heretical, Ionesco attempts to prove the contrary. This is not the kind of almost gratuitous battle that he waged in *Nu*. What principally motivates his quarrel is that, by the late 1960s, he has become in his own way an "engaged" writer, someone driven to preserve art as a metaphysical quest. (Unwilling to embrace a term with Sartrian connotations, he would no doubt have preferred the term "antiengaged"). Vigilant in his defense of the individual imagination and its spiritual requirements, he disputes the postmodernist dismissal of the creative "I" and represents language as "being in the image of the universal Manifestation which expresses the thought, pre-existent, of God" (*D*, 44).

It is not Ionesco's linguistic "theories" that are compelling here but the intensity of his yearning for spiritual "proofs" (which he does not expect to materialize) and the eloquence of his plea for the freedom of the imagination. What can be explained did not engage him. Writing, he believed, is "an absolute solitude which questions itself," a theme he expanded upon in his inaugural address to the French Academy (*D*, 121). From the work of Jean Paulhan, whose Academy "chair" he was elected to fill, he quoted to the assembly that it is not " 'to be elegant and witty . . . nor to be right, nor to give plausibility to theses that are palpably false' " that one writes but " 'to be understood . . . to be saved.' "[5] Literature for Ionesco was too precious a source of "original" truth to be delivered over to political or "historical" ends, or even to professional writers, a category distinct from artists in his mind. "What would literature be if it were only a telegram or an editorial?" he asks (*D*, 103). Certainly not what he both wanted and needed it to be: "the restitution of the inexpressible" (*D*, 96).

La Quête intermittente (The Intermittent Quest)

Ionesco's last published personal journal was written during the summer and autumn of 1986, much of which he spent in a convalescent home. It is the work of a depressed man, panicked at the approach of death, who is attempting to explain why "it is less and less ridiculous to believe in God" (*QI*, 89). The earlier intuitions of plenitude, or the "universal presence" as he sometimes calls it, have yielded to the void. The catastrophe of age and memory loss is experienced as an unsettling confrontation with transparent faces, "empty face surrounded by oval frames" (*QI*, 33). Contrasted with depictions of the Edenic fullness of La Chapelle-Anthenaise where "everyone, and everything, had a face. . . . Everything was personalized, concrete," the description in *Quête* takes on particular poignancy (*CP*, 17).

At the end of *Découvertes*, Ionesco tells how his first childish questions about what was all around him and who he was had turned into the more tormented question "Why am I here, surrounded by all this?" (*D*, 121). Secular answers had been unsatisfying and by the time of *Quête* the "strange and dramatic or tragic sentiment that everything is illusion, that there is not reality" that has tortured him for so long leads him to address those same questions to God (*QI*, 96). The religious quest in these pages is sometimes as childishly awkward as it is intermittent. Fully aware of this, Ionesco, at one point, ridicules his efforts as beating with a shovel on what he thought was the heavenly ceiling only to discover that it was merely "the floor of the next level" (*QI*, 154). He does not minimize the need for the effort, however: "If I didn't want Heaven, then why these incomprehensible, bitter and profound nostalgias that destroy my life?" (*QI*, 155).

Once his primary means of "salvation," writing has become only "therapeutic" and is meant to yield to faith. The change was not made easily, perhaps, finally, not at all. He was determined to concentrate on his soul and the problem of eternity—"Eternity. Not Immortality. It's not enough, immortality" (*QI*, 137). Much of the journal consists, nonetheless, of "intermittences," the reflections of a writer "more preoccupied with literary glory, with what I want to leave to the living, the dying of tomorrow" (*QI*, 165). Ionesco plays halfheartedly with words and phrases and describes suffering from boredom, jealousy, and a myriad of physical complaints. He worries about his finances and his diminishing creative capacities, fearing that he will never be able to write another play and that the colors of his paintings will grow dim. Several anecdotes, some of them heartbreakingly trivial, some a familiar refrain, bear witness to frustration at no longer being a major participant in the literary fray. He expresses irritation at having to spell his name for a telephone operator, whereas once the automatic response to the name would have been to ask, "Like the author?" Comparing himself to Gide, he portrays himself as a victim shunted aside for his anticommunism. He claims a plot by political enemies (a list now including not only familiar foes but even British drama critic Martin Esslin) to minimize his role in the history of the theater of the absurd. Desperate to prove that absurdist theater started with him, he occasionally denigrates both the art and character of its other major voices: Arthur Adamov, Edward Albee, Harold Pinter, Tom Stoppard, and, especially, Samuel Beckett, whom he accuses of being "too lucid, too cold, too calculated, and of "creating style" with the misery of the world" (*QI*, 73). In a discouraged state, he reflects with apprehension rather than pleasure on an upcoming revival of *Amédée*, apprehensive that critics will find it "outdated," and "not nearly as good as Beckett" (*QI*, 97). He also fears comparison of Amédée's unpleasant spouse to his own wife, to whom many pages of *Quête* are addressed in an act of contrition and affectionate praise. Rosette Lamont has astutely interpreted this book as "a deeply touching public love letter" to Rodica Burileanu in the form of a journal (Lamont, 1993, 170).

In his last years, Ionesco was still anxious to affirm his uniqueness, hoping that "when I no longer exist, the world, after me, will be a little altered, it will be missing what I reflect or what I refract" (*QI*, 52). By this time, however, his individuality required a stronger reconciliation with his desire that his existence also have a universal meaning. The resolution offered in *Quête* is a pessimistic one: "Each one is alone (or solitary), all are alone (solitary), each one is thus like everyone else" (*QI*, 64).

Chapter Four

Essays on Literature, Politics, and Art

Rosette Lamont and Melvin Friedman gave the very fitting title *The Two Faces of Ionesco* to a collection of scholarly articles addressing both Ionesco's well-known prankish side and his affinity for polemical metaphysics.[1] The "second" Ionesco, more familiar to the leftist critics and intellectuals whom he vigorously castigated than to the general public, emerges sharply in the collections of his essays on literature, politics, and art published as *Notes and Counter Notes, Antidotes, Un homme en question,* and *Le Blanc et le noir (White and Black)*. Most of Ionesco's polemical pieces could be given the title of one of his successful short plays: *Délire à deux autant qu'on veut (Frenzy for Two or More)*. "First-person" documents, they round out the material in the personal journals and clarify the extent to which his artistic development reflected the preoccupations of a passionately engaged world citizen.

Notes and Counter Notes: Essays on the Theater

The speeches, interviews, critical essays, newspaper articles, and program notes gathered in *Notes and Counter Notes* were written between 1958 and 1961. When it was published, Ionesco had been a "man of the theater" for roughly a decade. He gives a synopsis of his career as progress from "a tiny failure, a minor scandal" with *The Bald Soprano,* to something "a bit more resounding" with *The Lesson,* to even greater importance after the performance of *The Chairs* for a nightly audience of "eight disgruntled people," then 10 successful "flops" permitting him to predict confidently that such "failures" should soon lead to "a positive triumph" (*NCN*, 224).

These "notes" coincide with Ionesco's liveliest years in the theater. The phenomenon of theater of the absurd was still new and Ionesco's version of it still controversial enough to be provocative to conservative audiences and Brechtians alike, a satisfying situation for a writer who proclaimed that the "two dictatorships that threaten us" are "routine" and "dogma" (*NCN*, 231). The political left had challenged him to write "committed" theater. In 1958, when Kenneth Tynan urged him to move beyond "that bleak new world from which the humanist heresies of faith in logic and belief in man will forever be banished," Ionesco responded that "art is the realm of passion, not pedagogy" (*NCN*, 32, 89). He viewed theater as a kind of survival kit for the individual "cut off from his most deeply repressed desires, his most essential needs, his myths, his indisputable anguish, his most secret reality and his dreams" (*NCN*, 223–24). The essays in *Notes and Counter Notes* range across a broad personal and literary terrain but are all anchored in the conviction that there can be no art without metaphysics.

Ionesco examines the links between tragedy and comedy on the one hand and reality, dreams, and the imagination on the other, attempting in the process to salvage language and theater from didactic warping. He defines his themes as "obsessions, or anxieties. They are the same for everyone. Art is only possible because it is founded on this identity" (*NCN*, 129). As much a self-portrait as an analysis of the theater, *Notes* is also a lively introduction to these anxious obsessions by an Ionesco still quick to remind both himself and his critics that "to take things too seriously is to build prisons, to be inquisitorial, didactic or boring, to make wars and to kill" (*NCN*, 125). Much of the material constitutes a "Defense and Illustration" of an illogical, physical theater. Sharing the disdain for psychologically oriented drama that Antonin Artaud (1896–1948) had so forcefully expressed in his revolutionary manifesto, *Le Théâtre et son double (The Theater and Its Double)*, Ionesco cites the need for theater to find its domain in the realm of dreams, paroxysmal violence, and extravagance. Words must be worked up to a frenzy, "language should almost break up or explode in its fruitless effort to contain so many meanings" (*NCN*, 29). Acknowledging that "Artaud had something to say about that," he also calls for a theater which can be compared to an architecture, "a moving structure of scenic images" (*NCN*, 29). Unlike Artaud, however, he is fundamentally a man of words for whom a play emerges "more like a linguistic idiom than action, since it springs from a lyrical state of mind" (*NCN*, 137).

Ionesco's challenge to the theater, as to all of society, is to get rid of "language that congeals as soon as it is formulated" (*NCN*, 92). "Lessons," he claims, "are given in order to lead us by the nose and conceal from us the complexity of truth and all its contradictions" (*NCN*, 127). In the name of their various revolutions, the "intellectuals" with whom he contrasts himself had fostered alienation by masking human pain with labels, slogans, and dehumanizing historical theories. "No society," he reminds his readers, "can abolish human sadness, no political system can deliver us from the pain of living, from our fear of death, our thirst for the absolute" (*NCN*, 91). His definition of "revolutionary" excludes ideology: "Any new artistic expression enriches us by answering some spiritual need and broadens the frontiers of known reality; it is an adventure, it is a gamble, so it cannot be a repetition of some already classified ideology" (*NCN*, 102).

Antidotes

By the late 1960s and early 1970s, Ionesco's literary and critical contexts had broadened considerably. The speeches, interviews, journal excerpts, and articles (many of which originally appeared in the conservative *Le Figaro,* the newspaper whose critic had repeatedly lambasted his early experimental theater) published in 1977 in a volume entitled *Antidotes* touch upon a considerable portion of the globe. The subjects considered range from politics to religion, euthanasia, theater, and language. Whether he is deploring the Chinese destruction of Tibet or Russian hegemony in eastern Europe, or criticizing contemporary literary trends, Ionesco's fundamental message remains the same. From the opening essay "Oser ne pas penser comme les autres" ("To Dare Not to Think Like the Others") through such typical entries as "Le Fascisme n'est pas mort" ("Fascism Is Not Dead"), "Le Mirage de la révolution" ("The Mirage of the Revolution"), and "Toute la culture a été faite par les ennemis de la culture" ("All Culture Has Been Created by Enemies of Culture"), he vents his frustration with his growing isolation and condemns politicians and artists who "in the name of so-called revolutionary or counterrevolutionary ideologies prevent creative liberation, the free development of the imagination" (*A,* 178).

    The pieces in *Antidotes* correspond to a time when Ionesco's widely broadcast contempt for the revolutionary styles and ideologies of the 1960s and 1970s had inexorably distanced him from the leftist Parisian avant-garde. Although he defends his position with a familiar litany, insisting that he was "born disobedient," that "solitude is not isolation. . . . it's a shield," and flaunts his "bitter satisfaction at never having been a dupe," he is nevertheless distressed (*A,* 76, 274, 11). With characteristic candor, he admits, "Literary success, if I have it I scorn it. If I don't have it, I suffer" (*A,* 195). The humor and self-irony that balance *Notes and Counter Notes* is noticeably absent from most of these essays. The hyperbole is as unappealing as it is unsubtle. He lashes out at youth, repeatedly accusing them of being hypocritical, ignorant, spoiled, and even fascist. He cynically imagines the restoration of a monarchy and defends the right of the Jews to commit atrocities. *Notes and Counter Notes* is a lively work, driven by an enthusiastic individualism. *Antidotes* is to a considerable extent a cold war document reflecting the tunnel-vision combativeness that journalistic debate tends to elicit.

Antidotes is interesting primarily for the light it sheds on the increasing politicization of Ionesco's theater in the 1960s and 1970s and as an attempt to define what might be truly revolutionary in literature if that term could be separated, as he insisted it must be, from ideology. Wondering why others refuse "to dismantle these systems of clichés . . . which constitute their ready-made philosophy like ready-to-wear clothing," he pursues the argument begun in *Nu* that imagination can only be liberated when language is free (*A*, 11). More earnestly than many of his critics in the 1970s were willing to acknowledge, Ionesco was still searching for "a new surrealism . . . more powerful still, more liberating," having rejected "an irrational or an absurd that had become comfortable" (*A*, 257). Although he did not generally respond favorably to the revolutionary events of May 1968, the dadaist poetic anarchy and spontaneous theatricality of the student revolt struck resonant chords. He tells of being drawn by the "beauty" of one of the students' slogans: "It is forbidden to forbid" (*A*, 151). His rallying cry, from a 1976 speech, is "No orders to be given to those who create" (*A*, 178). It is a message that retains its urgency, given humankind's appetite for "tidy" political solutions.

The fundamental question in *Antidotes* is a metaphysical one: "Why the horror?" (*A*, 325). The deepest human need, he insists, is for religion. "Otherwise, it is catastrophe, despair, death" (*A*, 191). To support his argument, he seeks to reclaim Beckett from the "young philosophers" who have dismissed Ionesco but identify Beckett as one of their own.[2] Noting the importance for both himself and Beckett of the metaphysical weight of Dostoevski and Kafka, he objects, not unjustly, to characterizations of Beckett as a kind of schizophrenic victimized by a capitalistic modern society. Contending that it is not from a social or political condition but an ontological one that Samuel Beckett suffers ("a favorable social condition could only attenuate a little the fundamental malaise of being in the world"), Ionesco defines the thrust of his own best theater as well (*A*, 189).

Un homme en question (A Man in Question)

Un homme en question, published in 1979, brings together previously published interviews and journalistic pieces. The self-righteous negativity that characterizes much of *Antidotes* is tempered here by a growing spiritual crisis. Ionesco, who was struggling with medical problems and a severe depression and had turned to autobiography, dreams, and psychoanalytic themes in his theater, minimizes the importance of his political plays. He argues that humanity has not been thoroughly "despiritualized" and that it remains "eschatological" in spite of an excess of politics (*HQ*, 45). Articulating his own situation as a conflicted sense of betrayal and longing vis-à-vis God, he assumes the role of a modern Job, the virtuous *Old Testament* figure seemingly capriciously singled out by God for a cruel test of faith. "I feel like Job," he announces in the interview that opens *Un homme,* "and I am stopped at the fundamental question of 'what is wanted of me?'" (*HQ*, 12). In the final essay he asserts that "we are all 'Jobs'" (*HQ*, 213).

Job has been a recurrent figure in modern literature as a symbol of the alienated individual faced with a multitude of incomprehensible afflictions. Like Sartre and Camus before him, Ionesco is not far from Job when he proposes that "our first reproach to our Creator should be " 'Why don't we understand? Why are we obliged to accept this game? . . . Why are we made to not understand?' " (*HQ*, 19).[3] Sartre and Camus, convinced that there would be no answer from on high, elaborated philosophical responses that challenged each individual, not God, to create and validate the rules of existence. Ionesco and Beckett, more typical of the generation of absurdist playwrights, remained in their different ways obsessed with the absent Creator. Beckett, whose entire work Ionesco had aptly described as "agony, a long groan, the image of human impotence, our refusal to assume the Creation and our state," refined that "long groan" into works that became increasingly tight and inhuman (*A*, 209). Ionesco, ever ready to engage in combat, issues a challenge to both the Creator and his creation. He identifies not with the Job who finally submits to God's will but with the outraged Job who resisted conventional wisdom, the temptation of suicide, and the overwhelming clout of authority, insisting on bringing God to trial.

The overarching theme of *Un homme en question*—reflected in titles such as "Délivrons-nous de nos idées" ("Deliver Us from Our Ideas"), the ideas in question being Marxist ideology; "J'accuse" ("I Accuse"), charging French intellectuals with betraying fellow writers; "Contre les metteurs en scène" ("Against Directors"); and "Le Monde est invivable" ("The World is Unlivable"), a black account of spreading world violence—is that of betrayal. Ionesco objects to the "modern heresy" that accords more importance to the director than to the author. He is infuriated by the treacherous conduct of UNESCO, the French Writers Society, and the International Theatre Institute, which he believes have betrayed dissident eastern European writers in the name of an abstract solidarity with Marxism. Contemplating his long career as a writer, he feels betrayed by literature and even by success. "I always had false goals. Adolescent, it was the absolute I was looking for . . . some kind of hidden, comforting evidence, and I was swallowed up in literature" (*HQ,* 92). He also recognizes, in a return to one of his earliest themes, that language is also to blame for the "betrayal" of his literary vocation: "The words that I pronounce are simple and banal and cannot capture this profound and authentic anguish that, paradoxically, only the astute and sublimated artifices of literature can express. I am caught in the inexpressible" (*HQ,* 92).[4]

There is presumption in Ionesco's identification with Job. There are also legitimate parallels, particularly with Job's stand when, abandoned and stigmatized by his friends and even his formal Advocate for refusing to espouse their conventional wisdom, he remains defiant. Although he flaunts it less than in other contexts, Ionesco was already savoring the left's progressive disaffection for the repressive policies of communist governments which was vindicating his unpopular political predictions. The fact that the opening interview was conducted by Philippe Sollers and Pierre-André Boutang, among those referred to in *Antidotes* as "intellectual terrorists," is indicative of a significant evolution in his status among French intellectuals. Having first denied in this interview looking for answers in religion, he retracts the claim, but explains as he does so that religion as he has experienced it is "too much of this world . . . represented by Job's three friends who tell him 'you have committed a sin, you are proud. Bend yourself to the law' " (*HQ,* 15). *Un homme* illustrates Ionesco's continued skepticism about getting a fair hearing. It also emphasizes his unwillingness to capitulate. Reflecting on the contributions of Rimbaud, Baudelaire, and Tristan Tzara, and of dada, futurism, and surrealism, he observes that the more cultural traditions are denied, the more they are enriched.

Le Blanc et le noir (White and Black)

Late in his life, weary of words which could neither assuage his anguish nor fulfill his spiritual needs, but still clinging to "the insane hope" for some kind of epiphany, Ionesco turned to painting, an activity he had not pursued seriously since illustrating *Découvertes*.[5] *Le Blanc et le noir*, published in 1981, is a meditation on this new vocation, which accompanies a series of his lithographs. Examining his totemlike renderings of pathetic clowns, guignolesque kings and tyrants (there is even a rhinoceros), moribund figures, unearthly trees, and occasional, triumphant flowers, he recognizes familiar struggles in the images and the play of light and color on the canvas: "Politics, ideology, faith, without words, abstracted. What bothers me is that I cannot draw a woman's head. Only the heads of men, so very monstrous. Too masculine, my drawing, the demonic and the dreadful reign there. How can one describe, without figures, grace?" (*BN*, 14). The preoccupation with good and evil that dominates much of his writing in the 1970s and 1980s emerges in his paintings in the aggressive roles he assigns to colors. "I have learned," he explains, "that in the confrontation between black and white, white resists, but a little black in a corner is more violent than the white. . . . The brutality of black is terrible. If, in the middle of a black page, I put a blue circle or design, the blue is swallowed up by the black tide. . . . Orange resists better. If I do a black head, I have to make the eyes red, a dark, wicked red, it goes with the black, but at a great price, it sustains it, becomes its slave" (*BN*, 9–10).

Ionesco's interest in the plastic arts dated from his student days when he wrote art criticism for his lycée magazine. During the 1930s he contributed several articles about artists to Romanian periodicals, including two enthusiastic essays on Van Gogh in 1937, the first of which bore the title "A Madman Who Could Have Been a Saint." In Paris, Ionesco's many artist friends included André Masson (1896–1987) and Joan Miró (1893–1983), both of whose influence is evident in his drawings. The art criticism that he continued to write in Paris tended to single out qualities matching his own ambitions for theater. An "anecdotal portrait" of the sculptor Constantin Brancusi (1876–1957), a fellow Romanian expatriate, pays high tribute to the imperviousness to history and intellectualism evidenced in the seeming simplicity of Brancusi's sculptures: "He had assimilated the whole history of sculpture, had mastered, transcended and rejected it: rejuvenated, purified and reinvented it. He had extracted its very essence" (*NCN*, 262–63). Writing about the painter Gérard Schneider, he extolled "an objective vision of the world, discovered through his own deeply subjective experience, in other words in a spirit that reflects the world or is itself in the world's image" (*NCN*, 271). A 1980 essay on the paintings of Saul Steinberg (1914–) and Richard Lindner (1901–1978) highlights in Steinberg's work "an essential irony, both acid and melancholic," and in Lindner's its forceful-ness as an act of protest. His description of Lindner's painting mirrors much of his own stage imagery: "Heavy, terrifying, tragic, ugly, carica-ture going beyond caricature. . . . the world, humanity is there, ponder-ous, weighing on him, the painter has discovered a kind of true beauty in ugliness."[6] An exception to Ionesco's denigration of the post-1960s generation of experimental directors was his unstinting praise for Robert Wilson. In his enthusiasm for Wilson's capacity to transform the stage into a painting where the physical imagery becomes a language com-plete in itself, Ionesco declared that "every director ought to be a painter."[7]

His claim that he had "neither a master nor a manual" is suspect since he had art lessons as a student in Bucharest. It reflects nonetheless his resolve to return by means of painting to the creative spontaneity of his first experiments with antitheater (*BN*, 24). The lithographs in *Le Blanc et le noir* recall his early plays by their ironic, grating, comic effect and by the startling, dreamy blend of the figurative with the abstract. Comparing his drawings to his first play, which was meant to be "the tragedy of language" but turned into a black comedy, Ionesco acknowl-edges that he is a "naively comic artist": "With time and experience I would be tempted by the tragic, happily it is only comical, . . . comical forms of evil" (*BN*, 44).

In *Present Past Past Present*, Ionesco spoke of being "lost in the thou-sands of words and unsuccessful acts that are my life, which take my soul apart and destroy it" (*PP*, 168). During his last years, substituting colors for words, he achieved at least an intermittent respite from this anguish. His painting, which he described as an odd carnival, "a greased pole with surprise favors attached to each branch," revived his capacity to return to a state of naive wonder at the forms and colors of the world. (*BN*, 44). "Colors, and nothing but colors, are the only language I can speak," he wrote in *La Quête intermittente*. "They are of this world and it seems they link me to the Other World. I rediscover in them what the word has lost" (*QI*, 13).

Part 2. Antitheater

Chapter Five
Ionesco and Theater of the Absurd

In an essay in *Nu* entitled "False Causality," Ionesco dismisses the theater because plays are created from effects he compared to the strong beat in music. They eliminate all the empty, inessential, or "wasted" moments that constitute a real existence. He summarizes a "typical" tragedy: "Act I: The toe is exposed. Act II: They show the knee. Act III: We get to the navel. Act IV: Unveiling of the chest. Act V: And here we are at the bald spot" (*N*, 259). Two "strong beats," he argues, are effective only when connected by the "creative vitality of . . . those moments when nothing happens" (*N*, 258–59). By the early 1950s Ionesco had figured out how to create effective theater almost entirely from such moments. Along with a number of other playwrights, most notably Samuel Beckett, Arthur Adamov, and Jean Genet, he was transforming the French stage with plays that eschewed plots, psychology, identity, coherent dialogues, linear time, traditional distinctions between comedy and tragedy, and concern with either instructing or amusing the audience.[1] These plays have become widely known as "theater of the absurd," after the title of a groundbreaking study published in 1961 by British drama critic Martin Esslin. An understanding of Ionesco's links to this revolutionary theater of the 1950s and 1960s is critical to an appreciation of his evolution as a playwright. It was as an author of this kind of theater that he became best known. He wrote his most exceptional plays during his "absurd" period and later gave a unique dimension to his more serious theater by carrying absurdist elements into it.

Esslin's book, *The Theater of the Absurd,* underscores the striking resemblance of this theater to depictions of existential alienation and despair by Sartre and Camus, encapsulated in the latter's definition of the absurd as "that divorce between the mind that desires and the world that disappoints, my nostalgia for unity, this fragmented universe and the contradiction that binds them together."[2] Although Esslin's is the most widely recognized label, many others have been applied, correcting to some extent the overly philosophical connotations of his description. In France these plays are typically referred to as "théâtre nouveau" (new theater) or "avant-garde theater." The military connotation of the latter term appropriately emphasizes the combative nature of exploratory dramatic works which were detached from the theater mainstream by means of aggressive application of irony, parody, and disarticulated language. Ionesco's contention that "every work is either aggressive or else demagogic, commercial," reflects the guiding spirit behind much of this theater (Bonnefoy, 1971, 91). These plays have also been referred to as "theater of cruelty," a recognition of the link with the dramatic theories of Antonin Artaud, as "metaphysical farce," and as "theater of derision."[3] Ionesco found "theater of derision" a particularly appropriate label, although he adopted the appellation "antitheater" for his early plays and offered the only partly facetious insight that the essential characteristic of the new drama is its newness."[4] It may be George Wellwarth's term "theater of protest and paradox" that best describes Ionesco's theater as a whole.[5]

Sartre, who referred to these plays as "critical theater," maintained that the label "theater of the absurd" was itself absurd because none of its practitioners "regards human life and the world as an absurdity."[6] Sartre's dismissal notwithstanding, there are significant links between these plays and the existentialist notion of the absurd. When Ionesco says, for example, that it is because his characters "are given no clue as to the road to take" that "they wander in the dark, in the absurd, in incomprehension, in anguish," he is both describing essential elements of the new theater and speaking in a Camusian voice (*A*, 316). He expressed admiration for Camus's work on many occasions, although he came to believe that the latter's nonspiritual humanism could not work because it had no roots. Principally, however, it was his esteem for Sartre's 1938 novel *La Nausée (Nausea)* that prompted his acknowledgement that "perhaps, in certain aspects of our writing, we link ourselves to Existentialisms."[7]

Roquentin's existential crisis in *Nausea* is portrayed as a stripping away of the immunity provided by routine and linguistic convention. He makes the humiliating discovery that his existence is superfluous, that he is isolated in an amorphous, viscous, obscene—because it is unjustifiable—brute existence. Ionesco's characters, many of whom, like their author, can never quite get used to existence, and thus struggle in the metaphorical mud of psychic conflicts, could easily accommodate Roquentin in their midst. In one of his most frequently cited descriptions of his theater, Ionesco explains, in almost Sartrian terms, "All my plays have their origin in two fundamental states of consciousness . . . an awareness of evanescence and of solidity, of emptiness and of too much presence, of the unreal transparency of the world and its opacity, of light and of thick darkness" (*NCN*, 162). This statement points at the same time, however, to a fundamental difference in perspective. Ionesco's anguish was susceptible to leavening by a state of astonishment. He once cited as his two "strongest" reasons for writing "that others should share my amazement and my wonderment at life, at the miracle of the world; and that our cry of anguish should be heard by God and by our fellow men, so that they should know we have existed" (*Plays, XI*, 134). His penchant for the fantastic and inclination toward mysticism, contrasting with the despiritualized world of Sartre and Camus as well as the theater of Beckett and Adamov, allies him more closely with the surrealists than with the existentialists.

One of the most significant differences between absurdist theater and existentialism lies in the response to the apparent gratuitousness of existence. In *Nausea*, for example, Roquentin's experience of the absurd as a "frightening and obscene nudity" is ultimately intellectualized.[8] Tamed, then covered over with words which allow him to both understand and possess his nausea, it becomes a springboard for revolt. In absurdist theater, the endless physical and psychological humiliation that constitutes human existence has eliminated the dignity fundamental to revolt. Adamov's expressed goal: "to tear way all the dead skin, to strip oneself to the point of finding oneself at the hour of the great nakedness," is central to the theater of the absurd.[9] When Estragon's pants fall to his ankles in *Waiting for Godot* or when Adamov's Professor Taranne slowly undresses on stage as the curtain falls, unable to find the word that could successfully defend him against the charge of appearing naked on the beach, neither the character's nor the spectator's reaction is cerebral. It is a very gut-level embarrassment and discouragement. Ionesco places the theme of existential nakedness in a slightly different context. Rejecting Kenneth Tynan's contention that human existence is primarily defined by social function, he draws an example from his military service, supposing that "when my lieutenant and my boss are back in their homes, alone in their rooms, they could, for example, just like me, being outside the social order, be afraid of death as I am, have the same dreams and nightmares, and having stripped themselves of their social personality, suddenly find themselves naked, like a body stretched out on the sand, amazed to be there and amazed at their own amazement" (*NCN*, 108). It is in this solitude, according to Ionesco, that they would most resemble him.

Promoting commitment as an "antidote" to the absurd, Sartre and Camus used their theater as a moral showcase. "The most moving thing the theater can show," Sartre wrote in 1947, "is a character creating himself, the moment of choice, of the free decision which commits him to a moral code and a whole way of life" (Contat and Rybalka, 1976, 4). Absurdist theater, in contrast, is peopled with somnambulists: vulnerable, confused, interchangeable, Everyman figures not destined to complete their journeys. Freakish metamorphoses and cyclical structures substitute for emotional and intellectual development. Ionesco's first plays, for example, end where they begin. The guests in *The Bald Soprano* replace their hosts at the end of the play, ready to regurgitate the string of banalities that has just been played out. The end of *The Lesson* replicates the opening moments, as the young pupil who will be the professor's next murder victim rings the doorbell. The frequency in this theater of repetitive patterns and inconclusive endings reflects the pessimism that was widespread in postwar Europe. During the war years there had appeared to be "wrong" and "right" sides and an identifiable goal. The less easily categorized hostilities of the cold war and the toll taken by propaganda, clichés, and the endless doublespeak of modern politics and commerce sapped a vital confidence in the communicative powers of language. Words became increasingly alienating, if not alien, objects. The absurdist theater, which Ionesco referred to as a "revised version of the adventure of the Tower of Babel," reflects this linguistic debacle (*NCN*, 249).

An experience linking several of the absurdist playwrights was that of being a linguistic outsider. Beckett, who wrote in both French and English, was an unhappy self-exiled Irishman. Adamov was an Armenian whose family had been frightened into exile during his youth. Ionesco was a Romanian citizen during his first years in France. Too much can be attributed to their foreignness, particularly because all were extraordinarily fluent in French. Ionesco insisted, moreover, that he would have felt as much an outsider no matter what culture he had been attached to "because it is in this entire strange, incomprehensible universe that I feel like I don't belong."[10] Nonetheless, these "Parisians" by adoption kept French at an emotional distance by treating it as a writers' language.[11] Because their passion for French literature had been nourished in part by revolt against fathers and fatherlands, they preserved a wary eye for potential fraud in both ordinary language and literary monuments. At the same time, as writers, they confronted the dilemma of loving and needing words but finding them fragile and subversive. Beckett's characters wait and talk endlessly in a world that their words can neither arrange, change, nor interpret. Genet's characters act out murderous charades in unsuccessful attempts to achieve authenticity. Adamov's characters operate on such different affective planes that they are deaf to one another although their words run on and on. In Ionesco's plays, matter and words proliferate in a bludgeoning, geometric progression.

Suspicion of linguistic conventions led these playwrights to translate the experience of alienation into a stunningly physical, instinctive theatrical experience, communicating the visceral quality of loneliness and anguish with a force that intellectual analysis could not match. They supplemented or replaced the spoken word with a "stage language," inspired by mime and the physicality of commedia dell'arte, Punch-and-Judy shows, the circus, vaudeville, and silent cinema. Because their theater required an acting style described by Ionesco as "at once more natural and more exaggerated, something between a realistic character and a marionette . . . something strange and unusual about the natural, something natural about the strange and the unusual," they also drew upon a half-century of rebellious dramatic and literary experimentation largely precipitated by *Ubu roi (Ubu the King)* by Alfred Jarry (1873–1907) and then sustained by the spirit of dada and surrealism (*NCN,* 250).

In 1896, Jarry staged the grotesquely fat Père Ubu and his equally large and ignominious wife as "real-life" marionettes. Joyously lying, blaspheming, murdering, and pillaging their way through a parody of *Macbeth,* the characters savaged the mores and politics of the French Third Republic. Jarry held up Ubu to spectators as a mirror image, "an ignoble creature, which is why he is so much like us all (seen from below)."[12] Speaking a language that wraps stupidity and crudity into a kind of outrageous Rabelaisian poetry, as hilarious as it is alarming, the Ubus created a liberating blueprint for undermining naturalistic theater. Jarry also put Elizabethan stage techniques to revolutionary parodical use. He hung a horse from an actor's neck, for example, to designate equestrian scenes because he found crowd scenes "an insult to the intelligence," and he adopted exaggeratedly stylized gaits, masks, and voices for the Ubus. Ionesco had been "spellbound" by Punch-and-Judy shows as a child, finding there "the very image of the world . . . strange and improbable but truer than true, in the profoundly simplified form of caricature, as though to stress the brutal nature of the truth" (*NCN,* 20). As an adult, he had been put off theater by flesh-and-blood characters on stage because "their physical presence destroyed the imaginative illusion" (*NCN,* 17).[13] The *Ubu* plays offered him a compatible and fertile model for revolutionizing the theater.

Jarry's attack on conventional theater dialogue and imagery was renewed in 1917 by Guillaume Apollinaire (1890–1918) in *Les Mamelles de Tirésias (The Breasts of Tirésias),* a play that has echoes in many of Ionesco's early sketches and short plays.[14] *Tiresias* is set in Zanzibar, the entire population of which is represented by a single character. Tirèsias's wife, the cubist-inspired, blue-faced Thérèse, departs to pursue traditionally male-associated occupations as her red and blue balloon breasts fly off into the auditorium. Her husband takes over for her. Dressed in Thérèse's clothing and amid much clowning and animation of stage properties, Tirésias announces that he has given birth in a single day to 40,049 children. Apollinaire's refusal in the Preface to decide whether or not his play is serious pointed the way to the theater of the absurd. So did his seminal definition of a "surrealist" act, which he proposed as a model for a new theater: "When man wanted to imitate walking he created the wheel, which does not resemble the leg."[15]

The surrealists appropriated and then expanded the meaning of Apollinaire's evocative term. Surrealism had its early roots in Dada, a confrontational, nihilistic, artistic movement born in neutral Zurich during World War I. Heavily influenced by Nietzsche, the dadaists, led by Ionesco's compatriot Tristan Tzara and the German Hugo Ball, revolted against the supposedly rational society responsible for the horrors of this war. Unleashing the creative forces of unreason and anarchy, by means of prankish black humor, outrageous exhibitionism, and an irreverent approach to language and artistic subject matter, they sought to accomplish what Ionesco would later claim as the ultimate goal of theater: the revelation of the monstrous. As dada's capacity to be shocking and spontaneous wore out, the surrealist movement, officially founded in 1924 by André Breton (1896–1966), took over much of its revolutionary agenda. The surrealists were more concerned with freedom than with destruction, however, and they steered away from dada's nihilism. Spurred by Freud's discoveries about dreams and the unconscious and by their interest in the marvelous and the occult, they charted a course into psychic domains where the boundaries between conscious and unconscious worlds dissolved into a richer reality, revealing the fantastic lurking beneath the mundane. They promoted chance encounters among words, images, and objects; the irrational creativity of dreams and madness; eroticism; and the anarchic potential of humor.

Because the surrealists "officially" rejected theater after brief early involvement with ephemeral dadaist productions, the two writers who most directly contributed surrealist dimensions to the absurdist theater, Antonin Artaud (1896–1948) and Roger Vitrac (1899–1952), were officially expelled from the movement.[16] Vitrac's *Victor, ou les enfants au pouvoir (Victor, or the Children in Power)*, unsuccessful in 1929, ultimately became the only surrealist play to survive as a French "classic." *Victor* provided a model for the unsettling combination of tragedy and comedy in absurdist theater. Vitrac's precocious, 6-foot-tall Victor, who dies of disgust with adult hypocrisy on his ninth birthday, attempts to shield himself against a sleazy world by "speaking surrealist," poetical nonsense that unmasks with stinging comedy the clichés and moral mendacity of "normal" adult conversation.[17] He has a fleeting physical accomplice in the ethereal Ida Mortemart, a mysterious creature as extraordinary for her flatulence as for her beauty. Her inexplicable appearance intrudes on the vulgar world of Victor's parents with the same revelatory force as Victor's subversive language. There are avatars of both Victor and Ida Mortamort in Ionesco's theater.

Artaud sought a stage revolution as far-reaching and uncompromising as any surrealist demand for altering the notion of reality. True theater, like the plague, he claimed, "invites the mind to share a delirium which exalts its energies . . . impelling men to see themselves as they are, it causes the mask to fall, reveals the lie, the slackness, baseness and hypocrisy of our world."[18] In *The Theater and Its Double,* a series of essays published in 1938, he envisioned theater as a ritualized "poetry of space which will be resolved in precisely the domain which does not belong to words," a language composed of "all the means of expression utilizable on the stage" (Artaud, 1958, 38–39). He wanted to end theater's dependence on dialogue and psychology, calling instead for a modern version of the Wagnerian *Gesamtkunstwerk,* a "total spectacle by which the theater would recover from the cinema, the music hall, the circus and from life itself what has always belonged to it. . . . One does not separate the mind from the body nor the senses from the intelligence" (Artaud, 1958, 86).[19] Such a spectacle would make room for "real humor," which Artaud defined as "a sense of laughter's power of physical and anarchic disassociation" (Artaud, 1958, 42). Above all it would have the capacity to confront the theatergoer with the "true precipitates of his dreams" (Artaud, 1958, 92).

The absurdist playwrights objected to critics' attempts to place an Artaudian grid over their work. They had not needed Artaud to discover in popular entertainments and ritual the almost hallucinatory pratfalls and rhythms which they transformed into such convincing depictions of human disconnectedness. The influence of *The Theater and Its Double* was nonetheless pervasive, particularly its emphasis on the mise-en-scène as a concrete language and the demotion of theater dialogue from the position of a realistic centerpiece to that of a tragicomical, reified object. Reissued in 1944, Artaud's manifesto caught the attention of a new generation of playwrights and young directors eager to break with the prewar theater. Ionesco described his own theater as an attempt "to exteriorize, by using objects . . . the anguish of my characters, to make the set speak . . . to translate into concrete images terror, regret or remorse, and estrangement, to play with words (but not to send them packing) and even perhaps to deform them—which is generally accepted in the work of poets and humorists" (*NCN*, 104). His definition of the essence of a new theater and rationale for its existence were also Artaudian: "farce, the extreme exaggeration of parody. . . . Everything raised to paroxysm, where the source of tragedy lies. . . . we need to be virtually bludgeoned into detachment from our daily lives, our habits and mental laziness, which conceal from us the strangeness of the world" (*NCN*, 26).

The absurdist playwrights, as was also true for Artaud, did not share the surrealists' optimism. "Contemporary art," Ionesco observed, "is in great measure, the reserve, the museum of our despair" (*HQ*, 67). Nevertheless, their rejection of logic and "normal" linguistic behavior in favor of dreamlike or hallucinatory language and stage properties, and their reliance on subversive humor to effect an explosive reaction between the physical and the metaphysical made their theater "surrealizing" in effect if not in direct intent.[20] Sounding much like Breton in one of his *Manifestos,* Ionesco proposed that "freedom of imagination is not flight into the unreal, it is not escape, it is daring and invention. . . . The way is barred only when we find ourselves within the narrow confines of what we call some dreary 'thesis' or realism" (*NCN*, 82). In 1951, Breton saw *The Bald Soprano* and proclaimed that Ionesco had achieved what the surrealists had attempted to create 20 years earlier.[21]

Chapter Six

Surprising Truths

La Cantatrice chauve (*The Bald Soprano*)

In 1948, according to a story which Ionesco enjoyed retelling, he was diligently copying phrases from an English-language manual when he became distracted by the "surprising truths" being uttered by its very English protagonists, the Smiths and the Martins: that there are 7 days in the week, for example, that the ceiling is above the floor, and "an Englishman's home is his castle" (*NCN*, 175–76). Such revelations, not rare in language manuals, were not the sort of thing to be shrugged off by someone with as many misgivings about language as Ionesco. He found the apparently empty phrases pregnant not only with fantastic humor but with "all that is automatic in the language and behavior of people . . . talking because there is nothing personal to say, the absence of any life within, the mechanical routine of everyday life, man sunk in his social background, no longer able to distinguish himself from it" (*NCN*, 180). The verities of the conversation manual took on an increasingly alarming existence, evolving into *The Bald Soprano*, where "the words had turned into sounding shells devoid of meaning; the characters too, of course, had been emptied of psychology and the world appeared to me in an unearthly, perhaps its true, light, beyond understanding and governed by arbitrary laws" (*NCN*, 179).

With a temerity reminiscent of *Nu*, Ionesco showed his manuscript first to the administrator of the Comédie Française and then to an editor at a major publishing firm who assured him that it would never reach the stage (*HQ*, 187). Fortunately, a friend put it into the hands of Nicolas Bataille, a very young and talented director whose small company fell immediately under its spell. *The Bald Soprano*, whose performances would number in the tens of thousands by its twentieth anniversary, opened in the unprestigious 6:30 P.M. time slot at the Théâtre des Noctambules in the Latin Quarter. The theater had been lent rent-free for the occasion. The actors were in borrowed costumes and the skimpy set consisted of second-hand furniture. Other than the surrealists, only a few open-minded critics appreciated its wild black humor and the discomfort it caused the scattering of "serious" spectators who had bothered to come. "I never remember without pleasure," wrote Jacques Lemarchand, "the murmurs of discontent, spontaneous indignation, insults, which greeted the appearance of *The Bald Soprano*. I had spent an extraordinarily pleasant evening, made all the more agreeable by the grunts and ironic laughter of the notables in the audience."[1] As no funds were available for publicity, the play was largely ignored in spite of the heroic efforts of Ionesco and his friends to advertise by parading in the streets with sandwich boards. It closed almost immediately, and the playwright and his actors stood accused by a drama critic writing for the conservative newspaper *Le Figaro* of driving potential audiences away from the theater.[2]

The "serious" French theater at the time was dominated by the highly literary plays of Sartre, Anouilh, and Henri de Montherlant (1986–1971), in which moral and intellectual theses held sway. This is not the case for *The Bald Soprano,* where the curtain rises on a conventional middle-class living room to the sound of an "English clock" striking 17 "English strokes." Mrs. Smith, who is darning "English socks," announces in a monotonous, self-satisfied tone to Mr. Smith, who is sitting in an "English armchair" wearing "English socks" and reading an "English newspaper": "There, it's nine o'clock. We've drunk the soup, and eaten the fish and chips, and the English salad. The children have drunk English water. We've eaten well this evening. That's because we live in the suburbs of London and because our name is Smith."[3] The clock, which becomes increasingly cavalier in its approach to linear time, is more spirited than Mr. Smith. He responds mostly by tongue clicking to several more such utterances by Mrs. Smith, who reports, for example, that "yogurt is excellent for the stomach, the kidneys, the appendicitis, and apotheosis" (*FP,* 10). Mr. Smith does come to life when he reads an obituary notice for a Bobby Watson. This event launches one of the most comical examples in Ionesco's theater of depersonalization by means of repetition and proliferation. A contradictory tangle of vaudevillesque non sequiturs lasting for nearly three pages in which the name Bobby Watson is mentioned repeatedly, reveals that all the many Watsons, young and old, male and female, are named Bobby Watson and that they are all commercial travelers. The deadpan exchange introduces a distinctly Ionescan world where the outlandish is accepted without question; only the utterly mundane elicits astonishment.

The Smiths are relayed on stage by the Martins who arrive, too late in any case, in response to a dinner invitation that may or may not have been extended. Endowed like the Smiths with a surname so common as to drain rather than sustain identity, the Martins are younger versions of their hosts but are situated at the opposite pole of an absurd compass. Mrs. Smith knows exactly what her middle-class world holds and she can list it: not only English soup and a pipe-smoking husband with a newspaper, but two children, a boy and a girl of course, a maid named Mary, greengrocers, and a whole universe of Bobby Watsons that eliminates the necessity for pondering existential dilemmas. The Smiths are so excessively ensconced in their "English" existence that their "reality" oozes into an uncomfortable, meaningless mass. The Martins, on the other hand, seem to issue from a vacuum. In what has become a classic absurdist scene, left alone on stage awaiting the return of the Smiths, they conclude with agonizing laboriousness and with the stiff uncertainty of a couple on a blind date that, because they have taken the same train car (on which they had facing seats) from Manchester, because they live at the same address in London and in the same apartment, because they sleep in the same bedroom, and especially because each has a daughter with one red eye and one white eye, they must be Donald and Elizabeth, husband and wife. The recognition scene, a parody of the climactic moment in melodrama, is punctuated by an exaggeratedly monotonous chorus of "How strange," "How curious," and "How bizarre," and by Mrs. Martin's affectless refrain: "It is indeed possible but I do not recall it, dear sir." The scene ends abruptly when they embrace without passion and fall asleep in the same armchair. This is the cue for the entrance of Smith's maid, Mary, who is also, as she informs the audience, Sherlock Holmes. She tiptoes on stage to whisper that Elizabeth and Donald are not in fact husband and wife, because Donald's daughter has a white right eye whereas Elizabeth's daughter's white eye is her left one. "Thus," she announces directly to the audience, "all of Donald's system of deduction crumbles when it comes up against this last obstacle which destroys his whole theory" (*FP,* 19). The Martins' identity disintegrates in a paroxysm of nonidentity as effectively as the Smith's did in platitudinous convictions.

When the Smiths return, the couples face one another, first in a long "embarrassed silence" broken by hemming and hawing and Mr. Smith wetting his pants—proof, he claims, that "the heart is ageless," then in a conversation that becomes a comically appalling reflection of boredom, hostility, and absurdity (*FP,* 20). They are rescued by an unexpected hero. After Mrs. Smith has opened the door three times in response to a ringing doorbell, to find no one on the landing, and has deduced—with the kind of specious logic Ionesco loves to parody—that "experience teaches us that when one hears the doorbell ring it is because there is never anyone there," Mr. Smith, triumphantly proving her wrong, opens the door after a fourth ring and produces a Fire Chief in full regalia (*FP,* 23). Fires being in short supply, the Fire Chief stays to entertain. His stories, typified by his Aesopian "experimental moral fable" told with inflated emotion, about a dog who swallowed his trunk because he thought he was an elephant, are no less nonsensical than those of his hosts. The Fire Chief recognizes Mary as the one who "extinguished my first fires," prompting a second, but this time exaggeratedly emotional, melodramatic recognition scene. Mary, oblivious to the menacing objections of her employers and in a highly comical literalization of the "heat of passion," stands firmly out of her place as a maid in this very English living room and passionately recites a dadaist poem entitled "The Fire" in honor of the Fire Chief. She is finally pushed offstage by the indignant Smiths, but her poetic conflagration has released language from its halter of habit and cliché. Mary's poem achieves the kind of linguistic liberation that the dadaists and surrealists admired in *The Songs of Maldoror,* by Lautréamont (a pseudonymn for Isadore Ducasse [1846–1870]), where, according to André Breton, "it is all over for the limits to which words can enter into a relationship with other words or things with things."[4]

Expected at a fire that will be breaking out in "exactly three-quarters of an hour and sixteen minutes," the Fire Chief takes his leave, thanked by Mrs. Martin for a "truly Cartesian quarter of an hour" (*FP,* 37). His parting inquiry about the Bald Soprano provokes embarrassed silence, finally broken by Mrs. Smith's reply that she always wears her hair the same way. It is at this point that the blaze sought earlier by the Fire Chief breaks out, not in smoke and flames but as an explosion of words. Left to their own devices, the Smiths and the Martins are swept into a very post-Cartesian quarter of an hour. As the erratically striking clock marks the tempo for the breakdown of language and logic, the conversation breaks up into a hostile crossfire of nonsensical aphorisms, neologisms, non sequiturs, puerile obscenities, the days of the week recited in English, "choo choo train" noises, and the grunted sounds of empty but menacing letters and syllables. When the stage lights are finally extinguished, the Smiths and Martins, all furious, are screaming at each other, repeating in an accelerating rhythm: "It's not that way, it's over here" (*FP,* 42–43). The lights come on again and the play starts over mechanically with the Martins, who have replaced the Smiths, reciting the opening lines from the first scene. In a world where language is reduced to nonsense and contradictions, "over here" can just as easily be "over there."

Language, and all the human qualities it represents, has turned into a dehumanized mechanism which assaults the spectator. This process has been captured with remarkable congruence in a typographical "performance" of *The Bald Soprano* created in 1964 by Henri Massin.[5] Massin depicts the verbal exchange between the Smiths and the Martins immediately following the Fire Chief's departure first as parallel lines of absurd aphorisms that go off from each character's head at an angle without intersecting. As the violence comes closer to the surface, Massin enlarges the type and fires the lines across and on top of each other, but keeps the text legible. Just before the communicative ability of the two couples disintegrates, Massin levels a single line of text which effectively blasts into bits the remnants of language. Images of the detached heads of the four characters appear to be exploding from a dysfunctional centrifuge. A note from Ionesco, printed in the corner of the last page of Massin's text, applies to stage performances as well. The playwright affirms that what might appear to be simply a linguistic disaster should be experienced as an all-encompassing catastrophe (*TC,* 1928).[6]

The Bald Soprano was unique in Ionesco's career. Created in collaboration with a gifted director and innovative actors at perhaps the only time in his career when he was truly open to others' experiments with his work, it evolved considerably during the rehearsals, which he regularly attended. According to Bataille's recollections, the actors first approached it as a farce but discovered that a serious tone intensified its unsettling combination of humor and anguish. In the original version, the play had no ending. Ionesco proposed that a dadaist ruckus of protest be created in the audience, which would bring on first the theater manager and then the Superintendent of Police, who would open fire on the spectators. This was rejected as too complicated and too expensive (since it would require more actors). It would also require a "certain amount of courage" (*NCN,* 185)! His suggestion that he appear on stage himself to insult and threaten the audience was deemed inappropriate to the "stylized production and 'dignified' performances desired by the actors" (*NCN,* 185). Since no solution could be found, they decided to simply begin again. After some 100 performances, the Martins were substituted for the Smiths as the play ended to accentuate the depersonalized state of these cliché-bound automatons (*NCN,* 180–81). The title also emerged from a rehearsal. When Ionesco gave Bataille the script, it was entitled *L'Anglais sans peine (English Made*

Easy), but he and Bataille agreed that this would be too suggestive of a simple pastiche. A slip of the tongue by the actor rehearsing the role of the Fire Chief turned "a very blond prima donna" into "a very bald prima donna." The laughing cast recognized an ideal title.

The Bald Soprano rapidly became a model for experimental French theater in the 1950s, a "pure drama," according to Ionesco, "anti-thematic, anti-ideological, anti-social realist, anti-philosophical, anti-boulevard-psychology, anti-bourgeois, the rediscovery of a new free theatre" (*NCN*, 181). His later claim that he was surprised to hear spectators laughing when this play was first performed, because he thought he had written "something like the tragedy of language," was disingenuous: the rehearsals had been punctuated with laughter (*NCN*, 179). *The Bald Soprano* remains one of the most popular and effective absurdist plays precisely because it loosens hilarious laughter before it produces the embarrassing apprehension that, like Jarry's *Ubu* plays, it is holding a mirror up to the spectators. Its continuous run since 1957 in tandem with *The Lesson* at the Théâtre de la Huchette provides a rare opportunity to experience theater in one of the tiny, shoestring theaters, now nearly all defunct or converted to movie houses, where the theater of the absurd came into existence. At the same time, turning it into a monument ritually performed by a formally constituted actors' association with enough members to simultaneously create exactly the same production anywhere else in the world, has done some disservice to a play intended to be a satirical undoing of conventional theater. *The Bald Soprano* may one day require an irreverent dada mustache like the one Marcel Duchamps applied to the "Mona Lisa," but the continued full houses at the Huchette prove that it is not yet in danger of losing its fascination.

La Leçon (The Lesson)

When "thought is made in the mouth," as Ionesco's dadaist compatriot Tristan Tzara argued had become the norm, there is much license for satirical humor.[7] There is also peril, as *The Lesson* illustrates. It was written in 1950 shortly after the opening of *The Bald Soprano,* at the request of Maurice Cuvelier, director of the small, underfunded Théâtre de Poche in Montparnasse, who needed a play requiring very few actors and minimal staging. When Cuvelier staged it in February 1951, the response was much the same as to *The Bald Soprano.* A friendly critic predicted: "When we are old, we shall bask in the glory of having seen performances of *The Bald Soprano* and *The Lesson.*"[8] The public, however, stayed away from both.[9] Those who did find their way to *The Lesson* anticipating the parodies and crumbling logic of *The Bald Soprano* were not disappointed, but they were also confronted by a more somber vision. *The Lesson* introduces the tyrannical distortions of language, physical violence, degraded sexuality, and the fascist father figure and hybrid mother-mistress-maid characters that would become increasingly familiar to Ionesco's public.

At the beginning of the play, a confident 18-year-old girl (in the dramatis personae she is designated as "the young pupil" and is typically played as very young and naive) arrives at the home of an aging, provincial professor to prepare for the "total doctorate." The lesson, which takes place in a nondescript study that contrasts comically with the startling events, soon founders. The young pupil can do addition without difficulty and can multiply 3,755,998,251 times 5,162,303,508 in an instant, because she has memorized "all products of all possible multiplications" to compensate for her unreliable powers of reasoning. She cannot learn to subtract, despite the professor's repeated efforts with imaginary chalk on an imaginary blackboard and his comically sinister warning: "It's not enough to integrate, you must also disintegrate. That's the way life is. That's philosophy. That's science. That's progress, civilization" (*FP,* 55). The pupil must settle for the "partial doctorate." The preparation launches the professor, who becomes progressively lewd and abusive, into a philology lesson as wildly distorted by preposterous facts and mangled clichés as the conversations in *The Bald Soprano.* Sounds, the professor explains, must "become filled with warm air that is lighter than the surrounding air so that they can fly without danger of falling on deaf ears, which are veritable voids, tombs of sonorities" (*FP,* 62). The fundamental principle of the linguistic and comparative philology of the indistinguishable "neo-Spanish languages" that he has promised to teach in 15 minutes, is that they are so closely related as to be "considered true second cousins. Moreover, they have the same mother: Spanishe, with a mute *e*" (*FP,* 64).There is no innocent language in Ionesco's theater. "Philology," as Marie, the professor's maid, warns repeatedly, "leads to calamity." The linguistics lesson is increasingly eroticized. "To project words," the professor informs the pupil, "sounds and all the rest, you must realize that it is necessary to pitilessly expel air from the lungs, and make it pass delicately, caressingly, over the vocal cords, which, like harps or leaves in the wind, will suddenly shake, agitate, vibrate, vibrate, vibrate or uvulate, or fricate or jostle against each other" (*FP,* 63).

The lesson degenerates into undisguised sadism as the professor comes brazenly to life, taking over language like an unscrupulous politician. Enraged by the increasingly passive pupil's agonized chorus of "I've got a toothache," he seizes a "Spanish, neo-Spanish, Portuguese, French, Oriental, Rumanian, Sardanapali, Latin and Spanish" knife (either real or imaginary) and initiates what the stage directions describe as a kind of scalp dance as the exhausted, weeping pupil moans and clutches caressingly at her body, her hand descending graphically from her neck to her stomach. His back to the audience, he stabs the girl and shudders in orgastic relief.[10] Fending off his attempt to attack her with the knife, Marie scolds him into a state of childish contrition and takes charge of the burial arrangements.[11] She quiets his fears that 40 coffins might arouse suspicion, assuring him that "people won't ask questions, they're used to it" (FP, 77). In the original version she offers the professor a protective armband like those worn by the Nazis. This gesture was eliminated by Ionesco when the play was performed.[12] After several moments during which the stage remains empty, the maid reappears, exactly as she was at the beginning of the play, when she ushered in the now defunct fortieth pupil. The forty-first is already ringing the doorbell.

The violence is forecast by a physical metamorphosis that adds a nightmarish dimension to the humorous dialogue. The pupil, initially confident and animated, becomes increasingly morose. By the end of the play, according to the detailed stage directions, "her face must clearly express a nervous depression . . . she comes to have a manner vaguely paralyzed . . . almost a mute and inert object, seemingly inanimate in the Professor's hands" (FP, 46). As the pupil "disintegrates," the timid old professor grows steadily more offensive until "the lewd gleams in his eyes . . . become a steady devouring flame in the end" (FP, 46). Watching a Swiss production of The Lesson in which the director projected the shadows of the actors against the wall to heighten the effect of ritualized savagery, Ionesco realized that what he had at first conceived as a rape was more than that: "it was vampirism. . . . As the action progressed, he was devouring the girl, drinking her blood. And as he became stronger, her life was being sapped away, until in the end she was nothing but a limp rag" (Bonnefoy, 1971, 103).

Already in The Bald Soprano, language gone amok had taken on a vampirelike quality as it drained the signifying capability of the Smiths and Martins. In Ionesco's second "tragedy of language," among the most Artaudian of his plays in its violence, words are endowed with a truly deadly potential. Like the first signs of the plague, or fascism, this is not noticed in time because, as Marie observes, "they're used to it." *The Lesson* was subtitled "A Comic Drama" by Ionesco who found in the comic "an intuitive perception of the absurd . . . more hopeless than the tragic" (*NCN*, 27).

Jacques, ou la soumission (Jack, or the Submission); L'Avenir est dans les oeufs, ou il faut de tout pour faire un monde (The Future Is in Eggs, or It Takes All Sorts to Make a World)

The events of Ionesco's thirteenth year became a pivotal dramatic subject for the first time in *Jack, or the Submission,* written about the same time as *The Lesson.* The first of Ionesco's plays to contain elements of his dreams and to emphasize stage imagery conceived "in color," *Jack* is the most surrealistic of Ionesco's plays. It was written in 1950, and its sequel, *The Future Is in Eggs,* was completed a year later. *Jack's* subtitle, "A Naturalistic Comedy," and Ionesco's description of the play as "primarily a family drama, or a parody of family drama. It could be a moral play" were only partially paradoxical (*NCN*, 194). *Jack* is a phantasmagoric family drama with an antifascist moral.

The play opens with its eponymous young protagonist at center stage, sprawled in a rickety, soiled armchair in an ill-lit room. He is surrounded by family members, all named Jack. In a torrent of contorted language and logic, they alternately cajole, insult, and threaten him, for reasons not immediately made clear to the audience. Mother Jack reminds this "mononster" that "more than a mother to you, I've been a true sweetheart, a husband, a sailor, a buddy, a goose" (*FP*, 81). Father Jack, harshly modeled after Ionesco's own father, recalls Jack's impeccable upbringing "in a family of veritable leeches, of authentic torpedoes," and denounces him as a "murderer" and a "patricide" (*FP*, 83). The sulking Jack stands out from the others because he is silent. He is also the only one not wearing a guignolesque mask or makeup, although he does wear a cap, which will be removed, after his submission to the freakish familial canon, to reveal green hair. Symbolically naked in his isolation, as Ionesco described feeling as a child, he sits in rebellious silence until he is informed by his sister Jacqueline that he is "chronometrable" (*FP*, 86).

Faced with the unacceptable mortality that haunted his creator, Jack engages in a debate with his conscience in a scene reminiscent of Jarry's

Ubu. Like Père Ubu, he ultimately yields to his basest instincts. Protesting, "Oh words, what crimes are committed in your name," he signals his capitulation to familial duties by announcing, "Oh well, yes, yes, na, I adore hashed brown potatoes!" (*FP,* 86–87). Jack's bride is immediately produced. The veiled Roberta enters flanked by her two enormous parents, Mother Robert and Father Robert. She is sniffed and pawed by the Jacks while Father Robert, with the enthusiasm of a cattle auctioneer, catalogs her Picasso-like charms. They include truffled feet, a hand, toes, armpits, calves, and "green pimples on her beige skin, red breasts on a mauve background, an illuminated navel, a tongue the color of tomato sauce, pan-browned square shoulders, and all the meat needed to merit the highest commendation" (*FP,* 91–92). Rejected by Jack because she has only two noses, she is promptly replaced by the Roberts' second "only daughter," who has three noses.

Jack, a combination of Vitrac's precocious Victor and the young Ionesco forced to move to Romania, confesses to Roberta II that he has understood too much and has been deceived: "When I was born, I was almost fourteen years old. That's why I was able to understand more easily than most what it was all about" (*FP,* 103). He fell for the promised compensations: "assorted prairies, assorted mountains, assorted oceans . . . maritime, naturally . . . one star, two cathedrals chosen from among the most successful. . . . But everything was fake. . . . they all had the word goodness in their mouths, a bloody knife between their teeth. . . . They deceived me" (*FP,* 103–104). Roberta, who has been told that Jack will be interested in what she has to say "if it is the truth," tells nightmarish tales (*FP,* 102). Inflamed by her story of a wild horse burning in the desert, Jack becomes the galloping horse as a blazing mane crosses the stage. When the tale ends, he is exhausted and thirsty. To quench his thirst, Roberta, whose mask makes her resemble a grotesque fertility goddess, leads him into swampy psychic recesses. She recites a litany of her moist charms and the powers of her "drizzling," "trickling" body: "My necklace is made of mud, my breasts are dissolving, my pelvis is wet, I've got water in my crevasses. . . . I wrap my arms around you like snakes; with my soft thighs. . . . you plunge down and you dissolve" (*FP,* 107–108). Her "true name," she says, is Liza, homophonous with the French verb *"enliser,"* to get something stuck. As she speaks, the stage is bathed in a greenish, aquatic light contrasting with the monochrome gray of the opening and closing family scenes. Eroticism is usually equated with degradation in Ionesco's writing, although it is rarely presented as graphically as in *Jack* and *The*

Future Is in Eggs. "Here," according to Ionesco, "the characters escape from psychology and logic, they escape from the everyday mentality. And from dreams, too. Jack escapes from society and loses his soul to sink into a reality that is purely biological. He is dominated by the material world" (Bonnefoy, 1971, 135).

Jack's sexual submission coincides with a dissolution of language. Like pupils of the Professor's reductionist, libidinal philology in *The Lesson,* Roberta and Jack engage in a long dialogue in which all the lines contain either the sounds of "cat" or the word "cat," finally becoming nothing more than a mindless repetition of "cat." Roberta's proclamation that "all we need to designate things is one single word: cat. . . . It's easier to talk that way" gives an ironic, sexually charged twist to Camus's contention in *The Myth of Sisyphus* that the deepest desire of the mind is for familiarity and clarity (*FP,* 109; Camus, 1955, 13). Roberta, described by the playwright as having "not just three faces but an infinity of faces, since she is all women," becomes a misogynistic parody of the surrealist *femme-enfant,* the inspirational "woman-child" (Bonnefoy, 1971, 136). For Ionesco, as for the surrealists, the pinnacle of human existence is a state of wonder. In a world where everything can be reduced to "cat," there is no room for the marvelous. As the stage lights are extinguished, Jack and Roberta, buried beneath her wedding gown, are squatting at center stage, meowing and locked in an embrace. Surrounding them, all the other Jacks and Roberts are also squatting, moaning, and making grotesque animal noises. The final stage instructions indicate that "all this must produce in the audience a feeling of embarrassment, awkwardness, and shame" (*FP,* 110).

The Future Is in Eggs opens with a purring Jack and Roberta still embracing three years later and still chanting "cat," oblivious to their incensed families' insistence that they procreate because the white race must be expanded. Time has brought few changes other than a more oppressive abundance of the militaristic and racist sentiments that surfaced intermittently in *Jack* and the death of Grandpapa Jack. His face peers through a picture frame from which he will later descend to add his lewd song to the melee. Distracted finally by servings of hash browned potatoes, Jack again capitulates. He remains onstage astride a hatching machine and puffing like a steam engine. Offstage, with great piercing clucking sounds, Roberta produces enormous quantities of eggs which are delivered to Jack by an assembly line of the other Jacks and Roberts. As the stage fills with eggs, the two families shout in triumph: "Production, production, production!" and "Long live the white race!"

The proliferation of eggs is Ionesco's first use of the encumbering stage matter that became one of his hallmarks. Ionesco very probably had in mind Apollinaire's Tirésias, who claimed to have given birth to tens of thousands of children in one day. By making his eggs visually concrete, however, Ionesco creates an asphyxiating atmosphere that is both more comical and more horrifying than in Apollinaire's play. The eggs, symbolic of undifferentiated existence and degraded fertility, are for all practical purposes dead on arrival. Mother Roberta's inquiry as to what will be done with the progeny elicits an absurdly long list of possibilities, which is constantly punctuated by grandmother Jack's refrain: "And omelettes, lots of omelettes."[13] A recurrent alchemical symbol of the universe in surrealist works, the egg becomes in Ionesco's work an antiuniverse.[14]

Neither *Jack*, not staged until 1955, nor *The Future Is in Eggs*, first performed in 1957, was a success for Ionesco.[15] The shock effect of mechanical, dislocated language was beginning to diminish, although the proliferation of matter in *The Future Is in Eggs* was a startling compensation.[16] Because Ionesco's first published personal journals did not appear until the 1960s, the surrealized autobiographical elements and the depth of the antifascist sentiments were easily lost in the nonsense. Both plays, moreover, probably raised the discomfort level of the audiences beyond tolerable limits. "Boulevard theater going bad, gone mad," was the way Ionesco described *Jack* (*NCN*, 194). The boulevard theater, like Broadway theater in the United States, had long served spectators as a familiar mirror. Ionesco's mirror images increasingly held more than audiences wanted to see. Anticipating a blackly humorous reduction of language and bourgeois mores to absurdity, they were confronted with a bestial reduction of familial ties and "love" to a marketable carnality in the service of war machines and nationalistic goals.

Chapter Seven

Absurd Apotheoses

Les Chaises (The Chairs)

The command "chairs for all" in *Le Misanthrope (The Misanthrope)*, by Molière (1622–73), launches the famous "Portrait Scene," in which Célimène, cued by the wits in her salon, brings to imaginary life a gallery of courtiers as vividly present in their absence as the characters on stage. Nearly three centuries later, with a stage full of chairs signifying "multiplication and absence, proliferation and nothingness," Ionesco accomplished an even more extraordinary tour de force (Bonnefoy, 1971, 73). With three actors, a set consisting of circular walls with 10 doors, and limited stage properties (two windows, two stools, a dais, a blackboard, a gas lamp, recorded sound, and as many empty chairs as the director could muster), he conjured up a whole society, complete with an emperor. *The Chairs*, written in the spring of 1951 and subtitled a "tragic farce," is an extraordinary illustration of the littered "ontological void" that constitutes the contradictory experience of the absurd.[1]

The action is situated in a caretaker's apartment in an isolated, round tower surrounded by a stagnant sea. This Ionescan version of a circle of hell, bathed in a greenish light from the gas lamp and a cold, gray light from the sea, is inhabited by a 95-year-old man working on a final message to humanity and a 94-year-old woman wearing thick red stockings and implausibly named Semiramis, like the legendary queen of Assyria and Babylonia. Married for some 75 years, they are mired in buried memories and lost dreams and bound by a carping affection. Like contradictory echoes, their memories—and their memory lapses—stretch improbably back to a lost paradise as old as Paris, "the city of light . . . extinguished for four hundred thousand years" (*FP*, 116). Semiramis, designated in the list of characters as "The Old Woman," speaks of their child who ran away, accusing them of betrayal and cruelty and of leaving the streets running red with the blood of dead birds. The Old Man maintains they were childless. She describes her husband as an exemplary son. He remembers abandoning his mother to die alone in a ditch: "I know, I know, sons, always, abandon their mothers, and they more or less kill their fathers. . . . Life is like that . . . but I, I suffer from it . . .

and the others, they don't" (*FP*, 135). One thing is certain: this couple has gone on for a long time, sustained by endlessly repeated anecdotes, charades, and puns whose details and significance have been reduced to fragments of sense and sound accompanied by the refrain of "if only."

With oneiric freedom, roles and personalities shift at a dizzying pace: his from infantile states to messianic bravado; hers from nagging maternity to senile lasciviousness. "Mamma, Mamma, where are you, Mamma . . . hi, hi, hi, I'm an orphan . . . an orphan, dworfan," the Old Man wails from the lap of the Old Woman, who is rocking and crooning, "Orphanly, orphan-lay, orphan-lo, orphan loo" (*FP*, 118). Moments later, tears dried and nose wiped by Semiramis, who encourages him to carry on with his message, he jumps off her knees. Acknowledging the importance of his mission, he extols his virtuous service as a "general factotum," emphasizing the military portion of the term rather than the element of the hired odd-jobber. The dreamlike slippage of this word play, which allows conflicting "realities" to sustain as well as contradict each other, is characteristic of these old, baffled dreamers, specialists, as the Old Man says of himself, in absurd apotheoses. "I am not myself. I am another. I am the one in the other," the Old Man tells his invisible guests in a garbled rendition of Arthur Rimbaud's poetic adventure (*FP*, 145). Semiramis's existential recipe makes her more sympathetic than many of Ionesco's female characters. "It's easy once you begin," she assures the Old Man, "like life and death. . . . it's enough to have your mind made up. It's in speaking that ideas come to us, words, and then we, in our own words, we find perhaps everything, the city too, the garden, and then we are orphans no longer" (*FP*, 120–21).

The Old Man's message, which he has engaged an orator to deliver, summarizes a lifetime as a "collector of injustices, the lightening rod of catastrophes" (*FP*, 151). A guest list that might have hatched from Jack's eggs—janitors, bishops, chemists, tinsmiths, violinists, delegates, presidents, police, merchants, buildings, penholders, chromosomes, proletarians, functionaries, militaries, revolutionaries, reactionaries, alienists and their alienated, in fact "everybody who is a little intellectual, a little proprietary"—has been invited to hear it (*FP*, 121). With a premonition, perhaps, that enlisting another to take over their dialogue presages death, Semiramis begs her husband to invite everyone for another night, but it is too late. There is a sound of boats gliding through the water followed by the ringing of the doorbell.

In *The Bald Soprano,* just when the audience is nearly as persuaded as Mrs. Smith that "when one hears the doorbell ring it is because there is never anyone there," a fourth ring produces the Fire Chief (*FP*, 23). In *The Chairs,* when the doorbell rings, as it does at a quickening pace for most of the duration of the play, there is indeed no one there. Nevertheless, by means of mimed social niceties, logistical arrangements, a comically one-sided "dialogue" that gives the first arrivals distinct personalities, and the rapidly multiplying number of real chairs that fill the stage, Ionesco vividly creates the suffocating presence of the invisible guests. Alternately hobbling decrepitly and springing with improbable litheness over the increasingly cumbersome furniture, Semiramis produces chairs through a whirlwind of slamming doors. The rhythm of her deliveries, capturing Ionesco's seminal image of "a sort of whirlwind of emptiness," is matched by the accelerating pace at which the Old Man ushers guests in through his own set of wildly swinging doors, accompanied by the sounds of waves and boats, and the incessant ringing of the doorbell (Bonnefoy, 1971, 83).

A spate of coquettishness, turning the Old Woman into an unlikely siren, interrupts her hostessing. With dirty petticoats lifted over her ragged undergarments and thick red stockings, old breasts bared, and pelvis thrust forward, she flirts grotesquely with a photoengraver until, as alarmed by spontaneity and novelty as by infidelity, she suddenly recalls that she is her husband's "poor mamma" and bursts out in kaleidoscopic fragments of metaphors: "For me the branch of the apple tree is broken. Try to find somebody else. I no longer want to gather rosebuds" (*FP*, 134). Moments later she is hawking programs and Eskimo pies. During her flirtation, the Old Woman is back-to-back with the Old Man, who is courting a long-lost love, now old and ugly, named Belle. Remembering a time in their youth when "the moon was a living star, when they might have loved if they had dared," he too despairs: "Those days have flown away as fast as the wheels of a train. Time has left the marks of his wheels on our skin" (*FP*, 132). The invisible presence of the photoengraver invites speculation about just what kind of image might actually be captured here. As the voices of the Old Man and the Old Woman connect in their recitations of past failures, memory and affect disconnect. Neither recalls the story of the other. An increasingly bright light illuminates the stage.

With the arrival of the Emperor, also invisible, the center door opens wide with a great crash. The "cold, empty" light that has been invading the stage reaches a maximum of intensity, and the crowd noises cease. The Old Man and the Old Woman are separated by a stage filled with empty chairs. They stand beneath opposite windows, awaiting the

advent of the Orator, who is, unexpectedly, real, a caricatural version of
a romantic artist dressed in a smock and a wide-brimmed felt hat. His
arrival—heralded, like that of a savior, by 13 echoing lines proclaiming
"He will come" and "He is coming," which plunge into an alarmed "He
is here"—puts the Old Man into an even more feverish state (*FP,* 154).[2]
Eyes lifted heavenward, he thanks the audience, the Orator, and, at
great length, all those imaginable and unimaginable who have contributed to this "end in apotheosis." Semiramis, dreaming at her separate window of becoming a legend, is roused sufficiently to proclaim,
"What will be will be" (*FP,* 158). Affirming their trust in the Orator and
reassuring themselves that they will "leave some traces, for we are people and not cities," they leap to their death (*FP,* 158). There is a sudden
moment of silence intended to make audible the sound of an "Ah" coming from both sides of the stage and "the sea-green noises of bodies
falling into the water" (*FP,* 159).

The Orator is entirely taken up with signing autographs until the
moment of the double suicide. After several moments of silence, he
turns to address the rows of empty chairs, which have been reversed
midway through the play, making the real and invisible theater audiences into one. He signals that he is a deaf-mute. Uttering incomprehensible sounds, he scribbles a message on a chalkboard in which
"ANGELFOOD" and then "ADIEU" are among the few comprehensible
elements. Angered by the lack of reaction from the invisible spectators,
he stalks off through doors opening onto darkness. The curtain remains
up on the stage, which is bare of everything but empty chairs and "useless confetti" meant to convey an impression of "sadness, emptiness and
disenchantment such as one finds in a ballroom after a dance" (*NCN,*
191). As this image of emptiness is etched on the minds of the spectators, the voices of the invisible audience are finally heard again, along
with the sounds of the waves and wind. The void, according to Ionesco,
comes inexplicably to life, "an effect beyond reason," as the lighting
again becomes "pale and yellowish . . . for it matches the action, and
now the jamboree is over" (*NCN,* 191).

Ionesco did not want the play interpreted "in the usual dull way" as
either the contents of the senile old couple's hallucinations or a symbolic
representation of their remorse. In his program note for the 1952 performance, he explains that it is a "search for some essential reality,
nameless and forgotten—and outside it I do not feel I exist—that I have
tried to express through my characters, who drift through incoherence,
having nothing of their own apart from their anguish, their remorse,

their failures, the vacuity of their lives" (*NCN,* 186). "The further one goes, the deeper one sinks," the Old Man observes, sounding like one of Beckett's characters but, in fact, echoing lines attributed in "Spring 1939" to Marie, the old farm woman with whom Ionesco revisited La Chapelle-Anthenaise in 1939. "It's because the earth keeps turning around, around, around, around" (*FP,* 114).[3]

Ionesco believed that tragedy and comedy are inevitably linked for anyone who can stand apart, at least momentarily, from the derisory spectacle that is contemporary society (*NCN,* 121). The old couple is often as humorously guignolesque as the Smiths and the Martins, but they are not merely that. Their Job-like isolation and incomprehension at having suffered so unjustly render them tragically human. When *The Chairs* was first performed in 1952, critics tended to focus too narrowly on its nonsense and guignolesque dimensions to recognize that Ionesco had just furnished extraordinary proof of Artaud's contention that "the stage is a concrete physical place which asks to be filled and given its own concrete language to speak" (Artaud, 1958, 37). With the empty rows of seats in the theater mirroring the empty chairs on stage, the play closed almost immediately. After Jacques Mauclair's prize-winning revival in 1956, however, it continued to be one of the most performed of Ionesco's plays. Not long before his death in 1994, it was playing to full houses at a theater in Paris.

Victimes du devoir (Victims of Duty)

In *The Lesson* the Professor alleges that "by themselves, words charged with significance will fall, weighted down by their meaning, and in the end they always collapse" (*FP,* 63). In *Victims of Duty,* a "pseudo-drama" written in 1952, it is the protagonist, a victim of language as well as of duty, who is felled by the "weight of meaning." Choubert, climbing a phantasmagoric mountain, briefly ascends beyond his existential encumbrances, but words, leaden with the menace of banality, bring him crashing down into a wastebasket.

The curtain rises on the middle-aged Choubert. Seated in his armchair, he reads the newspaper to his sharp-tongued, sock-darning wife Madeleine, giving equal weight to comets, cosmic disturbances, and dog messes on the sidewalk. It appears to be a return to the world of the Smiths and the Martins. When he turns, however, to an "official announcement" urging citizens to "cultivate detachment" as a "last hope of finding an answer to the economic crisis, the confusion of the spirit and the problems of existence," Choubert is, in fact, in the process of slipping into Oedipal tangles, literary theory, and serious political themes. *Victims* is the first of Ionesco's staged excursions into oneiric autobiography.[4]

The conversation drifts from politics to the theater, with Choubert opining that "all the plays that have ever been written, from Ancient Greece to the present, have never been anything but thrillers. Drama's always been realistic and there's always been a detective about" (*TP,* 119). A knock at the door produces the requisite detective, a shy young officer searching for someone named Mallot or Mallod. When Choubert volunteers that it is Mallot, the detective suddenly becomes ruthless with Choubert and inappropriately familiar with Madeleine. Assuming multiple guises, police interrogator, psychoanalyst, Choubert's/Ionesco's father, Madeleine's seducer, theater critic, torturer, and the first in the play to offer the excuse that he is simply a "victim of duty," the Detective substantiates Choubert's dramatic theories. He bullies him through a psychodrama presented as a surrealist "thriller."

Madeleine promptly succumbs to the detective's authority. In a series of onstage metamorphoses that parallel those of the detective, she becomes his accomplice. Her housedress falls away to reveal a low-cut outfit. Her shrill voice temporarily turns gentle and musical as, her extended arm miming a stair rail, she steers Choubert into his memories. As he flounders in his past, her role shifts from youthful seductress to decrepit, old wife. She becomes his mother, the detective's lover, a beggar woman, and, finally, another of the "victims of duty." Choubert, unable to remember Mallot or identify the detective's photo of a beaten-up face above a prison number, is stripped of necktie, shoelaces, and belt. A classic image of a police interrogation, it is also a "flashback" to Ionesco's description of himself in *Découvertes* as a young boy "naked" in his isolation and his difference. Alternately cajoled and browbeaten by the detective and Madeleine, he makes an increasingly infantile descent into the recesses of his psyche.

Choubert begins his odyssey sloughing through mud, a negative symbol of sexuality as in *Jack.* Suddenly, Madeleine and Choubert are old. Choubert sings in a cracked voice of lost love and an enchanted garden that "has folded into night, has sunk into the mud" (*TP,* 130). Forced to go further down, he mimes a deeper descent in which he is swimming up to his eyebrows in the mud. Gone beyond "the sight barrier," he crosses the stage unseen by Madeleine and the Detective, who emerge from the wings to play the parental roles in Ionesco's childhood memory of the quarrel during which his mother attempted to take poison. Standing at a distance, Choubert wrings his hands muttering, "Father, mother, father, mother" (*TP,* 134). In the role of Choubert's father, the detective, whose evil deeds have approached the level of the cosmic disturbances mentioned at the beginning of the play, becomes a cartoonish example of the soldier simply following orders. Echoing the short-lived reconciliation scenes that marked Ionesco's tempestuous relationship with his father, the detective's voice calls out remorse and excuses in a lawyerly flood of words from which he remains both physically and emotionally distant. He stands motionless, his face without expression, while his recorded voice comes from the opposite side of the stage. A conflicted Choubert, alternately accusing and seeking forgiveness, is unable to hear him and begs him to speak.

Resuming their previous roles, the Detective and Madeleine take theater seats in a humorous concretization of Freud's description of the unconscious as the "other stage." Choubert, groping blindly like Oedipus, mounts a small platform. At the beginning of his "performance," he is old and timidly incoherent. As his language becomes increasingly free, the muddle of reminiscences yields to surrealistic adventures. "I feel myself," he announces, as he takes off on a mimed voyage across seas, continents, deserts, and forests, to the foot of a mountain, briefly encountering bright sunshine and blue skies (*TP,* 143). A passage in *Découvertes,* in which Ionesco proposes that "perhaps . . . it is still this light which nourishes me, keeps me alive, which is stronger than my depressions and which guides me in the abyss . . . and which allowed me to rediscover the path if not to the summit, at least to the upward slope," captures what must be made to seem to propel Choubert during this portion of his voyage (*D,* 60–61).

At the insistence of the detective, hands bleeding and gasping for breath, Choubert ascends the mountain. There is no sign of Mallot, but he announces from the summit that he has lost his fear of death. Resisting threats and bribes meant to bring him down, Choubert discovers that he can fly. From a darkened stage his voice calls back, "the light is seeping through me. I'm so surprised to be, surprised to be, surprised to be" (*TP,* 151). The detective predicts with triumphant accuracy, "He'll never pass the surprise barrier." Moments later, reminded of his habitual "giddiness," Choubert becomes frightened. When the stage lights come up again, he is sprawled like a derisory Icarus in a large wastebasket.[5]

Determined to plug the holes in Choubert's memory, the detective stuffs his mouth with enormous pieces of barklike bread. Madeleine, with a kind of mechanical impassivity, brings cup after cup of coffee; untouched, the cups fill the entire sideboard. The "human" gesture is transformed by indifference into useless, encumbering matter. Two other impervious witnesses arrive, heightening the irony of Choubert's discussion of the policy of detachment early in the play. A strange lady reminiscent of Vitrac's Ida Mortamart, suddenly onstage when the lights come back up after Choubert's fall, stands by silently like a dysfunctional muse.[6] A poet friend, Nicolas d'Eu (the name is homophonous with the Russian emperor), materializes with the same dreamlike inexplicability. Ignoring Choubert's suffering to discourse on the theater, he insists that theater should be "surrealizing . . . in so far as surrealism is oneirical" and that the phoniness of plot and motivation must be abandoned: "no more drama, no more tragedy: the tragic's turning comic, the comic is tragic, and life's getting more cheerful . . . more cheerful" (*TP*, 158–59). There are elements of humorous self-parody in this Ionescan manifesto, but it also reflects the playwright's disgust with the propensity of intellectuals to be blinded to real suffering by theoretical ardor. The detective, combining conservative critics and totalitarian order in one of Ionesco's broad, mocking sweeps, prefers to "remain Aristotelically logical, true to myself, faithful to my duty and full of respect for my bosses. . . . I don't believe in the absurd" (*TP*, 159).

Only when the detective prepares to shove his fist down Choubert's throat does Nicolas d'Eu react to his choking, bleeding friend who has been wailing for his "Ma-ma-ma-de-lei-ne." In an abrupt role reversal, he becomes the knife-wielding father figure. He stabs the detective, unmoved by the latter's blubbered excuses: "I'm only a pawn . . . a soldier tied to his orders. . . . I'm only twenty" (*TP*, 164). The detective dies echoing the rallying cry of the Jacks and the Roberts: "Long live the white race," and protesting that he is a "victim of duty" (*TP*, 165). Suddenly remorseful, Nicolas takes over the search for Mallot. The stuffing of Choubert recommences. As the curtain falls, all the characters, even the previously silent woman and Choubert with his mouth full, all "victims of duty," are mechanically chanting "Swallow, chew, swallow, chew" (*TP*, 166). The scene is a grim echo of the violence and depersonalization of totalitarian regimes and of Ionesco's bitter conflict with his father.

According to Artaud, the important question is not whether physical stage language can equal the psychological impact of spoken language "but whether there are not attitudes in the realm of thought and intelligence that words are incapable of grasping and that gestures and everything partaking of a spatial language attain with more precision than they" (Artaud, 1958, 71). Mime, he suggested, was the most powerful ingredient of the "poetry in space." When Jacques Mauclair staged *Victims* in 1953, Choubert's mimed ascent, a nightmarish condensation of time, space, and contradictory emotions, captured "that dream-like state, that state of astonishment in the face of an increasingly disjunctive and dislocated reality" in which the play was rooted (Bonnefoy, 1971, 94). Ionesco acknowledged not having known how to present Choubert's imaginary voyage. Mauclair created the scene with a simple table in the center of the stage. As Choubert crossed the forest, he crawled under the table. For the ascent, he climbed on the table. When the climb became more difficult, a chair was put on the table, which he just managed to climb. He was standing on the table when he reached the mountaintop. Ionesco called it "one of the fairly rare moments when I've understood what the theater is, what it ought to be: a real, living experience, not just the illustration of a text. . . . That was a moment of real theater because it was true and false at the same time" (Bonnefoy, 1971, 98–99).[7] Heavily charged with messages, theorizing, and literary inside jokes, *Victims* is not an evenly crafted play, but it is one of Ionesco's most interesting. It was greeted with mixed reviews, a sign that his theater was gaining acceptance.

Victims of Duty is the first of several of Ionesco's plays to be created from one of his short stories.[8] Although more spare and less humorous, the basic plots of these oneirically autobiographical tales, most based on actual dreams, do not differ substantially from the plays. They contain substantial portions of dialogue that Ionesco used again in the dramatizations. Interesting as abstracts for the later theater, these stories are also engaging contributions to the genre of the fantastic tale, weaving the absurd and Ionesco's particular brand of surrealism into personal and political statements. In the stories, as in the plays they engendered, Ionesco circumvents the inadequacy of language by turning to the realm of the fantastic. There, as Tzvetan Todorov has persuasively argued, ambiguity becomes a conduit for questioning "the existence of an irreducible opposition between real and unreal."[9] Ionesco's protagonists, all first-person narrators (the voice most conducive to the fantastic, according to Todorov, because, belonging to everyone, it facilitates identification and rational explanations for the bizarre), are all to some extent outsiders or misfits. Vaguely guilty and not quite adequate to their circumstances, they are clearly heirs to Kafka's fictions.

In the very brief story entitled "A Victim of Duty," there is more emphasis on a political agenda than on the Oedipal themes central to the shifting poles of the Choubert-Madeleine-Detective triangle in the play. The narrator's wife's immediate attraction to the shy young policeman appears to be primarily the effect of his gold watch, fine suit, and stylish shoes, which suggest that he might be a well-rewarded, loyal party member. The identification is accentuated when, demanding that his host identify a missing Mallot or Mallod, he provides a mug shot of a face too battered to be recognizable. In this context, the barklike bread that is shoved down the protesting narrator's throat to stop the gaps in his memory has connotations that are primarily political. At the end of the story, however, when Nicolas, his face distorted by an inexplicable hatred, pulls out an enormous knife and stabs the young detective whom the narrator suggests might be his son, it becomes clear that the notion of a "victim of duty" has oedipal as well as political dimensions. The oedipal-political amalgam is particularly brutal in the short story, which is not leavened by the distancing, satirical humor of the play.

Amédée, ou comment s'en debarasser (Amédée, or How to Get Rid of It)

In 1953, Ionesco wrote his first three-act play. Like *Victims,* it was adapted from a short story based on a dream and written "in a nightmare state or at least in a state of astonishment" (Bonnefoy 1971, 71). "Oriflamme," the source for *Amédée,* is a harsh tale. Whereas the play is centered on the tragedy of a disunited couple, the short story emphasizes a political context for the nightmarish horror of the corpse's presence in their apartment. In *Amédée* the origin of the expanding corpse is never made explicit. Thus the guilt, odd loyalties, and sense of loss it provokes lend themselves to a host of symbolic possibilities. In "Oriflamme" it is identified as Madeleine's former lover, killed by the narrator in a burst of passion that seems to have left him with a soul nearly as dead as the corpse. The process of its ejection is less conflicted in the short story. Unlike the play where it is presented in terms of a monstrous birth entailing loss as well as gain, in "Oriflamme" the expulsion is treated as a politicized Gargantuan purge: "as if I was tearing out my own inside through my mouth—my guts, my lungs, my stomach, my heart, a whole heap of vague feelings of insoluble wishes, of evil-smelling thoughts, of musty, stagnant images, a depraved ideology, a decaying moral code, poisonous metaphors, noxious gases that clung to my organs like parasitic plants" (*CP,* 20). When the transformed cadaver suddenly lofts the narrator to freedom, "Oriflamme" becomes a kind of fantastic sequel to "Anywhere Out of This World," by Charles Baudelaire (1821–1867). Baudelaire's poem, prophetic of modern ennui, compares life to a hospital where each patient wants to change beds.

Amédée is subtitled "A Comedy," but, according to the playwright, like *Victims* it was written during an oppressive state when "the horizon closes in and the world becomes a stifling dungeon. Language breaks down in a different way and words drop like stones or dead bodies; I feel I am invaded by heavy forces, against which I can only fight a losing battle" (*NCN,* 163). The curtain rises on another living room. This Parisian apartment differs from Ionesco's familiar petit bourgeois settings by being more explicitly a prison metaphor. Even before the first mushroom is plucked from the carpet and a corpse afflicted with "geometric progression" is introduced, this room with its large shuttered window at center backstage, furnished only with a very visible clock, a table with a switchboard, an old armchair, and a small table strewn with writing materials, is disconcerting. A combination living room–dining room-office, it turns out to be a fragile fortress where Amédée and his wife, another unpleasant Madeleine, have been hiding for 15 years, obsessed with the presence of a corpse. The graying, bespectacled Amédée is a dreamy playwright, deficient in both inspiration and energy. In 15 years he has written only two lines of a play that sounds much like *The Chairs*.[10] Madeleine supports the two. The replacement of her housewifely kerchief with a proper hat transforms her into a switchboard operator. Her switchboard connections are a source of nonsensical comedy. The president of the Republic, the king of Lebanon, and even Charlie Chaplin (a grocer) require her services. Madeleine's generally negative responses are also a commentary about human disconnectedness. The president is inaccessible, and firemen cannot be reached on Thursdays.

The corpse remains unseen during Act I, still confined "in the best room, *our* bedroom when we were first married," according to Amédée, who wonders if it has forgiven them yet (*TP,* 21). Both Madeleine and Amédée inspect it obsessively. He finds it alarming but strangely attractive with its "great, green eyes shining like beacons." She dusts and polishes it. His memory as leaky as Choubert's, Amédée can remember neither how the corpse got there nor who it was. Unwilling to accept Madeleine's claim that it was her lover murdered by him in a fit of jealousy, he suggests it might be a neighbor's baby, temporarily in their care, or even a woman he left to drown. Whatever its origin, fear of the secret's being discovered has taken over the couple's lives. They are terrified by a postman who knocks at the door with a postcard for Amédée Buccinioni just as the sound of cracking walls from the bedroom and a crop of mushrooms springing up from the carpet announce the expansion of the corpse into the living room. The postman is warded off by Amédée's claim that nearly half the people in Paris have the same name and that he is not Amédée Buccinioni anyway but "A-mé-dée-BUCCINIONI." The moment is as tense as it is zany, a reminder that fear of authorities in uniforms is not always unwarranted and that anonymity pervades modern existence. Act I ends with a strong image of the helpless misery so characteristic of theater of the absurd. Completely at a loss, Amédée stands at center stage holding his hat and staring into space. Then, hunched up and exhausted, he sinks into his armchair murmuring wearily: "I can't understand how we got into such a mess. It's so unfair. . . . And in a case like this . . . no-one to turn to for help and advice" (TP, 30).[11]

The rapidly growing corpse invades the living room in Act II. Propped on stools, the corpse's enormous feet and legs jerk in the direction of the panicked couple, who are nearly buried by the bedroom furniture the feet push in their path. Poisonous mushrooms proliferate, as do Madeleine's venomous accusations. Threatened by Madeleine, the habitually procrastinating Amédée agrees to act at midnight, "the witching hour. . . . Not before . . . like a thief" (TP, 45). During the interminable wait, while the clock hands move slowly in tandem with the jerking progression of the cadaver toward the door to the landing, Amédée tries to write. As he tugs at images with an invisible piece of rope, he pulls onstage two actors dressed in wedding clothes who look and sound exactly like Madeleine and Amédée. Unseen by Madeleine and Amédée, they reenact the unhappy couple's wedding night. A rapturous Amédée II speaks of love and light, green valleys, "gravity abolished . . . no more weariness . . . world without weight" (TP, 50). Madeleine II, admonishing him not to come near her, speaks of pain, eternal night, mud, suffocating marshes, and mushrooms. She misechoes his refrain, "house of glass, house of light" as "house of brass, house of night" (TP, 51). Madeleine II rushes off screaming. Amédée II runs after her, begging her to wait. Ionesco stipulates that the roles of Madeleine II and Amédée II be played "quite naturally in this unnatural and unreal situation—just as naturally as Amédée and Madeleine play theirs" (TP, 47). The blurring of distinctions between the real and the dream evokes powerfully both the fantastic possibilities accessible through dreams and the imagination, and the tremendous loss sustained when the possibilities are thwarted. The shutters are finally opened on a dazzling night, reflected indoors by the mushrooms, which are shining like glowworms, and by the glowing green corpse, which is emitting strange music. The elaborate stage directions indicate that the atmosphere in the apartment "must definitely suggest the mingled presence of horror and beauty at the same time" (*TP,* 59). The act of "getting rid of it" becomes a breech birth of cosmic proportions. Madeleine, beside herself, her heart beating so loudly it shakes the set, shouts "pull . . . tear him out," while Amédée, suddenly calm and making a superhuman effort, tugs the corpse's feet toward the window (*TP,* 62). Chairs tumble and clouds of plaster fall from the ceiling, creating the impression that the corpse is "dragging the whole house with it and tugging at the entrails of two principal characters" (*TP,* 62).

In Act III, Amédée emerges into a night lit by huge clusters of stars, comets, and fireworks. The cadaver becomes a symbol of lost love. As Amédée struggles toward the Seine, where he intends to dump the corpse, he encounters a drunken American soldier to whom he explains it as "a great misfortune, the tragedy of our life . . . the skeleton in our cupboard" (*TP,* 68). To make Amédée's burden less cumbersome, the soldier winds the corpse around him. Suddenly, as a carnival atmosphere pervades the square below, the cadaver opens out like a gigantic sail or parachute. The plays ends with Amédée shouting nonsensical excuses to Madeleine and the "Keystone cops" characters who have been chasing him, and making comments about social realism, immanence, and transcendence. His comments parody philosophers in general and Sartre in particular, as he drifts into an increasingly brilliant sky.

Amédée is a rarity in Ionesco's theater, because he remains aloft. His surprising flight was something of a desperate expedient for author and character alike. Ionesco acknowledged that he too got stuck staring at the corpse, not knowing how to get rid of it (Bonnefoy, 1971, 85): "The logic and the truth" of the situation required that it continue indefinitely to the point of complete suffocation.[12] Pleased, however, that audiences relished this unlikely ending, he interpreted the ascent in a spiritual context: "I found these characters weightily present . . . and suddenly I was watching the transformation I had hoped for, the disgrace transformed into grace, salvation coming from this fundamental guilt" (Benmussa, 1966, 100). The euphoria of the comically apologetic Amédée is tainted nonetheless with loss and cruelty: his play is unfinished, his wife abandoned. In many respects *Amédée* depicts the same kind of failure to communicate as *The Bald Soprano,* but Ionesco has raised the stakes, linking it to the destruction of love. Increasingly in his theater, love will be presented as a chance for a second experience of luminous "eternity" otherwise lost with childhood. The opportunity is inevitably squandered owing to conflicting desires.

In a later interpretation, the corpse was defined by the playwright as "transgression, original sin" and the "growing corpse" as "time" (Bonnefoy 1971, 84). Complexly revolting and desirable, utterly impossible and yet believably domesticated, the corpse is a troubling and mysterious, perhaps even mystical, stage metaphor. It signals an alteration in Ionesco's approach to the theater. The first phase, according to the playwright, was verbal derision. The second phase is distinguished by the placing of characters in an extravagant situation in order to underscore the complex plausibility of the fantastic with realistic language.[13]

Le Nouveau locataire (The New Tenant)

Ionesco reported that he was never able to put *Amédée* away completely (Benmussa, 1966, 99). When he wrote *The New Tenant* just one month later, he gave it the kind of claustrophobic ending that *Amédée* had initially seemed to require. *The New Tenant* ends with a suicidal entombment. The main character, a catatonic gentleman costumed like Charlie Chaplin, the consummate animator of silence, has piece after piece of furniture delivered to his apartment. As he silently orchestrates what becomes a frenzied dumb show, the furniture blocks the entries and stairways; then, reportedly, it blocks the subway, and, finally, it malignantly invades the whole country. As the last items are lowered onto his head from an opening in the ceiling, the gentleman is buried by his belongings.

The play corresponded to a time when, for Ionesco, "the presence of other people had become unbearable. . . . It was horrible to listen to them, painful to speak to them, terrible to have anything to do with them or feel them around me. . . . And their machines, their machines! Great trucks, motorcycles, motors of every kind, electric appliances, elevators and vacuum cleaners all mixed up with their aspirations and their expirations" (*NCN,* 222). The action consists almost entirely of burgeoning matter, first the reified language of a grotesquely verbose concierge which is echoed by the cacophony in the street, then the furniture. This tragicomical rendering of the dehumanizing flood of materialism comes remarkably close to realizing Ionesco's wish to strip from dramatic action the didactic potential of plot and characters and "all the justifications, explanations and logic of the conflict" (*NCN,* 217).

After the first deliveries, the gentleman draws a large circle at center stage, and places his armchair in the circle. From there he silently choreographs the action of what the stage directions characterize as a "ponderous ballet." Circles figure as prominently in Ionesco's early theater as armchairs. Mr. Smith's caveat in *The Bald Soprano,* "Take a circle, caress it, and it will turn vicious," leads to the circular scalp dance in *The Lesson* (*FP,* 38). For the Old Man in *The Chairs,* the perfect circle is the shape of absolute silence, a state the New Tenant is desperate to achieve.[14] Like the semicircular space in *The Chairs,* the New Tenant's circle suggests a Dantesque circle of hell. In a lighter vein, it parodies Brecht's message in *The Caucasian Chalk Circle:* that property should belong to those who can use it well. The circle is also a very effective means of highlighting the theatricality of the gentleman's willed disappearance from his own spotlight. Just before closing off the ceiling, one of the movers tosses in a bouquet. The flowers, usually interpreted as a funeral bouquet, could as easily be the flowers tossed onstage at the end of a notable performance. That this first and rare instance of an Ionescan character taking charge of his own "performance" by freeing himself from familial and social constraints and the babble of language is an orchestration of a suicide makes a singularly pessimistic statement.[15] One way or another, Ionesco's major plays, written during his "absurdist period," are variations on the theme of death—if not a "real" death as in *The Lesson, The Chairs, Victims, Amédée,* and *The New Tenant,* a symbolic death of the imagination and dreams, annulled by mechanized language or the smothering of the individual spirit.

Short Plays: *Scène à quatre (Scene for Four); Le Maître (The Leader); Le Tableau (The Picture); L'Impromptu d'Alma (Improvisation, or the Shepherd's Chameleon)*

Ionesco wrote several other dramatic pieces during the early 1950s, aptly characterized by Emmanuel Jacquart as Ionesco's "practicing his scales" (*TC,* 1603). These plays are highly comical, but intimations of tyranny, physical brutality, and depersonalization give the humor a characteristically Ionescan dark twist. With the exception of *Scene for Four, The Leader, The Picture,* and *Improvisation, or the Shepherd's Chameleon,* they are minor, ludic experiments with the disintegration of language and identities.[16]

Scene for Four, like most of Ionesco's early short sketches, is based on out-of-control language.[17] It stands out, however, in a manner that was to become increasingly characteristic of Ionesco's best theater, because the effect of the language play is significantly enriched by a choreography that mimics the tone of the dialogue. Rhythmic manipulations and repetitive patterns replace dramatic development. Moving about a table in a carefully orchestrated dance, a Mr. Durand and a Mr. Dupont, later joined by a Mr. Martin, quarrel in a stream of echolalia which even the arrival of a beautiful woman claimed by all three as a fiancée is powerless to interrupt. The play ends with a startling stage picture resembling the sadistic surrealistic vision of the painter Hans Bellmer (1902–1975). The woman, passed from one man to the other as the three men circle the table, loses a shoe; a glove; her cape and fur; her skirt; and finally her arms, legs, and breasts. According to Jorge Lavelli, who mounted a student production of this little-known play, the challenge of representing a flesh-and-blood character losing limbs like a puppet led to a critical discovery that use of theater space must be as free as the act of writing: although "theater is certainly the art of the concrete, there is nothing more profitable than to confront it with non-representable ideas; the imaginary is always nourished by sensations."[18]

The Leader was written in 1951 and re-created in an operatic version by Radio France in 1960. The Announcer and two Admirers, a young man and a young woman representing an entire crowd of followers, await the Leader. His arrival is repeatedly heralded with biblical solemnity by the Announcer, amid a din of offstage "hurrahs" and cries of "long live the leader," echoed by the characters on stage. When the Leader finally appears, he turns out to be a "man-in-an-overcoat-with-a-hat-without-a-head." This is not a problem, the Announcer assures the admirers, because "he's got genius."[19] The term *"le maître"* can be applied to a political chief, a lawyer, or a literary "master." Ionesco's headless leader symbolizes mindless demagoguery. The observation that he is changing his shirt behind a "red" screen, an allusion to the politics of Ionesco's father, serves more broadly as a reminder of how similar fascism and communism were for Ionesco. This self-mythologizing creature, mistaking himself for God, fatuously immersed in nature, and temporarily trouserless (like Ionesco's Hugo), is also a parody of the literary establishment.

The choreographic development of the action is what is particularly notable in *The Leader,* as also in *Scene for Four.* The comings and goings of the Announcer and the Admirers, who repeatedly rush offstage each time they are confronted by the Leader's failure to arrive, are duplicated by the taglike mating game of two other characters, the Girl Friend and the Young Lover. The commotion of entrances and exits is suggestive of Artaud's frenetic *Le Jet du sang* (*Jet of Blood*). In the feverish excitement preceding the Leader's arrival, all the characters run in from separate points and intersect in an embrace that leaves the couples scrambled. At the end of the play, flattened against opposing walls like the Old Man and the Old Woman at the end of *The Chairs,* the male Admirer embraces the Girl Friend, as the female Admirer embraces the Young Lover. The fact that the play ends with interchangeable couples and a five-way chorus of "What's your name?" makes as forceful a statement about depersonalization as the headless leader. Rosette Lamont has observed that the pattern of the lovers' encounters is an early example of the brevity of love in Ionesco's dramatic universe, a recognition of the human dimension that nearly always enriches even the most guignol-esque of Ionesco's plays (Lamont, 1993, 180–81).

The Picture, a one-act play completed in 1954, was subtitled "Guig-nolade" by Ionesco. He states in the Preface that the actors must avoid a realistic style at all costs, and must play their roles like circus clowns. In spite of its buffoonery and its half-lampoon, half–fairy-tale surprise ending, the play hovers close to social criticism. The principal character, designated only as the "Large Gentleman," is a self-made man who has "advanced over the bodies of the fallen."[20] This hybrid of Père Ubu and Molière's Monsieur Jourdain wants to buy a picture to compensate for the ugliness of his one-armed, housekeeper sister and his inability to find a wife. Offered a portrait of a handsome woman for 400,000 francs, he manages, by dint of verbiage as much as philistine unscrupulousness, to reduce the down-and-out painter to paying for the privilege of leaving behind his painting.

Left alone, sniffing, kissing, and flattening himself against the paint-ing, the Large Gentleman indulges in a scene worthy of the Jacks and the Roberts. A textual annotation indicates that the actor must be "either as erotic as the censors or the spectators will bear or else ridicu-lously lyrical and emphatic. But always guignolesque" (*TC,* 412).[21] Interrupted by his deformed sister, he shoots her, bringing about a star-tling metamorphosis. As her white wig, her glasses, and the shawl that made her appear one-armed fall off, she is transformed into a replica of the attractive woman in the portrait. More shots alter an ugly neighbor woman and then the Painter, who turns into "Prince Charming." At the end of the play, even the decor is transformed by the firing gun: flowers and confetti fall from the ceiling and fireworks light up the stage. Only the Large Gentleman remains in his original grotesque state, waving his pistol at the spectators and begging for someone to fire on him.[22]

First staged in 1955 on a double bill with *Jack, or the Submission, The Picture* was a critical failure. Ionesco blamed the failure on its being interpreted too seriously as a critique of capitalism. Underscoring his antipathy to theater as thesis, he insisted that the characters not be given psychological dimensions and that any social significance the critics saw in the play was coincidental. The same message, in fact, had already been humorously incorporated into the play, in a broadside at critics who judge a work of the imagination by its social relevance: The principal objection offered by the Large Gentlemen to the Painter is that "in your work one has to imagine, and even that is not always possible, what one cannot see" (*HT,* 132).

In 1956, Ionesco attacked his critics much more directly, staging them as identifiable pedantic buffoons. *Improvisation, or the Shepherd's Chameleon,* modeled after Molière's reply to critics and rivals in his *L'Impromptu de Versailles,* was written at the height of the controversy over the social significance of Ionesco's theater. In this satirical play-within-a-play-within-a-play, a character playing Ionesco is confronted by three of his adversaries, Roland Barthes, Bernard Dort, and Jean-Jacques Gautier, who are caricaturally rendered as Bartholomeus I (Barthes), Bartholomeus II (Dort), and Bartholomeus III (Gautier). Barthes and Dort are ridiculed as blindly voguish theorists. Gautier, a conservative critic whose articles on Ionesco's theater had been venomous from the first, is pilloried for his ignorance and stupidity. Bartholomeus III is an "unpedantic fool" who cannot distinguish between a platypus and a Platonist, and who blames Shakespeare for being a foreigner—a Russian, he thinks, until he looks in a dictionary and discovers that Shakespeare is Polish. Bartholomeus I and Bartholomeus II resist Bartholomeus III's xenophobia but agree that he has "every right to blame [Shakespeare], you're a critic. . . . You can be full of blame, for everything, that's your mission in life."[23]

Bartholomeus I, arriving to announce that he has found a theater that will produce Ionesco's next play "according to the latest dramatic theories . . . worthy of a people's theater in this ultra-scientific age," is the first to importune the dozing playwright (*K,* 111). "Ionesco" explains that his latest play was inspired by a touching scene he saw in a provincial square: a shepherd embracing a chameleon. Bartholomeus I interprets this gibe at a Brechtian context as "the reconciliation of the

Self with the Other," and wonders whether Ionesco will be the shepherd or the chameleon. "Definitely not the chameleon," the latter insists, "*I* don't change color every day. . . . I'm not always being towed along by the latest fashion" (*K*, 113). He begins to read his play, which repeats what has just taken place. The opening scene is then repeated two more times, as Bartolomeus II and then Bartolomeus III enter, each dressed (like Bartholomeus I) in an old-fashioned academic gown and speaking the same lines.

Much of *Improvisation* is a farcical "re-education program" caricaturing Brecht's *Verfremdungseffekt,* an "alienation effect" sometimes referred to as the "V effect," and Sartre's *L'Être et le néant (Being and Nothingness).* Explaining how to extricate oneself from a vicious circle, for example, Bartholomeus I and Bartholomeus II propose, "You can only alienate yourself . . . by not escaping from it; whereas you can only escape from it by staying inside. . . . For the more alienated you are . . . the more involved you are . . . and the more involved you are . . . the more alienated you are. It's the electrical shock of alienation, or the Y effect . . . and dialectically speaking, its called: 'The Being-In-on-the-Outside-and-Out-on-the Inside.' . . . It's also the 'Being of not-Being and the Not-Being of Being in the Know' " (*K*, 117–18). The reform program includes weaning Ionesco from the influence of Molière, who "failed to express the social gestus of his age," and from poetry, "an enemy of our science" (*K*, 121–22).

While the three Bartholomeuses pontificate, the cleaning lady, Marie, a representative of the "people" the playwright stands accused of ignoring, is summarily shut out by her intellectual "defenders." Before she can be let in, the stage must be "historicized." In a parody of a Brechtian episode, a sign reading "A PLAYWRIGHT'S EDUCATION" is tacked to the wall "to indicate the action" and "summarize it and draw the public's attention to the fundamental epic attitude enshrined in each tableau" (*K*, 137). Other placards inform the audience that the scene has become one of "STYLIZED REALISM" and that this is a "FALSE PLACE." Wearing a dunce cap and hung with signs reading "POET" in front and "SCIENTIST" in back, the Ionesco character is nearly detrousered because Bartholomeus I, a doctor of costumology, has diagnosed his costume as not "costumic," suffering from "hypertrophy of the historical function. . . . It's veridical" (*K*, 141).[24] His clothing "historicized," he is declared ready to learn, although he insists he no longer has any desire to do so. At this point, the theme of brainwashing becomes more insistent. Already forced to confess, he is reduced to the plight of

Pozzo's manservant Lucky in *Waiting for Godot*. Ordered to "Dance, sing, talk," he brays like a mule. They are all braying when Marie breaks in. Not fooled by this "people's theater" nor impressed by Ionesco's "costumical costume and signaletical signs," she chases away the doctors with her broom.

Declaring the play over, the Ionesco character brings the other characters back for a final theoretical speech of his own. "For me," he explains, directly addressing the audience, "the theatre is the projection onto the stage of the world within . . . my dreams and desires, my anguish and my obsessions . . . are a part of . . . a very ancient deposit to which all mankind may lay claim. It is this which, surpassing the superficial diversity of men, brings them together and constitutes our deepest fellowship, a universal language" (*K,* 150). The long monologue addresses criticism of his theater as "uncommitted." More important, it reflects his growing admiration for the work of psychologist Carl Jung (1875–1961) and points to a new direction for his theater.

When the Ionesco character in *Improvisation* dreams of filling a 25-seat theater at a staging of his next play, Bartholomeus I replies that half-filling it would be reason enough for gratitude. In fact, *Improvisation* was the first of Ionesco's plays to have its premiere in an established theater. It opened in 1956 at the Studio des Champs Elysees, a theater with 250 seats and sophisticated lighting equipment, on a double bill with the revival of *The Chairs* that inspired Anouilh's laudatory article. *Improvisation* marks a time of transition in Ionesco's theater in several ways. His early "antitheater" was deeply rooted in Jarry's *Ubu*, Dada, and the age-old principles of farce. Ionesco's notes for *The Picture* are broadly applicable to these plays: "It is only by extreme simplification, unsubtle and puerile, that the meaning of this farce can be brought out and become plausible by means of its very implausibility and idiocy. Idiocy can constitute this kind of revelatory simplification" (*TC,* 382). During the late 1950s, however, his theater moved away from "revelatory simplification." His plays became considerably longer, somewhat more traditionally narrative, substantially more personal and political, and, ultimately, overtly autobiographical and metaphysical. Farcical and guignolesque elements did not disappear, but the role of such elements was diminished as elaborate visual effects took on increasing importance.

The shift in focus announced at the end of *Improvisation* corresponded to a moment when Ionesco's growing success provided him with access to more sophisticated staging and larger casts. The plays in his next "cycle" would be performed in major theaters in world capitals. Many of his early admirers regretted the loss of spontaneity and anarchy that accompanied the change. The small number of characters and the minimal sets that were necessary because of the physical and financial limitations of the tiny theaters where his plays were first staged had not necessarily been disadvantageous. The brevity of the texts and the economy of the staging, stretched by freewheeling language and imaginative use of simple props, had suited the haunting mixture of reality and unreality, and exuberant hilariousness and morbidity that gave theater of the absurd its peculiar force.

Part 3.
"Theater of My Anguish"

Chapter Eight
The Burlesque Mask Lowered

The plays that Ionesco wrote at a remarkable rate between 1948 and 1955 were subversive, not didactic. Charged with overinflated language, they were meant to explode the foundations of conventional boulevard theater and the hypertrophied mores of much of its public. They provided an ideal outlet for the sabotaging humor that had already framed the world as parody in *Nu* and *Hugoliad*. What this antitheater had not easily permitted, however, was for the playwright to present himself seriously. In 1957, by then in his mid-forties, he remedied this with the creation of the first of a series of four distinctly autobiographical characters, all named Bérenger. With the invention of Bérenger, as a drama critic noted, he "begins to speak in the first person."[1] The Bérengers are dreamy, angst-ridden composites of Everyman, Charlie Chaplin, and Don Quixote transplanted to the nightmarishly enigmatic world of Kafka. Ionesco described them as "sometimes myself, sometimes the caricature of myself, sometimes what I would not like to be . . . sometimes someone entirely different."[2] Although the four Bérengers are given very different roles, both an assessment made of the first Bérenger in *The Killer* and Bérenger's response hold true for them all. In this interchange, Bérenger is told, "You've always been dissatisfied, always refused to resign yourself." He responds, "That's because I'm suffocating. . . . The air I have to breathe is not the kind that's made for me" (*K*, 61). The four Bérengers share their author's determined individualism, his swings from euphoria to leaden despair, his obsession with death, and his solitude. In his welcoming speech to Ionesco at the Académie Française, Jean Delay observed, "You are a solitary man. The burlesque mask of your theater covers up solitude."[3] After the invention of the Bérengers, however, that mask was frequently lowered.

Tueur sans gages (The Killer)

The first Bérenger play, *The Killer*,[4] which was completed in 1957, is a three-act elaboration of the title story of *The Colonel's Photograph*, a collection of short stories published in 1962. A passage in *Nu*, in which

Ionesco states that "at the mere thought that the others go happily on their way, I feel a despair welling up in me, cold, nasty, implacable like a knife," indicates that the inspiration for both the story and the play dates backs to the years in Romania (N, 100). At the beginning of the play, an astonished Bérenger tours the Radiant City, a district of eternal blue skies and bright sunshine. His response duplicates a miracle of the playwright's youth, when a sudden luminosity filled him with "over-flowing joy . . . absolute presence. . . . for I had learnt that man does not die" (F, 68). For a long moment before Bérenger comes on stage, a daz-zling effect is created by a play of light on the empty stage, gray at first, then suddenly brilliant white and intense blue. When Bérenger enters in the company of the Architect, who designed the Radiant City, he describes invisible marvels, countering the Architect's dry insistence on technological explanations with surrealistic fervor: "Mirages . . . there's nothing more real than a mirage. Flowers on fire, trees in flame, pools of light, that's all there really is that matters" (K, 18). More than through Bérenger's words, however, it is by means of mime and lighting effects that the radiant city takes on a magical existence. Bérenger ecstatically touches invisible walls and responds to invisible flowers with a physical buoyancy. When he speaks of an ornamental pool, it materializes instantly by means of the stage lighting.

Bérenger believes that he has found the metaphysical antidote he has been seeking: "the projection, the continuation of the universe inside you. Only, to project this universe within, some outside help is needed: some kind of material, physical light, a world that is objectively new" (K, 19). As he speaks, however, he corrects himself: "Come to think of it, it's quite wrong to talk of a world within and a world without, separate worlds. . . . when there's not total agreement between myself inside and myself outside, then it's a catastrophe, a universal contradiction, a schism" (K, 19). The light mimics his confession, going gray again when a defeated Bérenger heads home from the Radiant City. Just as Ionesco's luminous vision had darkened, Bérenger's dream of a transforming light is quickly destroyed. The Radiant City has a tragic flaw, the Killer. Dis-guised as a beggar, the Killer hawks the trifles in his briefcase and entices his victims with a photograph of a uniformed colonel. Although his ploy is well known, the image of the uniformed officer proves irre-sistible. When his victims bend down to examine the photo, the Killer pushes them into the ornamental pool. Even as Bérenger learns of the Killer from the surprisingly indifferent Architect, bodies of a young boy, his mother, and a civil servant are floating in the pool. The Architect's former secretary, whom the excitable Bérenger has just fantasized as his fiancée, becomes the latest victim.

The Architect, who also totes a thick briefcase, is a protean official resembling the policeman in *Victims of Duty*. Substantiating Choubert's claim that in drama "there's always been a detective about," he doubles as the superintendent of police and also presents himself as a general practitioner, a former surgeon, a psychoanalyst, and a sociologist (*TP*, 119). Bérenger treats him like a confessor. This "father figure" is indifferent to everything except the conservation of his authority. He flips through files and conducts his official business on a telephone he produces from his pocket (a "conjurer's trick" that elicited much laughter in the days before cellular phones), while Bérenger excitedly recounts a cherished dream, magically revived by the Radiant City, of "a spring no autumn could touch; a source of light, glowing wells that seemed inexhaustible" (*K*, 20).

In Act II, Bérenger returns in a wintry light, amid hostile street noises, to his dark apartment. The stage is bathed in an unpleasant yellowish-ray light, projecting, according to Ionesco, "the paralysis bred by habit . . . a gray cover beneath which we hide the world's virginity; that's what original sin is about" (Bonnefoy, 1971, 31). Bérenger is astonished to find his apartment occupied by a funereal-looking friend named Edouard, who insists that Bérenger himself had given him the keys. Unmoved by the news of the killer and Bérenger's dead "fiancée," Edouard huddles over a bulging briefcase, which eventually bursts open. Photographs of the colonel, the Killer's identity card and diary, and a strange collection of boxes within boxes spill from it.

Act III introduces a large cast augmented by mannequins and puppet figures, as well as an elaborately visual "magical realism," the kind of cast and visual effects that were to become regular features of Ionesco's theater. Unconvinced by Edouard's claim that the criminal had sent him the materials in the briefcase for publication in a literary journal, Bérenger struggles to drag his friend to the police station before it closes. Their progress is repeatedly blocked by a series of nightmarish impediments. They are stalled by a mob led by Mother Peep, whose flag-carrying, goose-stepping troops rally to distortions of political slogans. "To disalienate mankind, we must alienate each individual man . . . and there'll be soup kitchens for all. . . . We won't colonize, we'll occupy the countries we liberate," she shouts, assuring her followers that "while they're demystifying the mystifications demystified long ago, the intellectuals will give us a rest and leave our mystifications alone" (*K*, 77,

79). Ionesco's quarrel with the left had intensified with the Soviet Union's invasion of Hungary shortly before he began writing *The Killer.*[5] A drunkard in top hat and tails, also carrying a briefcase, argues from an Ionescan point of view that the real revolution is being carried out by the artists and scientists. The list he cites is a strange one, however. Robert Oppenheimer, a developer of the atomic bomb, and Pavlov, whose name is typically associated with dehumanizing consequences, are mentioned, along with Einstein, Breton, Kandinsky, and Picasso. The drunkard is denounced by the crowd as an "enemy of history." It is Edouard who speaks most clearly for Ionesco and "interprets" the play by replying: "We're all going to die. That's the only alienation that counts" (*K,* 83).

Once past Mother Peep, Bérenger's trajectory becomes increasingly phantasmagoric, as space stretches and time condenses. He discovers that Edouard's briefcase is missing but then becomes disoriented when several others exactly like it turn up all around him. Edouard is sent back for his briefcase. Bérenger attempts to go on but is blocked by a traffic jam and a confrontation with two larger-than-life policemen. They brutalize passersby but are indifferent to the news of the Killer. Alone on a darkening stage from which the decor begins to disappear, Bérenger appears to walk a long time without advancing, as if in a nightmare. As he walks he confronts the cold laughter of the Killer. According to the stage directions, the Killer is a puny, one-eyed derelict. He may either appear on stage or simply be hallucinated.

Anticipating that the scene with the Killer would be found too long, Ionesco specifies that it should be treated as a separate act, "interpreted in such a way as to bring out the gradual breaking-down of Bérenger . . . and the vacuity of his own rather common place morality, which collapses like a leaking balloon" (*K,* 9). Bérenger's cliché-ridden attempts to disarm the Killer, involving a seemingly endless series of naive appeals to humanitarian instincts, fraternal bonds, Christian love, logic, and, finally, mercenary impulses, elicit only derisive laughter. Overwhelmed by the inadequacy of language, Bérenger loses his resolve. He takes out two pistols, as old-fashioned as the humanism he has just brandished, but lays them on the ground. In the play's final image he is on his knees, head bent in submission, while the Killer advances, chuckling, his knife poised to strike. With his last words—"Oh God! There's nothing we can do. What can we do. . . . What can we do"—Bérenger swells the ranks of absurdist figures whose existential "why?" has brought only the echo of their anguish in response (*K*, 109). Albert Camus, present on opening night, reportedly applauded wildly.[6]

Bérenger's language, having descended from poetic ecstasy in the first act to melodramatic declamations in the second, becomes the equivalent of suicide in the third. According to the prefatory stage directions, faced with the Killer's silence, he "finds within himself, in spite of himself and against his own will, arguments in favor of the Killer" (*K*, 9). In this Kafkaesque ending, the presumed "innocent" dies as guilty perhaps as the Architect and Edouard or any other in the briefcase-wielding crowd have been conjectured to be. *The Killer* is a clever detective story; the clue indicating that Edouard must be the guilty one becomes increasingly problematic as the play progresses. The enigmatic treatment of the keys in the second act, which links Edouard to Bérenger as a kind of negative alter ego, is solved in the final moments of the play when Bérenger assumes the Killer's guilt.

Comparison of the play with the story entitled "The Colonel's Photograph" highlights the degree to which Ionesco's political agenda and themes of guilt and punishment were enriched by the invention of Bérenger and by the physical elements of the stage. The emphasis in the short story falls more heavily on the condemnation of political manipulation and violence. The oversized, abusive policemen elicit from the narrator a directly historical-political comment: "In my opinion, a country's done for when the police has the upper hand over the army" (*CP*, 38). This is a silent observation that is somehow "read" by one of the policemen, a blurring of mental boundaries that contributes a jarringly eerie quality to the otherwise generally flat affect of the narration. In the condensed space of the short story, the killer very quickly looms against the darkening horizon. The narrator estimates the hideous, cylopian derelict to be weaker than himself but does not, ultimately, resist his "implacable eye . . . gratuitously murderous": "I felt defenseless, desperate; for what use were bullets, or my own feeble strength, against the cold hatred and stubbornness, against the boundless energy of that absolute cruelty, devoid of reason as of mercy" (*CP*, 41). The story suggests the effect of terrifying paralysis common to nightmares, but the ending, unsustained by the mime and lighting effects made possible by the stage, collapses into moralizing.

When *The Killer* opened in Paris in 1959, many critics responded to it as a wordy rehashing of familiar avant-garde themes, failing to appreciate that the play is most essentially a meditation on the inevitable triumph of death. All the tramways, as the Architect informs Bérenger,

lead to the same terminal. The nested boxes that emerge so oddly from
Edouard's briefcase become symbolic of coffins within coffins. The
theme is amplified, not interrupted, by political attacks and displays of
perverted language, which signal the death of the imagination. In an
advance notice for *The Killer*, Ionesco asked, "Do we perhaps feel in a
confused sort of way, regardless of ideology, that we cannot help being,
at one and the same time, both killer and killed, governor and governed,
the instrument and the victim of all-conquering death?" (*NCN*, 162).
Increasingly in his theater, the answer to this question would be "yes."

Rhinocéros (*Rhinoceros*)

Ionesco's second Bérenger play, written in 1958, has had thousands of
performances around the world. In 1960, after a successful world premiere the previous year in Düsseldorf, it opened at the Odéon in Paris,
directed by Jean-Louis Barrault. A few months later, Orson Welles
staged it at the Royal Court Theatre in London. In 1961, it was the first
of Ionesco's plays to reach Broadway. The "case study" of rhinoceritis—
whether understood as a depiction of Nazism, the excesses of Stalinism,
the evolution of communism, or (by American audiences) the rage of
McCarthyism, was a powerful theatrical event. Ionesco's interpretation
of the phenomenon was broadly inclusive: "*Rhinocéros* is certainly an
anti-Nazi play, yet it is also and mainly an attack on collective hysteria
and the epidemics that lurk beneath the surface of reason and ideas but
are none the less serious collective diseases passed off as ideologies"
(*NCN*, 199).

The animal metaphor and the image of a nightmarish transformation, which Ionesco developed in a short story entitled "Rhinoceros,"
before he created the play, first took shape during Ionesco's experience
with Nazism in Romania. "Imagine," he wrote in his journal in 1941,
"that one fine morning you discover that rhinoceroses have taken power.
They have a rhinoceros ethics, a rhinoceros philosophy, a rhinoceros universe" (*PP*, 67). This is the situation that confronts the second Bérenger,
a bored, lethargic middle-aged employee of a provincial legal publishing
firm who, like the author, is inclined to submerge his discouragement in
alcohol. "I feel out of place in life, among people. . . . I can't seem to get
used to myself" is the excuse Bérenger offers for his dissipated state (*R*,
17–18). He echoes Ionesco's "I have never quite succeeded in getting
used to existence, whether it be the existence of the world or of other
people, or above all myself" (*NCN*, 157).

The curtain rises on an intentionally stereotypical setting: a café in a sunny provincial French square, where a hungover Bérenger meets his friend Jean. The scene—with its blue sky, harsh light, white walls, and church bells—recalls the radiant city of *The Killer.* Jean, dressed with exaggerated impeccability (although Ionesco also assigns him clownlike yellow shoes and capacious pockets from which, like Harpo Marx, he can produce the necessities of the moment), is reminiscent of the Architect. Intransigent and unsympathetic, he flaunts himself as a "superior man who fulfills his duty," and counters the existential plaints of his friend, as the Architect did those of the first Bérenger, with admonitions of "Will-power, my good man!" Like the radiant city, a defective technological paradise planned by an architect working entirely "by order of city council," the town in *Rhinoceros* is flawed by a deficiency of imagination. There has been no zoo since the animals were destroyed by the plague; traveling circus performers have been banned by the council. Instead, this town has a card-carrying "Logician." The mental gyrations involved in the Logician's demonstration of the powers of the syllogism, which intersects and echoes Jean's hypocritical sermon on how to become cultured in 4 weeks, reduce the humanistic tradition, absurdly touted by both, to farcical rubble.

What appear to be rhinoceroses thunder by in a great cloud of dust, disrupting the Sunday calm. When this happens, the rigid inanity of Jean and the Logician proves to be contagious. The other characters, a "slice of life" including a grocer and his wife, a housewife with her cat, an old gentleman, the café owner, a waitress, and a young secretary from Bérenger's office named Daisy, react in an echoing, unimaginative chorus: "Oh, a rhinoceros!" and "Well, of all things!" (*R,* 25–26). There is heated argument about the number of animals and whether they were bicorned or unicorned, but general indifference to the significance of the event. Bérenger, more concerned that Daisy will see him in his unkempt state than about the rhinoceroses, is nevertheless roused from his apathy to quarrel with Jean. In the heat of an argument over whether the rhinoceroses are Asiatic or African, and whether they have one horn or two, Jean, who has just advised his friend to arm himself with "the weapons of patience and culture, the weapons of the mind," explodes inexplicably: "If anybody's got two horns, it's you! You Asiatic Mongol!" (*R,* 21, 30). Accused of racism, Jean can only shout irrationally, "They're yellow!" (*R,* 31).

The first scene of the second act takes place at the publishing firm. The curtain comes up on a *tableau vivant* with the boss, Monsieur Papillon, in his dark blue suit and the rosette of the Legion of Honor; his assistant, the intellectually patronizing Dudard in a gray suit with sleeve protectors; the clerk, Botard, a bristly former schoolteacher in a gray smock and a Basque beret; and Daisy, the pretty, blond secretary. The initial impression created by this conventionality is a humorous one. Even when the characters begin speaking, still arguing about the reliability of the rhinoceros sightings and all showing in their clichéd contentiousness symptoms of potential rhinoceritis, Ionesco maintains a burlesque mode as he did in the first act. Botard, a ranting stereotype of a rigidly Marxist schoolteacher who pretends to have "scientific" answers for everything and cries "conspiracy" when he is caught flat, is the most ridiculous. Bérenger, sneaking in late and hoping to hide the fact from his boss, stands outside their circle, initially shielded from rhinoceritis by irresponsibility. The first definite proof of the epidemic comes with the arrival of the wife of an absent colleague named Boeuf. Terrified by a rhinoceros who has pursued her through the streets and come crashing and snorting up the stairs after her, she suddenly recognizes the plaintively bellowing animal as her husband. Undeterred by pleas and physical restraint, the large Madame Boeuf leaps down to land astride her husband, who is trumpeting among the rapidly growing number of rhinoceroses in the street.

Ionesco progressively shrinks the dramatic space as Bérenger approaches claustrophobic isolation. The next *tableau* takes place in Jean's room, where Bérenger has gone to make amends for the previous day's quarrel. The two undergo a dual metamorphosis that begins farcically but becomes darkly earnest as the banalities and stereotypes that bounced comically through the conversations in the square and the office take on a menacing character. Bérenger finds Jean in bed, coughing and hoarse, a bump on his forehead, and wearing green pajamas distinctly suggestive of both army uniforms and storybook rhinoceroses. Jean steps in and out of his adjoining bathroom to check on his bump and his increasingly greenish complexion in the mirror, returning each time with thicker, greener skin and a more hornlike protrusion until finally he becomes a full-fledged, and particularly nasty, rhinoceros, threatening to trample Bérenger.

Bérenger's simultaneous transformation is less visible but more surprising. He changes from a listless slouch to an ardent defender of "an irreplaceable set of human values" (*R*, 67). His sudden new role is only minimally plausible, but the extraordinary piece of stage business that brings about Jean's metamorphosis distracts the spectator from ques-

tioning its credibility. The two friends quarrel again, Bérenger proffering unconvincing but heartfelt humanistic arguments, Jean countering
with Nazi-like deformations of Nietzschean formulations: "We need to
go beyond moral standards. . . . We've got to build our life on new foundations . . . get back to primeval integrity" (*R*, 67). Jean's ultimate
argument is brute force. Bérenger flees for his life, only to discover as he
calls for help that all the building's inhabitants have become rhinoceroses.

The final act, a nightmarish parallel to the preceding scene, takes
place in Bérenger's room, which resembles Jean's. Bérenger is also in
bed as the act begins, awakening, like Gregor Samsa at the beginning of
Kafka's *Metamorphosis*, from a bad dream. His head is bandaged to keep
a horn from sprouting. The noise of a large number of rhinoceroses is
heard from the street. Dudard comes to see Bérenger, followed by Daisy.
Proffering hypocritical "intellectual" defenses, Dudard succumbs to
rhinoceritis. He cites Monsieur Papillon's becoming a rhinoceros as "a
case of community spirit triumphing over his anarchic impulses" (*R*,
89). His own enlistment in their ranks, humorously forecast when
Daisy's lunch invitation is declined due to a distaste for tinned food and
a preference for eating on the grass, is justified with a hackneyed excuse:
"if you're going to criticize, it's better to do so from the inside" (*R*, 93).[7]
Feeling inadequate to debate with someone so well educated, Bérenger
urges Dudard to meet the logician. As he speaks, a rhinoceros wearing
the logician's boater hat runs by.

Left alone, Bérenger and Daisy bolster their resistance with declarations of love that quickly degenerate into a quarrel as Bérenger laments,
"In the space of a few minutes we've gone through twenty-five years of
married life" (*R*, 104). Abandoned by Daisy, who finds the rhinoceroses
and their increasingly musical trumpeting irresistibly godlike, he too
begins to break down. As handsome images of rhinoceros heads are projected against the walls and along the footlights, he looks in the mirror
as obsessively as Jean did in the previous act, longing to replace his
smooth brow with horns and his slack skin and white, hairy body with
"a hard skin in that wonderful dull green colour" (*R*, 107).[8] He imitates
rhinoceros sounds to no avail. Forced to acknowledge that he is physically incapable of becoming a rhinoceros and unable to learn their language, he cries out in despair "Now I'm a monster. . . . I've gone past
changing. I want to, I really do, but I can't" (*R*, 107). Then he abruptly
revolts, calls for his pistols, and shouts defiantly in the direction of the
projected rhinoceros heads: "Oh well, too bad! I'll take on the whole lot

of them. . . . I'm the last man left and I'm staying that way until the end. I'm not capitulating" (*R*, 107). Bérenger's visceral response contrasts sharply with the ineffective ratiocinations at the end of *The Killer*, just as his call for pistols (which has been left out of the English translation) differs pointedly from the defeated lowering of the first Bérenger's pistols. Ionesco had no doubt chafed at being accused by critics of nihilism, but, characteristically, he contradicted the epithet on his own terms.

Bérenger's resistance has been compared to the lonely heroics of Sartre's Orestes in *Les Mouches*.[9] He is intentionally made anti-intellectual, however. Bérenger is an anti-hero whose immunity to rhinoceritis, having begun as the cloud of a hangover, is an instinctive resistance to ideology and propaganda for which, according to Ionesco, "it is probably impossible to give any explanation" (*NCN*, 199). *Rhinoceros* won Ionesco few admirers on the left, to the point where a communist writer, Elsa Triolet, accused her colleagues of having succumbed to rhinoceritis in their collective determination to condemn the play (Bonnefoy 1977, 205–206). Perhaps that is why, in the Preface to an American student edition of *Rhinoceros*, Ionesco turned to the writing of Denis de Rougemont to illustrate his intent, rather than emphasizing his personal experience. In a 1936 journal entry describing a Nazi rally at which Hitler appeared, de Rougemont tells of standing in an enormous, saluting crowd as it was overtaken by a groundswell of hysterical adulation. He experienced his difference from the crowd as a kind of deep, physical repulsion, a "shudder and palpitations of the heart," and also as a rejection: "I am alone and they are all together."[10] "There, perhaps," says Ionesco, "is the starting point of *Rhinoceros* (*NCN*, 199). Unlike the play, the short story "Rhinoceros" concludes on a note of bewildered discouragement: "I dared no longer look at myself. I was ashamed. And yet I couldn't, no I couldn't" (*P*, 98). Had the play ended with this despairing ambiguity, which Ionesco stated that he believed to be "more subtle, more true," it might have been considerably less popular (Kamayabi Mask 1987, 142). The story conveys without comical embellishment, and perhaps more frankly than postwar theater audiences would have liked, the moral paralysis created by the fear of isolation.

Ionesco was more concerned in *Rhinoceros* with exposing the hazards of ideology than with revolutionizing the theater. Some of the play's success was due to its clarity as well as its timely topic. "Ionesco is writing in French," proclaimed an enthusiastic critic, extolling the play's "limpid symbolism, all the more forceful because it is more accessible and of a greater significance because everyone can grasp its meaning."[11] Ionesco's theater is never simple, however. The rhinoceros metaphor is a challenging one to stage. It must be made to shift from comic to tragic intent without allowing the moral fable to bury either the fantastic elements or Bérenger's clownlike appeal. Ionesco condemned as "intellectual dishonesty" the principally comical emphasis of the Broadway production. He accepted the tragic emphasis of the German production, but it was Jean-Louis Barrault's interpretation of *Rhinoceros* as a "terrible farce and fantastic fable" that he believed best "caught the meaning of the play" (*NCN*, 207–208).

Le Piéton de l'air (A Stroll in the Air)

Ionesco completed a sketch for a ballet, *Apprendre à marcher (To Learn How to Walk)*, a film scenario, *La Colère (Anger)*, and the short play *Frenzy for Two or More* during the 4 years that separated *Rhinoceros* from the next Bérenger play, *A Stroll in the Air*. Generally this was a period filled more with polemics and traveling as an acclaimed spokesperson for the "new theater" than with the writing of plays. Based on a dream of flying, *A Stroll* is a long one-act play divided into a dreamlike series of shifting tableaux with musical interludes. It represents a radical departure from the style of *Rhinoceros* or *The Killer*, consisting almost entirely of fantastic events and apparitions. A silver bridge suddenly appears, spanning an imaginary abyss. Pink ruins are smothered in flowers. Bérenger's cottage is inexplicably exploded by a bomber left over from the last war. A representative of the antiworld floats on and off stage and Bérenger also takes flight. John Bull, a gigantic figure, is transformed into an executioner. *A Stroll* requires elaborate sets and sophisticated stage machinery, all of which Jean-Louis Barrault, who had encouraged Ionesco to write this play, had at his disposal for the 1963 French premiere at the Odéon.[12]

Ionesco's emphasis on the fantastic did not eliminate polemics. Before Bérenger goes on his spectacular stroll, he is interviewed by a journalist. Asked for a message, he replies, "They've all been given before. . . . The cafés and the newspaper offices are swarming with literary geniuses who have solved everything. They believe in the straight and narrow path of Historical Necessity, but History is really round the bend. For them might is right, so Historical Necessity is the doctrine of the victorious party in power, whatever it may be."[13] *A Stroll* is primarily, however, a confrontation with Ionesco's fear of death. At the end of the

interview Bérenger confesses: "I am paralyzed by the knowledge that
I'm going to die. . . . I want to be cured of death." The journalist reduces
his long list of complaints and prescriptions to "down with the way
things are . . . neurosis . . . cafés . . . discrimination . . . courage . . . intuition . . . diseases . . . writers are stupid" (S, 22–23). Like Ionesco in the
early 1960s, the third Bérenger is a well-known French playwright at a
crossroads that is both spiritual and literary. When the journalist suggests that he has temporarily given up theater for fear of rivals, he counters: "I think it's rather because I need renovating inside" (S, 21).

Accompanied by his wife, Josephine, and his young daughter, Marthe,
Bérenger is recuperating from writer's block and existential disenchantment in a whimsically stereotypical English village, home to a series of
exaggeratedly "British" characters including a little, bewigged songstress
introduced as the Bald Soprano. The stage directions call for a set with a
house and a landscape in the manner of Douanier Rousseau, Maurice
Utrillo, or Marc Chagall, with a naive, dreamlike quality closer to primitive art than to surrealism. On the Sunday of Bérenger's stroll, the coun-
tryside, like Ionesco's memories of La Chapelle-Anthenaise, is resplen-
dent with bright sunshine, blue sky, and lush green grass. Bérenger
experiences the same heady lightness that overwhelmed his namesake in
the radiant city. Insisting that flying, is "as necessary and natural as
breathing" and that "all you need is the will to do it. . . . You only come
down when you lose confidence," he makes the leap dreamed of by the
first Bérenger (S, 73, 79). Tiers of seats suddenly appear, transforming
the stage into a circus. Bérenger demonstrates a beginner's technique for
flying from a white circus bicycle tossed from the wings. He then flies off
on a trapeze or invisible ropes to the antiworld. Earlier he had compared
the antiworld to "the sun's rays shining through a crystal prism, reflected
and broken up, disintegrating into a patchwork of colors and then put
together again" (S, 52). Returning from his flight in a gray twilight of
smoking ruins colored by blood-red explosions, he describes instead a
Hieronymous Bosch-like spectacle: "Men licking the monkeys' behinds
and drinking the sows' piss . . . columns of guillotined men . . . giant
grasshoppers and fallen angels, and archangels gone astray." When his
proper English audience finds the description indecent and boringly out
of date, he offers a more modern apocalyptic version: "continents of Paradise all in flames," knives, graves, "oceans of blood . . . of mud and
blood and mud," bombardments, vanishing universes, "deserts of ice,
deserts of fire battling with each other and all coming slowly toward us"
(S, 112–16). He has also seen the goose men of Mother Peep.

The world Bérenger leaves behind is a match in horror for his apocalyptic journey. During his absence, Josephine, protesting her innocence, is tried, perhaps because she has been unhappy, by a monumentally large, red-robed judge who advances on rollers, flanked by two adjuncts, one of whom is John Bull. The latter slaughters two small children with a machine gun, then requests their mothers to take their turn. Josephine's horror elicits an echo of the Nuremberg trials. Her uncle-doctor defends the murders as "preventative mercy killing": "In any case it was bound to happen. It's all over much quicker this way." To her protest, "You, you who've saved so many human lives, thousands of children," he replies in some of the blackest humor in Ionesco's theater to that point: "This is how I redeem myself" (*S*, 102–103). A man in white and a hangman are rolled in as replacements for the judge and his adjuncts. Josephine is invited to take her turn at the gibbet. Marthe insists that it must be a dream; Josephine is not persuaded. In the final lines of the play, Marthe holds out hope that sometime in the future there will be gardens. Nothing in this very pessimistic play supports the childish wish.

In a 1959 essay, reminding his readers that "Humor is liberty," Ionesco reiterates the need for humor and the revelatory power of fantasy. *A Stroll*, conceived as a "dramatic fantasy . . . more a spectacle than a play or an anti-play," was an attempt to wrest the theater from the "worldly spirit of the boulevard or the sordid 'literature' of commitment" which Ionesco blames in the same essay for banishing fantasy for the sake of a realism that "leads us on into a frozen dream" (*NCN*, 143).[14] The play founders, however, under its heavy dose of technical extravaganza and morbid obsession.[15] When *A Stroll* was first performed, many critics reacted negatively to what seemed a more lavish than innovative turn in Ionesco's theater. Later interpretations, some influenced by discussion in Ionesco's journals of his metaphysical struggles, emphasized the spiritual dimensions of Bérenger's ascension and fall. Mircea Eliade, for example, found a close parallel to a Hindu vision of cyclical creation and destruction (Hubert 1990, 165).

By the early 1960s, Ionesco and Anouilh were the most performed playwrights in Paris. Thus, even though *A Stroll* was a critical failure, it became the subject of two important symposia: a roundtable sponsored by the review *Arts* and a debate on the national radio. In both contexts it was treated harshly. The critics accused Ionesco of substituting elaborate stage machinery for the marvelous potential of language and gesture and replacing the profound comedy of the absurd with facile comic effects. Furious, Ionesco responded in a series of acrimonious articles. In the article "Critiques, vous vivez de moi!" ("Critics, You Feed Off Me!"), he suggested that since that was the case, they might be more polite. He also explained at length that he had purposely avoided rhetoric in *A Stroll* in order to present the grim evidence about the human condition with the force of a brandished knife. Words, Ionesco maintained, mask the horrors of reality and diminish their effect.[16]

The story "The Stroller in the Air" on which this play was based, is more effective than the dramatic work because it is more concentrated. It stands out among the stories in *The Colonel's Photograph* because Ionesco speaks so clearly in his own pessimistically comical voice, casting aside the Kafkaesque mold. He creates an atmosphere more like that of the fantasies of Jean Cocteau (1889–1963), an artist, poet, and playwright on the periphery of the surrealist movement whom he admired. The magical mirrors, a levitating protagonist, and clowning repartee in the story are evocative of Cocteau's plays and films, but what might have been a music hall apocalypse in Cocteau's hands takes on a tragic tone in "The Stroller." The narrator's return from the circuslike ascent to the fun-fair gates that falsely promise "PARADISE," becomes an existential metaphor: "Slowly, sadly, I came down, as a man comes down an invisible staircase. I brushed against the top of a tree and pulled at a single leaf, without thinking. It spun round and round as it fell" (*CP*, 63).

Le Roi se meurt (Exit the King)

Completed in the fall of 1962, just a few months after *A Stroll*, *Exit the King* had a much different reception. Quickly and widely acclaimed as a masterpiece, it inspired even such an inveterate detractor of Ionesco's theater as Jean-Jacques Gautier to refer to its poetic density and poignant comedy as "Shakespearian."[17] Written in two brief periods immediately following Ionesco's hospitalizations for a serious illness, it was meant to be "a lesson, a sort of spiritual exercise, a gradual progress, stage by stage towards the ineluctable end, which I tried to make accessible to other people" (*F*, 88).

Bérenger, in pajamas and slippers in his final incarnation, is the ailing King who, although he cries out again and again, "I'm dying," refuses to die. Hailed as "Majesty, Commander-in-Chief, Master, Managing Director," he has reigned for 277 years and 3 months; invented gunpowder; stolen fire from the gods; built the first airplane, with Icarus as a pioneer test pilot; written Shakespeare's plays; invented the Eiffel tower; and created the major capitals of the western world. He has split the atom, but "now he can't even turn the light off. Or on!"[18] Signs of his imminent demise are multiplying. The central heating is out; the walls of the palace are cracking; the cows are out of milk; all but a few old or unwanted subjects have died or fled; and the King's ministers, who had all gone fishing, have vanished into a bottomless pit. There are cigarette butts in the throne room and spiders in the King's bedroom. The sun, which is coming up late, has lost "between fifty and seventy-five percent of its strength," and planets are colliding. Even time has suddenly perilously condensed. In 2 hours and 30 minutes, according to Bérenger's doctor, the year has progressed from spring to November. Determined, nevertheless, to overlook the fact that even kings are only "provisionally" immortal, the King is caught at the moment of his death like a "schoolboy who hasn't done his homework" (*EK*, 36, 39).

Influenced by *The Tibetan Book of the Dead* and originally entitled *La Cérémonie (The Ceremony)*, *Exit the King* is less a dramatic action than a ritualized death agony. It is considered the most classical of Ionesco's plays, due to its powerful simplicity. In the tradition of the classical French drama, but also, as Ionesco might have insisted, like life itself, it begins at a point where the catastrophic mechanism is already engaged. Shortly after Bérenger limps on stage, his first wife, Queen Marguerite, echoed by the Doctor/Surgeon/Executioner/Bacteriologist/Astrologist, informs him that he is going to die. The King retorts, "You get on my nerves! I'll die, yes, I'll die all right. In forty, fifty, three hundred years. Or even later. When I want to, when I've got the time, when I make up my mind" (*EK*, 22), but Marguerite is relentless: "You're going to die in an hour and a half," she insists, "you're going to die at the end of the show" (*EK*, 24). Aided by the Doctor, whose costume combines the apparel of an astrologer and an executioner, Marguerite spends that hour and a half bullying and guiding the recalcitrant King toward his "ineluctable fate."

Her efforts are hindered by the ludicrous little "Greek chorus" that makes up the remains of Bérenger's court: his housekeeper-nurse, Juliette; a half-witted, jabbering guard, suffering, like many of Ionesco's comic figures, from a distorting echolalia; and especially by the young and beautiful Queen Marie, second wife to the King, "but first in affection." The recurrent wife-mother composite in Ionesco's theater is given a richer nuance than in his other plays, with the conflicting dual roles split between competing wives. Marie attempts to save Bérenger from

Marguerite's fatal itinerary, insisting that love will be a barrier and proposing surrealist remedies: "Dive into an endless maze of wonder and surprise, then you too will have no end. . . . Escape from definitions and you too will breathe again" (*EK*, 51). Love, imagination, and words prove as impotent as Ionesco's own attempts to counter the dreadful knowledge of mortality, which had been passed on to him as a small boy by his mother. Bérenger's old heart, gone berserk, is beating so hard it widens the cracks in the wall (the stage directions suggest that a section of wall might disappear at this point) and can be heard in the auditorium. Marie disappears because Bérenger can no longer see her, and all his imperial protests, threats, and blubbering appeals for immortality come to naught.

Bérenger's fitful transformation takes place in rhythmic shifts from the slapstick pace of a farcical "countdown" to a liturgical ritual. In the first part of the play, the lines are delivered in a vaudevillian cross fire; later the exchanges are essentially choral. Just past the midpoint in the play, an abruptly supplicant Bérenger, appealing for lessons from the "countless thousands who died before me," prompts a five-voice litany. As all the actors kneel, arms outstretched, Juliette invokes "statues . . . dark or shining phantoms, ancients and shades," and Marie the "morning mists and dews" (*EK*, 54–55). The tone of the supplication is kept comically unbalanced. The doctor's pedestrian contribution is to recommend euphoric pills or sleeping potions, until Marguerite points out that Bérenger would vomit them up.

Now at a ceremonial "first remove" from his existence, Bérenger is ready for the lesson about life that must precede the lesson about death. Seemingly aware for the first time that Juliette is a real person, but perhaps only hoping to gain time, he asks his maid what her life is like. Juliette replies, "A bad life sir," pouring out a catalogue of miseries: she is cold, physically ravaged by her housekeeping duties, isolated, badly dressed, bored, and, above all, "tired, tired, tired." Bérenger counters her laments with an existential eulogy: "It's wonderful to feel bored and *not* to feel bored, too, to lose one's temper, and not to lose one's temper, to be discontented and to be content. You get excited, you talk and people talk to you, you touch and they touch you. All this is magical, like some endless celebration" (*EK*, 63, 64).

Juliette's kitchen complaints remind the king that he loves the simple ingredients of stew, but stew is no longer allowed by the doctor. Bérenger decrees that there was never such a thing as stew, and the guard announces loyally, "Stew has been banished from the length and breadth of the land" (*EK,* 65). Only Queen Marguerite comprehends the magnitude of this pathetic bravado, rejoicing at his first sign of abdication: "Now we can begin. Gently, as you remove a dressing from an open sore, first lifting the corners because they're [farthest] from the center of the wound" (*EK,* 65) In an extraordinary mime scene, Marguerite peels away the barnacles of existence that Bérenger has mistaken for his real self. Become both midwife and mother to the old King, who is now blind and deaf to all the others, she releases him from the world. Marguerite cuts an invisible cord with an invisible scissors. She relieves Bérenger of an imaginary ball and chain, a heavy sack, a spare pair of army boots, a rifle and a machine gun, and a rusty old saber. She pries open his clenched fist, in which he is holding his entire kingdom "in miniature: on microfilm . . . in tiny grains" (*EK,* 92). When Bérenger, whose last words are "blue, blue," has finally given up even his colors, she leads him on a last ascent to his throne. Marguerite disappears, as the rest of the cast and part of the set have already done. The King is left alone, motionless for a long moment in a deathly, grayish light, and then he too fades from view. In the original production, Jacques Noël had the backdrops painted on the reverse side and lighted from behind so that the set could be made to disappear at the end of Bérenger's performance by simply extinguishing the lights. When Jorge Lavelli staged the play in 1976 at the Odéon, he used walls constructed of inflatable material and a sophisticated play of light to give the impression of a slowly progressing demolition. Bérenger's exit reproduces Ionesco's own reaction at a time when he believed that death was imminent: "I had lived for nothing. . . . Everything that I had lived, felt, said, crumbled with the entire universe. . . . behind me was the void, another void was there, before me" (*A,* 196). At the end of the play, nothing remains but the gray light, symbolic of the "ontological emptiness" Ionesco had sought to render earlier in *The Chairs.*

Exit the King and *The Chairs,* Ionesco's two masterpieces, are similar in their depiction of regret for a life not lived well and lessons inevitably learned too late, although Bérenger's agony is more terrible than the Old Couple's because he is relentlessly denied his illusions. At best he will be for a while "a page in a book of ten thousand pages in one of a million libraries which has a million books," but paper, as the doctor notes, turns to dust and "libraries often go up in smoke" (*EK,* 82). More cruel still, he discovers in a moment of despairing Beckettian lucidity that "What's got to finish one day is finished now" (*EK,* 50).

Appropriately, the set for the long ceremony is a "vaguely dilapidated, vaguely Gothic" throne room. The stage directions indicate that a "derisive rendering" of the music associated with the "levees" of Louis XIV is to be played as the curtain goes up and for a long moment afterward.

There is little that is majestic about either Bérenger's surroundings or his entourage. Satirically symbolic, the throne room could be one of Ionesco's familiar bourgeois living rooms. Juliette refers to it as the living room in spite of the Queen's impatient corrections. Queen Marguerite plays her role with the imperial severity of the Fates or an old-fashioned schoolmistress, but her language, especially when she addresses her rival, is often more appropriate to a pub than a palace. Queen Marie, accused by Marguerite of having delusions of triviality rather than grandeur, is too teary-eyed to be regal. If there exists a "royal" line for Bérenger, it issues from King Ubu. Bérenger's selfish practicality is distinctly Ubuesque when he cries out to the sun, for example: "If you're in need of some small sacrifice, then parch and wither up the world. Let every human creature die provided *I* can live forever. . . . It's better to miss one's friends than to be missed oneself. Besides, one never is" (*EK,* 52). Jarry used the gleefully destructive Ubu to satirize the militarism of the French Third Republic. Some of Bérenger's exploits are blunt reminders of the continuing legacy of cold war brutality. When Marguerite says: "you had my parents butchered, your own brothers, your rivals, our cousins and great-grandcousins, and all their families, friends and cattle. You massacred the lot and scorched all their lands," Bérenger, insisting on the term "executions" not "assassinations," invokes "reasons of State" (*EK,* 46–47). For the most part, however, the political preoccupations emerge in a very minor key. Unlike Ubu, Bérenger is not an entirely ignominious buffoon. Faced with his mortality, falling over and missing his throne (for which a royally inscribed wheelchair is eventually substituted, along with the nightcap that replaces his crown), or crying out, "Why was I born if it wasn't forever," he becomes a familiar, humorously derisory creature, not all that far removed from a Choubert or an Amédée or, especially, the Bérenger of *The Killer.*

The dosage of humor has varied considerably from one successful production of *Exit the King* to another. A critic praising a 1966 revival of Jacques Mauclair's original production emphasized what was still considered in the 1960s to be the essential ingredient of Ionesco's theater:

"This tragedy does not exclude laughter—and it's the Ionescan miracle to thus be able to push the clowning and the absurd between the black paving stones of this funereal path."[19] Lavelli's highly acclaimed production was an essentially tragic version, plunging, according to an admiring critic for *Le Monde,* "to the quick of the wound without anesthetic, without the diversions of the pathetic and the absurd."[20] Lavelli's interpretation reflected not only a trend away from absurdist perspectives in the theater by the 1970s but also Ionesco's own increasingly somber dramatic evolution.

Délire à deux autant qu'on veut (Frenzy for Two or More)

In the spring of 1962, a theater director challenged Ionesco, François Billetdoux (1910–) and Jean Vauthier (1927–)—all of whom were dramatists in the absurdist vein, although they scarcely knew each other at the time—to each produce a one-act play on the theme of a lovers' quarrel. He stipulated that the play should be set in a room with three doors and a bed. The three plays were then shuffled like playing cards to create a spectacle called *Chemises de nuit (Night Shirts)*. The experiment was not successful, but when Jean-Louis Barrault staged Ionesco's contribution as *Frenzy for Two or More* at the Odéon in 1966, it was an important theater event. This short play presents a couple barricaded in the bedroom of their apartment while a civil war rages noisily below. As stray missiles occasionally penetrate the bedroom wall, they argue in a *Bald Soprano*–like mixture of insults, ad hominem arguments, specious logic, and twisted language, over the woman's claim that a tortoise and a snail are the same thing. When the carnage in the street stops, or as the man puts it, "peace has broken out," a guillotine is installed in what remains of the apartment above. In a scene reminiscent of Artaud's *Jet of Blood,* headless bodies and bodiless dolls' heads fall through the couples' bombed-out ceiling. The couple notices, but their argument goes on, as it has for 17 years, while they rebuild their barricade on the "peacetime" pretext of shutting out drafts and germs.

In this linguistic rampage with its automaton-like couple sparring in a claustrophobic space, Ionesco returns to the domain of his short plays of the early 1950s. This is an angrier work, however, predictive of the apocalyptic dramas to come. Explicit ties to history, allusions to the neighbors being taken away by soldiers, and pessimistic references to the outcome of war as simply one murderous ideology or political leader replacing another, blacken the humor. When the woman, speaking of the gratuitous violence in the world, observes that people never behave as they should, the man replies that violence helps to pass the time. When she asks what would happen if neither side won, the pessimism of the answer overwhelms the humor of the contradictory clichés:

HE: Stalemate. Both sides bled white.

SHE: And then what happens?

HE: It's a gray world. Everyone's red with fury. (S, 149)

In the late 1960s, red and darkness, given both spiritual and political connotations, became the prominent tones in Ionesco's theater.

Chapter Nine
Apocalyptic Visions

One of Ionesco's principal objections to the "collectivist" theories of the 1960s was their dismissal of metaphysics: "Metaphysics can lead to God. But God alienates us, they say. . . . They want nothing to do with anything behind appearances. They would have us see only 'society.' . . . Thus for the individual—let us say the 'individual soul'—there is no recourse above and beyond social alienation" (*PP,* 145). During the 1960s the existential dilemma became, with increasing complexity, both political and a matter of the soul for Ionesco. Speaking of the "apocalyptic sentiment" that animates *Macbett* and *Killing Game,* plays in which death and solitude on a grand guignolesque political scale constitute the entire dramatic matter, he noted that this has always been a part of his vision. According to Ionesco, the origins of this sentiment lie in his Christian formation, but it has been exacerbated by the political events of the 1960s and 1970s (Bonnefoy, 1977, 168). To accommodate the apocalyptic nature of his politically driven metaphysics, the physical dimensions of Ionesco's theater were expanded considerably. After the Bérenger plays, the absurdist vignettes that had characterized so much of his theater evolved into lavishly staged epics. In these high-tech morality plays, "sound and light" spectacles, and even operatic interludes, increasingly replace the verbal exuberance of his theater of the 1950s and the early 1960s.

Le Soif et la faim (Hunger and Thirst)

In the early pages of *Fragments of a Journal,* answering the question, "What is life?" Ionesco replies, "For me it is, it must be, the present, presentness, plenitude. I have run after life so much that I have lost it . . . and yet I still run after life in the hope of catching it at the last minute, as one jumps on to the steps of the last carriage of a moving train" (*F,* 21). *Hunger and Thirst* consists of three loosely connected, dreamlike episodes completed in 1964, to which a fourth was later added. It depicts a similar pursuit of a vaguely defined "grace," described by the protagonist, whose words are mirrored by striking visual stage effects, as a quest for light. Sharing the playwright's longing for some kind of salvation, Jean, the alter ego protagonist who has replaced the Bérengers, is driven to ask, "Why this sudden hunger, this sudden thirst? This dissatisfaction and the anguish. . . . Why were there no more luminous days?" (*HT,* 98).[1]

In the first episode, entitled "The Flight," Jean chafes at existence in a dank apartment, which for him has become a tomb sinking into the mire. Fearing death and frightened by the rapid passage of time, envying people who, for ridiculously low rents, "live on magical hilltops, glistening peaks," he blames his wife, Marie-Madeleine, for his misery (*HT,* 10, 29). Accustomed to his chronic discontent—"if it's not agoraphobia, it's claustrophobia!"—she counters his complaints with a radically different vision. In the mildewed wallpaper where Jean sees an apocalyptic universe matching the antiworld of *A Stroll in the Air,* Marie-Madeleine finds welcoming shapes. She claims there is a cure for his neuroses, but Jean replies from a deep fund of despair: "I see things as they are and that's incurable" (*HT,* 25).

Jean's "reality" is drawn from Ionesco's guilt-laden phantasms. The dismal apartment was a recurring nightmare image for the playwright. "The image of the tomb itself," its source was a ground-floor apartment rented by his mother right before she died, a choice he interpreted as a premonitory resignation to her impending death (Benmussa, 1966, 9). The night of her death, Ionesco dreamed that he tried unsuccessfully to save a woman perishing in flames. In *Hunger and Thirst,* Jean cannot bear the fire, in which he sees an agonizing woman holding out her arms in an "eternal reproach." From the mirror of Jean's apartment emerges a delusional, haglike old aunt, modeled after one of Ionesco's mother's sisters who became mentally ill. Chased away by Jean, who forces her to acknowledge that she is long dead, she berates him for the selfishness of the living. With each apparition Jean grows more desperate to escape the intersecting traps of domesticity and remorse. His will not be the fate of the Old Couple in *The Chairs.* While Marie-Madeleine rocks the cradle of the couple's infant daughter, Marthe, singing a refrain about a love that cannot be ripped from the heart, he initiates a cruel game of hide-and-seek. (Ionesco's pity for his mother did not blind him to an unwelcome identification with his father.) Jean and Marie-Madeleine appear and disappear with improbable alacrity, achieved by having the heads and waving arms of extras appear at different points of the stage, until, unseen by his wife, Jean stops the game. He rips from his heart a branch of briar rose, lays it on the table, then disappears. As Marie-

Madeleine again sings the refrain, the back wall of the stage vanishes, revealing a blossoming garden and a very blue sky from which a silver ladder is suspended, its top out of sight.

The very brief second episode, "The Rendezvous," takes place on a terrace that is suspended in midair, brilliantly lit with a cold light, and surrounded by arid mountains. In the first episode, Jean longs to cast off the unbearable weight of his own memories for "memories I've never had, impossible memories" (*HT,* 25). In the second, dazzled by the light and giddy with freedom and anticipation, he awaits the arrival of a scarcely remembered woman who has promised to wake him from his lifelong nightmare "the same person and someone else at one and the same time" (*HT,* 45). He waits in front of an oddly situated museum, perhaps the repository of these memories. As time speeds by, he is forced to acknowledge that he is waiting in vain. His despair produces a hallucinatory version of the biblical refrain (in Matthew) that gives the play its title: "What if that's all there was! My heart's like a wounded beast, clawing me in its death-throes. . . . My stomach's a bottomless pit, my mouth a funnel of fire. Hunger and thirst, hunger and thirst" (*HT,* 49). The museum guards go off, anticipating with shouts of "Bon appétit" a very real evening's soup.

In the third and longest episode, "The Black Masses of the Good Inn," Jean arrives at a hall described in the stage directions as "a kind of monastery-cum-barracks-cum-prison," where he is greeted by a sinister monklike character named Tarabas (*HT,* 52). Jean has not escaped time. He is exhausted and visibly aged, but above all tormented by an insatiable hunger and thirst which copious portions of food and drink served in a frenetic relay by the brothers can barely relieve. Briefly satisfied, he recounts his travels to the curious monks under the silent gaze of the God-like Brother Superior, a mute, white-robed figure made inhumanly large by stilts. His desires, like an insidious ideology, are conveniently interpreted by Tarabas.

In the telling, Jean's adventures become insignificant. The monks anticipate surrealistic tales of "the crimson ocean . . . chinks in the blue vault of Heaven, the rape of the stars and those contraptions whirling round in the shimmering rainbow sky" (*HT,* 60). Jean speaks of gray, deserted plains and fog, lonely paths and empty crossroads, children not spoken to; and gates closed "because it was too early or too late, forbidden to enter" (*HT,* 65). He has ignored the one figure he did see repeatedly, a ghastly, ragged old woman: It was a figment of my imagination . . . old age itself" (*HT,* 66). Promising him pills that will improve his imagination and visionary drops for his eyes, Tarabas offers his own entertainment, "a play about education and re-education."

Two starving and thirsty old clowns—Tripp, dressed in black, and Brechtoll, wearing red—are delivered onstage in cages. Tripp represents not only the Church, but Ionesco himself, according to the playwright. Brechtoll, of course, with its Jarryesque suffix, represents Brecht and all his admirers.[2] Tarabas, who has donned a sumptuous, half-red, half-black cloak, tortures them both. Satirically distorting their already confused slogans, Tarabas proffers soup and proofs of the inefficacy of his prisoners' beliefs until Brechtoll proclaims his faith in God and Tripp denies his existence. Jean, made to watch the performance from center front, is flanked by red-robed monks bathed in a red light on Brechtoll's side and by monks in black on Tripps's side. The monks rhythmically applaud "their" prisoner and mime the words of Tarabas's "disintoxication" ritual. Like a spectator at one of Ionesco's early plays, Jean's first response is stupefaction; then he begins to laugh, taking the performance as a game. As the "comedy" progresses, however, he also begins to mime the drama, but it is the clowns' anguish that he apes. By the end of the spectacle, he is moving and speaking in mesmerized synchrony with the prisoners. Although Tarabas announces that this mock-Brechtian epic is just one of 30 episodes and that the next one will "demystify freedom itself," Marxism is no more Ionesco's villain here than any other orthodoxy (HT, 94). The moral of the "entertainment" is the promiscuous interchangeability of ideological zealotry. Tarabas explains that the two clowns have learned each other's lines and can play either role.

His travel chronicle deemed insufficient compensation for the monks' hospitality, Jean must pay with service in kind. While he mechanically serves bowls of soup, Brother Accountant's debt figures multiply wildly. They are chanted by the monks, appear magically on the blackboard, and light up on screens and on the walls. They are also repeated in alarm by Marie-Madeleine and Marthe, now 15 years old, who suddenly appear beyond the bars of the monastery in the luminous garden of the first episode. The suspended ladder is still there, but Jean remains a prisoner of dissatisfaction. Although he begs his wife and daughter to wait, he is equally anxious to find out about "that other one, she for whom I was neither father, nor son, nor husband" (HT, 100).

The added episode, entitled "At the Foot of the Wall," is composed of fragments from recorded dreams which serve as cryptogrammic summaries of the fears and obsessions in the earlier episodes. This episode also suggests that the closure to Jean's quest will not be fulfillment but death. It takes place on a stark set, on which a high wall stretches across the back of the stage and there are dying weeds in the foreground. For Jean, connected to the protagonist in the original episodes only by the fact that he is a vulnerable, questing figure, the wall looms, as it does in Ionesco's journals, as an impenetrable psychological barrier and a reminder of mortality. He will not simply go around it, the practical solution adopted by another character, nor is he equipped to scale it, having left his ladder at home. Ionesco interpreted the recurrent wall image in his dreams as symbolic of death and solitude, and also as what separated him "from the truth or from a more accurate and extensive knowledge" (*F*, 62, 77).

As Jean waits, stymied, a rabbi enters, followed by a line of chanting children. Behind the rabbinical disguise, Jean recognizes Schaeffer, the chameleonlike figure from Ionesco's nightmares who represents the playwright's father. Religion has been banned, but Schaeffer has hedged his bets: the children are not singing psalms, but chanting the *Communist Manifesto* in Hebrew. Caught and hurled with the children over a precipice, he survives and reappears, like an opportunistic phoenix, disguised as a tourist guide. Jean refuses to join his group. Schaeffer, who is also a magician, banishes the wall, warning as he does so that Jean will have to "go down." With Schaeffer's disappearance, the last sunlight disappears from the stage. The wall vanishes, replaced by an old kitchen presided over by a filthy old woman. A nightmarish mother figure in a dark dress, she points his way in the gray light, warning him of the mud.[3] Going down a sloping ramp as the episode comes to an end, Jean, like many of the autobiographical protagonists who have preceded him in Ionesco's theater, descends into the inevitable trap of physical existence: degradation, then death. He complains that he had not been warned that the way down was as difficult as the way up. It would be easier if he could sing, the old woman replies, but he cannot because he has lost his youth.

The omnipresent religious imagery in *Hunger and Thirst*, suggested by the title, the monasterial setting, the "Jacob's ladder" in the Edenic garden, the biblical names of Jean's wife and daughter, the rhyming similarity of Tarabas to Barabas, the condemned thief who was saved instead of Jesus, and the powerful light and color effects, focused critical attention on either the religious or the sacrilegious thrust of the play depending on the perspective of the interpreter.[4] When the play was first performed in 1966, scandalized patrons of the Comédie Française responded to what they perceived as a blasphemous, condemnatory mix of the sacred and the secular in the cage scene by shouting insults at the actors. During one particularly tempestuous performance, the actor playing the role of Jean turned on the booing audience with an exasperated obscenity. The succès de scandale created by this Ubuesque defiance infuriated Ionesco who responded angrily that this "satire of the Inquisition" was really a satire of all inquisitions (*A*, 276). He was by then far removed from the anarchic disposition that had prompted his suggestion that *The Bald Soprano* be brought to an end by the playwright's rushing on stage and yelling obscenities at the audience. In the interim, he had begun to take very seriously a theater in which the primary ingredients had become "stories, images, situations drawn from my dreams" (*A*, 280).

Interviewed in 1966, a few years after he completed the play, Ionesco said it was more or less inspired by Zen Buddhism, in which liberation is achieved by going beyond systematized thought (Tarrab, 1970, 103–104). Earlier he had remarked to Jean-Marie Serreau, who directed the premiere at the Comédie Française, that "the hero of my play . . . is hungry and thirsty. For what? He doesn't know himself. It is a useless quest, an irrational Grail without a goal. In any case, I am waiting for the critics to explain the play in order to explain it to myself."[5] Ionesco offered a much different perspective in 1987, one that corresponds to his struggle with Christian faith and the paean to his wife in *La Quête intermittente*, which was published that same year. Jean enters in the "Christian myths" of purgatory according to Ionesco's later interpretation: "He sees that his life is lost because he did not understand the celestial message incarnated by his wife and daughter. During his long wanderings, he looks for a stable, mystical, religious foundation but because of his spiritual deficiency, he sees nothing" (*TC*, 1753). The play can be fully effective, however, only to the extent that it is interpreted in a fashion that is neither too personal nor thematically reductive. "Do I really want salvation?" Ionesco asked in *Fragments of a Journal* (13). *Hunger and Thirst* is most convincing as a provocative stage version of that question.

La Lacune (The Gap); Exercices de conversation et de diction française pour étudiants américains (French Conversation and Pronunciation Exercises for American Students)

After *Hunger and Thirst*, Ionesco returned very briefly, in a comic vein, to the realm of absurd pedagogy where his dramatic career had begun. In

The Gap, first published in *Le Nouvel observateur* in January 1965, a middle-aged member of the French Academy—who is a doctor, a renowned author and lecturer on the world circuit, the subject of thousands of theses, the recipient of innumerable honorary degrees which conspicuously cover his walls, and the former president of the baccalaureat commission of the Education Ministry—fails the baccalaureat examination because he did not stick to the subject in French composition.[6] Certain that the examiners have humiliated him for personal reasons, he telephones his friend, the president of the Republic, only to learn that the latter's mother has forbidden him to play with students at the bottom of the class. As the play ends, he breaks his ceremonial sword and rips off his medals.

Inspired by a scandal involving stolen baccalaureat tests and the very common "examination dream," *The Gap* is a satire of the intellectual establishment. It is also a half-serious, half-self-ironizing portrait. Ionesco was an outsider when he returned to Romania as an adolescent and an interloper in the French theater when he began his dramatic career. At the time he was writing the play, he was distanced from former admirers by his less than fashionable politics. Not yet a member of the Académie Française but nearly as famous as his protagonist, he had a long history nonetheless of feeling rebuffed by those who, as the protagonist's wife admiringly portrays the examiners, "know what they are doing. . . . They have passed the examinations, their formation is very serious, they know the rules of composition."[7]

Exercises de conversation et de diction française pour étudiants américains was begun in 1964 as dialogues for a beginning French-language textbook in which two university students named Marie-Jeanne and Jean-Marie, a myopic classmate named Thomas, and their French professor confront the elusive quality of linguistic accuracy.[8] The dialogues were first read as theater sketches at the Comédie Française in 1966. Ionesco was one of the readers. The topics in both the textbook, which lists Ionesco's professional credential as the Grand Satrap of the College of Pataphysics, and the theater sketches cover the basic range of student needs from the classroom to restaurants, transportation, the hospital, the courtroom, and, of course, the theater. (A reference to *"baignoires,"* which are both theater boxes and bathtubs in French, leads to a mass shower when a falling chandelier sets fire to the seats and firemen arrive with their hoses.) Autobiographical conflicts are introduced, but with magical solutions. A tale intended to teach the past tenses is a first-person account of a 13-year-old's escape from a train when the conductor falls asleep. In the next lesson, he is brought to trial but found "not guilty" because the conductor had no right to doze off. As in Ionesco's *Stories for Children under Three Years of Age*, words delivered from the constraints of reason create humorous worlds of their own in these dialogues, which returned Ionesco to the mocking irreverence of his confrontation with an English-language manual: "I remembered the Assimil method which did not succeed in teaching me English. Perhaps with these dialogues and monologues the Americans won't learn French either."[9]

Jeux de Massacre (Killing Game)

In what may have been a reaction to the negative reception of his confessional *Hunger and Thirst,* Ionesco turned to other authors for inspiration for his next two major plays. *Killing Game,* which took 6 years of revision and many title changes to complete, was inspired by Daniel Defoe's *Journal of a Plague Year,* a novel about the epidemic in London in 1665.[10] *Killing Game* incorporates details from Defoe's account, such as the fire that swept London in the aftermath of the plague and the draconian measures that were taken to segregate and exterminate victims and their families. Unlike Defoe's novel, however, a first-person narrative so realistic as to seem an on-site report, Ionesco's depiction of a plague-infested town in which nearly every inhabitant falls victim to a gruesome, onstage death, is minimally concerned with historical facts. For Ionesco, *Journal of a Plague Year* served primarily as a depersonalizing model and a vehicle for enlargement of the scope of his perennial theme that the knowledge of death makes happiness impossible.

The 18 episodes of *Killing Game* are set in a generic town, neither modern nor ancient according to the stage directions, which propose a late-nineteenth-century style for the decor. The one consistent character is a medieval apparition, the silent, hooded "Black Monk," who is mounted on stilts, as is the Brother Superior in *Hunger and Thirst.* Crossing the stage unseen by the other characters, he reappears in each vignette, presaging the next round of carnage. The language and the preoccupations of the townspeople, in contrast to those of the monk, are distinctly modern. Anachronistic references to moon landings and computers create a comic effect. References to London and Berlin, on the other hand, are grim reminders that this "killing game" has a very real and recent antecedent. The anachronisms empty meaning from the notion of time, just as the inevitability of death renders existence meaningless. As the epidemic spreads, unmasking an elemental fear and greed, its "geometrically progressing" death toll is inflated by suicides and by a smorgasbord of murders ranging from hypocritically "justified" homicide to strangling, infanticide, and cannibalism. In the last scene, the crowd of greedy survivors is swept away by a raging fire. Proliferating corpses mirror the proliferating words in Ionesco's apocalyptic plays.

The opening scene presents a market crowd engaged in the kinds of trivial activities that numb people into indifference to mortality. When suddenly confronted with the inexplicable deaths of two infants, however, the crowd responds with a chain of recriminatory murders. By the end of the scene, corpses are strewn across the stage like bowling pins.[11] The "game" goes on for 17 more scenes, bringing down the wealthy and their servants; prisoners and hangmen; those with faith in science, religion, or politics and those without; the selfish and the brave; the guilty and the innocent; friends and enemies; and lovers young and old. The bedlam moves without logic or transition from day to night and from indoors to outdoors. Scene and character shifts take place at a feverish pace, capturing the cancerous breeding and delirium of both the physical and the moral plague. The play is a hallucinatory Punch and Judy show that depends on sophisticated stage lighting for its full effect. Among the most arresting episodes is a night scene in which, from five windows that are lit in succession, the shadows and sounds of mayhem—suicides, stranglings, thefts, screams of fear and hatred, appeals for help—are projected onto a darkened stage that has just been crossed by the Black Monk in the sinister light of his lantern.

Ionesco's rendition of the plague had two twentieth-century antecedents: Camus's *La Peste (The Plague)*, a novel published in 1947 which was also inspired by Defoe, and Artaud's essay in *The Theater and Its Double* entitled "The Theater and the Plague." Although Ionesco discounted similarities to Camus' novel, contrasting the metaphysical implications of his play with the more concrete moral issues addressed by Camus, there are significant parallels (Bonnefoy, 1977, 161). Camus used his allegorical portrait of Occupied France to denounce legalized killing and the murderous excesses of Stalinism. Several scenes in *Killing Game* exist for similar purposes. A politician calling for "Revolt! Terrorism! Violence!" acknowledges that he cannot promise that the plague will disappear but makes the Mother Peepish claim that its meaning will be changed. His ultimate solution is to "kill the undertakers."[12] He is followed by another orator whose vision of the world after the plague is a utopia with Stalinist overtones. The survivors in this "much improved consumer society" will gain from being part of a smaller population. All contradictions will be reconciled with a "twelve-point plan" (*KG,* 80–81).

There is also a Camusian echo in Ionesco's depiction of solitude. This theme is more compellingly rendered in *Killing Game* than is the horror of death, which tends to be diluted by a macabre humor inflated to the point of parody. In the eighth episode, simultaneous scenes on a divided stage depict two sets of lovers whose echoing lines diverge only at the end when the woman in one scene and the man in another fall ill with the plague.[13] The husband remains, faithfully holding his dying wife; the woman flees her stricken mate. It is not the loyalty of the one and the faithlessness of the other that is central, however, but that the cherished woman and the abandoned man die in an equivalent solitude. Near the end of the play, in an episode with appealing vestiges of the lyricism of *Exit the King,* Ionesco temporarily slows the accelerating carnage to stage an autobiographical old couple. For the bored old man, whose early capacity for wonder was long ago overcome by the threat of death, each moment has become "overbearing, and empty" (*KG,* 92). Yet, like King Bérenger, he finds life unbearably short: "I've been on this earth for centuries and yet only an instant. It's been so long and there's so little time" (*KG,* 94). Although she is staggering from the disease, the Old Woman can still speak of catching dreams and the saving graces of love and imagination. The Old Man, begging her not to leave him, understands too late that "We had joy and I didn't know it" (*KG,* 98).

A broad philosophical gulf does separate, however, Ionesco's cataclysmic vision in *Killing Game* from Doctor Rieux's assessment at the end of Camus's novel: "there are more things to admire in man than to despise."[14] Most of the events in *Killing Game* are unredeemedly vicious. Ionesco is closer in his treatment of the plague to Artaud, who compared the theater to the plague "not because it is contagious, but because like the plague it is the revelation, the exteriorization of a depth of latent cruelty by which all the perverse possibilities of the mind, whether of an individual or a people, are localized" (Artaud, 1958, 30–31). In his prize-winning 1970 production, Jorge Lavelli interpreted the rhythm of the play as "the organization of a series of wounds, of ruptures, of suffocations, and libidinous drives" (*TC,* 1449).[15] Ionesco had suggested the use of mannequins or puppets to augment the crowd scenes. Lavelli opted to use only real actors, requiring them to change costumes at a prodigious speed, because he wanted to remove any symbolism or fiction that would shield the spectator from the horror of a very real death (*TC* 1449–50).

Killing Game is the most hopeless and derisive of Ionesco's plays. It is not a quest for meaning but a commentary about the meaninglessness of any such quest. For many critics, Ionesco's obsession with the impossibility of escaping death was becoming a worn-out theme. What is different in this play is the almost unrelieved human blindness, depredation, and solitude generated by the threat of death. This was powerfully captured by Lavelli, whose use of giant garbage cans on wheels to dispatch the corpses underscored the mechanical rapidity which with death comes and the dreadful throwaway quality of human existence. In a world that remains plagued by civil wars and epidemics, the play continues to be relevant.

Macbett

Ionesco reportedly spent more than a year and a half rereading *Macbeth* and taking notes before writing his parodic version, which had its premiere in 1972.[16] His reading was profoundly influenced by a work entitled *Shakespeare Our Contemporary* by the Polish writer Jan Kott, in which Shakespeare's tragedy is compared to the kind of cyclical repression and violence that resurfaced in Stalinism after World War II. Kott opposed Stalinism from the position of a Marxist intellectual, but his perception of the "Grand Mechanism" operating in *Macbeth* supported Ionesco's bitter assessment of human existence: "If you have been everywhere a foreigner and a stranger, as I have, you find that cruelty and hatred are the dominant factors in human affairs. That's a discovery I've never got over—that people are out to kill one another; if not directly, then indirectly."[17] Kott writes of Macbeth that, having put down a rebellion that brings him near the throne, "he can become a king, so he must become a king. He kills the rightful sovereign. He then must kill the witness of the crime, and those who suspect it. He must kill the sons and friends of those he has killed. Later he must kill everybody, for everybody is against him. . . . In the end he will be killed himself. He has trod the whole way up and down the grand staircase of history."[18]

Macbett is a very free adaptation. It is infused with Jarryesque touches, beginning with the spelling change, which corresponds to the French pronunciation of Macbeth but also makes it homophonous with the French word *bête* meaning both "stupid," and "animal." Ionesco noted that between Shakespeare and Jarry, his play was "rather close to

Ubu roi."[19] He wrote *Macbett* because "power corrupts and one must rise up against that," but he claimed to have written it joyfully nonetheless, because "it is necessary to know how to laugh about the most atrocious things."[20] Scenes and characters have been altered and added for comic and spectacular effects. Macbett is not married. Lady Macbeth's ambitions are assigned by Ionesco to the unhappily married Lady Duncan, a New Age replica of Choubert's Madeleine, who also doubles as one of Shakespeare's prophetic witches. In *Macbett* the "grand staircase of history" of which Kott spoke begins with Candor and Glamiss plotting against Archduke Duncan. Their echoed grievances, which they recite like schoolboys pumping themselves up to take on the school bully, build to a justification of war, with a classic Ionescan stretch of logic: "A tyrant, a usurper, a despot, a dictator, a miscreant, an ogre, an ass, a goose—and worse. The proof is, he's in power."[21]

With the exit of Candor and Glamiss, the empty stage is taken over by a lengthy sound-and-light spectacle. Crackling flashes of machine gunfire and stormy lightning give way to a clear red sky. The noise of the battle diminishes to death rattles, isolated shots, and the screams and groans of the wounded. Bit characters cross the stage, continuing the mayhem on a minor scale as they variously profit or perish in the violence. They are followed by Macbett, who sits wearily on a milestone clutching his bloody sword. While worrying that he might have trod upon the toes of a fellow soldier, he gives an account of his battle feats so outrageous as to become preposterously humorous. The number of his victims—slaughtered by sword or by his bare hands; executed by firing squad at his command; roasted alive when he set fire to the forests; suffocated under the rubble of their blown-up houses; drowned attempting an escape across the Channel; or dead of fear, suicide, "anger, apoplexy or a broken heart"—builds from dozens and dozens to tens of millions. The few who are left are still fighting: "The severed heads of our enemies spit in our face and mock us. Arms shorn from their trunks go on brandishing their swords and firing pistols. Amputated feet kick up the backside. They were all traitors, of course" (*M*, 15).

Suddenly feeling "quite bucked" and concluding that "it's been quite a pleasant day really," Macbett goes off (*M*, 16). This clears the way for his counterpart Banco, who appears in the same costume and with the same beard. Multiplying both the humor and the horror of the previous scene, he repeats, word for word, Macbett's soliloquy. As Banco goes off, the sounds and light of battle start up again accompanied by a "pounding brutal music." Loud fanfares announce the Archduchess and the

Archduke who proceed with a serial guillotining as a "whole forest" of guillotines springs up in the background and heads pile up in a basket. Candor dies first, made worthy of his name with a bit of realpolitik: "If I'd been stronger, I'd have been your anointed king. Defeated, I'm a traitor and a coward. . . . I hope at least that my fate will serve as an example to you all and to posterity. Throw in your lot with the stronger" (*M*, 32). He is followed to the guillotine by a procession of his 137,000 men.

In this play of deadly duets, two hags (not three as in Shakespeare) accost Macbett, predicting that he, not Banco, will inherit Glamiss's title and replace Duncan as king. The scene is immediately repeated, with Banco as the prey of the hags. During the ensuing phantasmagoria, Macbett is seduced into treason by a mixture of crude brainwashing, Latin chants, a magic wand, and a high-tech striptease in which the First Witch is transformed into a Folies Bergeres version of Lady Duncan. Clad in a sparkling bikini and a red-and-black cape, bearing scepter in one hand and a dagger in the other, and mounted on a ladder as if she were a celestial vision, she persuades Macbett to kill her husband by offering to become his mistress. His last scruples are dissolved by her Shakespearean assurance that "no man born of woman" will be able to conquer him and by the more modern claim of the Second Witch, who has become the Lady-in-Waiting: "we want only to save our country. The two of you will build a better society, a brave new world" (*M*, 57).

Macbett, Banco, and Lady Duncan, disguised as a monk and sickly faithful, assassinate the Archduke as he exercises his royal healing powers. Macbett replaces Duncan, as both king and husband, while enthusiastic crowds in the background shout "Long live Macbett!" Overhearing the jealous Banco making plans to marry the Lady-in-Waiting, he murders him too. Lady Duncan dons her witch's rags and false nose and teeth, and flies off on her suitcase. The gullible Macbett is then murdered by Macol, Duncan's son by a gazelle, as shouts of "Long Live Macol!" mechanically replace the earlier cries of "Long live Macbett!" Macol disappears into the mist, announcing his intent to become "Super-highness, super-king, super-majesty, emperor of emperors" (*M*, 105).

Ionesco's own tragicomic vision allowed him to take full advantage in *Macbett* of the rich texture of the Shakespearian universe, where the tragic accommodates the comic, as well as visual and linguistic extravagance. The anchoring of his apocalyptic vision of history in one of the world's best-known tragedies was an attempt to move from the microcosm of personal obsessions to the political-historical macrocosm without destroying either the derisive irony or the fragile dramatic tension necessary to bind the two convincingly together. Audiences responded to the play enthusiastically, but it was the gags and the spectacular stage effects that they appreciated more than Ionesco's history lesson.

"La Vase" ("The Slough"); *Le Solitaire (The Hermit); Ce formidable bordel (A Hell of a Mess)*

With its episodic construction and depiction of human existence as an endless cycle of carnage, Ionesco's *A Hell of a Mess,* written in 1973, forms a trilogy with *Killing Game* and *Macbett. A Hell of a Mess* is an adaptation of his only novel, *The Hermit,* which Ionesco likened to *The Bald Soprano*: "It is an expression of the same sentiment: the unreality of the real. Of the fact that this unreality does not prevent the real from being overwhelming and aggressive. It is also about non-significance" (*A,* 217). He made a distinction, however, between his earlier attitude and his position in the midst of the political upheavals of the late 1960s and early 1970s: "I put myself at a distance and I watch people and everything they do seems astonishing, ridiculous, insane . . . but no longer comic" (Bonnefoy, 1977, 167).

The Hermit is an elaboration of an earlier short story, "The Slough," first published in 1956 and then reissued in *The Colonel's Photograph and Other Stories.* "The Slough" is a startling story, a vivid, gruesome portrayal of aging. As the rubble of the narrator's existence is progressively reduced to the perceptions of a delusional, fragmented consciousness, his body also disintegrates. At the end of the story he is stuck in a slough. While he struggles with useless bits of memories, perhaps not even his own, of childhood and adolescence and of a wife who might have been his mother, his scattered, rotting limbs and then his head dissolve. Like Gregor Samsa in Kafka's *Metamorphosis,* the narrator was once an energetic traveling salesman. A transformation, initially described as a nausea, is triggered by graying skies and the discovery that he "has a liver." Quickly reduced to a paralyzing torpor, he remains confined in his increasingly filthy room as days, months, then years flash by. Jolted by a terrifying premonition of death, he haltingly reenters the "real" world, where his derelict appearance makes him an object of astonished contempt. Nearing collapse on the road, he calls out to a passerby, but again he resembles Gregor Samsa in that his voice no longer serves to make a connection.

In spite of the obvious influence of Sartre and Kafka in the significant moments of cruelty that contribute to the narrator's isolation, the central issue in the story is not the alienating role of the other. Rather, the central issue is the unbearable loss of the capacity for astonishment, which disappears with the first recognition of physical decline. The rapidity of the change recalls Ionesco's descriptions of his childhood discovery of the inevitability of death. The sense of loss and decay is also connected to Ionesco's adolescent struggles. Grasping at memories of memories as he lies dying, the narrator recalls a failed attempt to scale a mountain which began on a bright morning when he was 13. Like Choubert's attempt, this alpine adventure ended with a fall.

In *The Colonel's Photograph,* "The Slough" is juxtaposed with "Spring 1939," the account of Ionesco's return to La Chapelle-Anthenaise. A rueful culpability pervades both texts. In "Spring 1939," Ionesco writes of an "intolerable nostalgia, an overwhelming sadness, a nameless longing, boundless regrets and remorse" (*CP,* 120). The narrator in "The Slough," suddenly compelled "to seek from a glass of alcohol the indispensable euphoria," explains, "My joy was no longer invulnerable, my energy flagged, the colors lost their brilliance. . . . For no clear reason I grew melancholy, inclined to pessimism. . . . I was overcome by a sort of repentance which had no apparent cause" (*CP,* 100–101). In his final moments, however, trapped in muck and reduced to "an eye, a skull, and a heart beating less and less fast," he nevertheless persuades himself that he will begin again (*CP,* 126). It is with "the blue vision of a clear washed sky" that he disappears, his stubbornness reflecting Ionesco's struggle in his writing and painting and in his psychoanalytic and religious quests to restore the fading echoes of youthful wonder and euphoria (*P,* 126).

The Hermit, published in 1973, is a more self-consciously literary and philosophical treatment of similar material. The depressive, nameless, first-person narrator, who tells his story in the form of a journal, observes at midpoint, "The deeper I go, the more I find only sludge. Silt and slime. A foul pond."[22] Cutting himself off from the world, whether by means of alcoholic numbing or by barricading himself in his apartment, like the narrator in "The Slough," he, too, is essentially reduced to "an eye, a skull, and a heart beating less and less fast" (*CP,* 126).

The narrator is a school dropout, a former clerk who has made lists for a living, and a heavy drinker who claims that he has never read in its entirety an article about national or international politics. Like Sartre's Roquentin, he maneuvers solitarily in a petty bourgeois milieu characterized by an infinite fund of bad faith, and loses his footing in a world where objects have lost their innocence and neutrality. Buffeted between states of lightness and "the nausea of nothingness" and then "the nausea of surfeit," he gives his Sartrian dilemma a humorously Ionescan twist: "Between the solid and the hollow, between plentitude and emptiness, I toppled over" (*H,* 95, 112). Enabled by an inheritance from an uncle in America to leave his job and his dismal colleagues, he attempts to withdraw from society by creating a comfortable cocoon in a nondescript suburban apartment. The surrounding revolutionary violence and the conversations of his concierge and fellow tenants, mostly as inane and intrusive as those of his former colleagues in Paris, quickly lead him to a recognition that is a reformulation of Sartre's definition of hell in *No Exit*: "There's no way around it, you have to take people into account. They do exist, since they bother me when they stick their noses into my business. That's all it takes for me to disconnect and sink back down among them. They draw you out of reality and enclose you in their own" (*H,* 75–76).

At midpoint in the novel, however, by means of a reported telephone conversation between the narrator and a philosophy student who is also a psychologist, Ionesco extracts his protagonist from the Sartrian mold. Informed by the philosopher-psychologist that his anguish about human misery, his manic-depressive mood swings, and his horror of death are nothing new and that he would do well to take up reading, the narrator rebukes his interlocutor for reducing questions that "take me and shake me," to emotional sterility: "for you the whole thing is files and catalogues. . . . it's part of your culture. Despair has been domesticated; people have turned it into literature, into works of art. . . . So much the better for you if culture has succeeded in exorcising man's drama, his tragedy" (*H,* 87–88).

As Ionesco also seems to recover his own narrative voice from Sartre in the second half of *The Hermit,* the novel grows increasingly hallucinatory. Toward the end of the novel, abandoned by his mistress and further isolated by inertia and despair in the midst of one of the endlessly recurring bouts of civil war, the protagonist finds himself suddenly unanchored in time and memory. Afraid that his past has been swallowed, and panic-stricken at the thought of death, he makes the discovery, so remarkably illustrated in *The Chairs* and *Exit the King,* that "the past is a death without a body to prove it" (*H,* 114). When his neighborhood is transformed into a bloody police state, even as its inhabitants are insisting, "Don't worry, nothing can happen," he recognizes that his mechanically reflexive refrain of "What's the use?" has suddenly become "fully conscious" (*H*, 125).

The novel ends with a luminous vision. Old and sour, self-imprisoned in his bedroom, and haunted by hallucinatory vignettes of past failures, the narrator sees a giant flowering tree that has sprung from the muck heap in the courtyard. His walls disappear, blending his flower-papered room into a bright flowering meadow, and a shimmering ladder appears just above his head. He takes this for "a sign" (*H*, 169). This last image was deeply symbolic for Ionesco. Comparing it to Amédée's flight, the Old Couple's fading memory of a luminous garden in *The Chairs,* and the silver ladder suspended in a bright blue sky at the end of *Hunger and Thirst,* he related it to his quest for the lost light of youth: "now and again I seem to chance upon it. This is not only why I *create* literature, but why I have always been nourished by it. . . . Generally speaking, it is not by deliberate choice that I have introduced these images of light: whether they are soon eclipsed or just emerge as a natural conclusion to my tale, they merely happen. . . . I have the feeling, in my plays or my prose writing, that I am exploring a dark forest, groping through the night" (*Plays, XI,* 120–21).

In *Nu,* comparing the artificiality of the novel unfavorably to his far more authentic journal, Ionesco described the novelist as someone who "lies," because the novelist "constructs, organizes, composes, orchestrates" (*N,* 258). He attempted to incorporate the authenticity of the journal into *The Hermit* by presenting the loosely structured vignettes as the narrator's diary. The result, unfortunately, is an undisciplined work, overcharged with words and with biographical, ideological, and metaphysical themes. Ionesco's novel is so laden with messages that the ultimate effect of the fusion of the fantastic and the mundane is more gratuitous than mystical. The final image is not as poignant as the image at the end of "The Slough," where it retains a kind of hallucinatory purity, nor as the image at the end of *A Hell of a Mess,* where it benefits from the mesmerizing power of stage effects. With the exception of his *Stories for Children under Three Years of Age,* Ionesco's prose writing, lacking the metamorphic freedom of the stage, was not widely appreciated.

In *A Hell of a Mess,* an enigmatic, nearly catatonic main character, identified only as "the Character," is substituted for the soliloquizing protagonist of the novel. The rare speech acts of this absurdist Zen hermit erupt from a repository for the loneliness, boredom, and violence churning around him. Describing the transformation from novel to play, Ionesco explained, "It is the others who speak for him. It is no longer only the solitude of the individual character that I wanted to demonstrate but also the solitude of the characters surrounding him. . . . My main character is there to hear the monologues of others and, so doing, receives their solitude" (Bonnefoy, 1977, 109).

In the city, the Character's wall of silence is assaulted by a voluble collection of former colleagues and neighbors. The suburban refuge to which he flees with his unexpected inheritance is invaded by the voices of neighbors, concierges, and revolutionaries. (The dramatis personae for *A Hell of a Mess,* who are supplemented by dummies and puppets, number 39.) His new neighbors, in what could be any of the massive, uniformly planned blocks of government-subsidized apartment buildings that have sprung up around Paris, appear in turn at his door. Each of their speeches, like the housekeeper's speech in *Exit the King,* is a litany of discouragements. One neighbor, "the Gentleman," a limping, grayhaired, White Russian émigré, becomes a spokesperson for the playwright. His explanation for the carnage and disasters filling the newspapers that he can no longer bear to read is a refrain from *Antidotes*: ideologies are "merely a pretext for violence. . . . The world is badly conceived. . . . we live in a closed-circuit economy. Nothing arrives from elsewhere and we must keep eating, eating ourselves."[23] He reiterates the message of *Hunger and Thirst*: "We are all hungry, thirsty, desirous, and as soon as we've gratified our hunger, like our thirst, like our desires, there are other desires, and hungers, and thirsts. . . . We ought to be able to commit suicide. But it's not easy because *HE* also gave us an instinct for self-preservation, the fear of death" (*HM,* 53).

The ninth scene effects a transition from the context of the anonymous individual to that of the anonymous crowd. The Character is alone on stage taking delivery of his furniture, which encumbers the stage as in *The New Tenant.* As the stage lights go down at the end of the scene, sounds of unpleasant street noises invade the theater, foreshadowing the pessimistic "historical commentary" that constitutes a major theme in the second part of the play. The next scene, set in a neighborhood café where the Character intends to become a "regular," begins with the hyperconventionality of the opening scene of *Rhinoceros.* In Ionesco's theater the stereotypical leads inevitably to the phantasmagorical. Seated before his steak and potatoes, The Character experiences the kind of illumination, or Zen Buddhist "satori," described by Ionesco in *Antidotes* (*A,* 218). A sudden spot of light beams on the Character. As the stage light grows more intense, his euphoria spreads to the others, who begin dancing and singing. Just as abruptly, the light turns gray and the diners return to their habitual forlorn silence. The Character has consumed such an unlikely amount of alcohol that his "satori" could be simply inebriation, but he observes, in a surprising speech, "They're all back in their glass coffin. Everything's dim and gray again. . . . Can't you understand? Someone put the lid back on" (*HM*, 74). The pain conveyed by this observation is wrenching.

The café is invaded by a group of young, fist-waving, slogan-spouting revolutionaries, preparing for a new round of bloodletting as though for a street festival. Their presence casts a spell, creating a dark counterpart to the earlier satori. It parodies the behavior of many French citizens during the events of May 1968. Eager to be youthfully chic, the diners begin to boast of revolutionary credentials. In a *Rhinoceros*-like transformation, they change clothes, disguise themselves with elaborate beards and wigs, and take up rifles. All are slaughtered at the doorstep, but there are replacements. Justifying the unending bloodshed as an antidote to tedium, an insurgent, briefly expanding his vocabulary beyond profanity and belligerently truncated clichés, recapitulates the pessimistic conclusion to *Frenzy for Two or More*: "*Things would be too boring. What would we do without the revolution*" (*HM*, 111). The Character's concierge makes a broader indictment, concluding as she goes on sweeping that "the human adventure has lasted long enough. Let it be over with and not worry us any longer. The creator put his foot in it with this one" (*HM*, 113).

During the chaos in the café, the Character emerges briefly from his habitual antisocial torpor to defend the waitress, an appealing, if tougher, version of Daisy in *Rhinoceros*. While the cyclical violence continues, the two remain barricaded in his apartment for several years, an ill-assorted liaison as his pitying but horrified reaction to the "deep bloody wound" of her sex makes clear. When the violence comes to a halt, the Character refuses to go out. The waitress leaves and he remains shut up. Time passes more and more rapidly, measured by stage light shifts from day to night, separated only by seconds, and by visits in quick succession from three generations of visibly aging concierges. When the last of the concierges announces the death of the waitress, he demands that the lights be extinguished. They go off and on again several times as the concierge delivers meals at a prodigious rate, turning out the lights after each dinner delivery. In one of the dark interludes, the Character is visited by apparitions from his past, among them his disillusioned mother, a disappointed schoolteacher, and a woman whose love he failed to recognize. From different corners of the stage they call out, "We loved you," but he responds in a fury of insults, flinging his brandy bottle at them and screaming for the lights to be turned on. The lights come on one more time, intensely bright, but the concierge no longer answers. The apartment building is deserted. The stage also empties. First the furniture, then the walls disappear until all that is left is the Character's armchair, where he sits facing the audience from center stage. As he predicts that he will die of hunger and thirst and asks "What's the meaning of all this," a huge tree in full bloom comes toward him from the illumination upstage. Looking at some blossoms that have fallen from the tree, The Character suddenly bursts into uproarious laughter, understanding the "joke" at last: "It's fantastic! What a gag! What a huge, overdone gag! And I worried and suffered, and . . ." (HM, 151). As the curtain comes down he is still laughing in the direction of the audience: "What a mess. . . . What a hell of a mess!" (HM, 152).

In the program notes for the first production, Ionesco writes, "I leave it to the audience to interpret the final image and the last lines" (TC, 1819). However, in "Why Do I Write?" he acknowledges the influence of a story about a Zen monk who, having spent his life trying to understand the meaning of existence, has a sudden illumination, realizes that it has all been an illusory trap, and bursts into laughter. According to Rosette Lamont, the play bears witness to Ionesco's "mature understanding" that life is a "series of tragicomic vignettes," and the "final laughter raises the play's finale to the level of transcendent merriment, like that of Homer's gods rocking with gentle amusement at the sight of human follies" (Lamont, 1993, 199). Less sanguine interpretations of the play have been more typical. "This 'Hell of a mess,' " according to another writer, is "life, this monstrous bric-a-brac, about which one knows neither where it has come from nor where it is going, nor how to manage with it."[24] The latter assessment is more consistent with the message that emerges from the play itself. The Russian gentleman, who tends to sound much like Ionesco, compares life to a prison on the model of a Russian doll, boxes enclosed within an endless series of boxes. Clearly an alter ego for the playwright, he comes to the profaned Pascalian conclusion that "we work at our trivia within the realm of the inexplicable. The inextricable. What a mess" (HM, 53–54).

A Hell of a Mess was enthusiastically received. Ionesco was particularly pleased to note that what drew praise was not the sound-and-light-filled second part but the monologue-filled first part of the play, because he had conceived of this part of the play as a risky "technical experiment" in which the spectators would become the confessors of the Character, the recipients of his silence.[25] "Thanks to the monologues, I noted that the public was able to welcome, to understand the solitude of others. Each character who recited his drama, his problems, complained in fact about his solitude. Perhaps I succeeded by means of the theater in arousing in people what is most intimate, most solitary. At least that is a hope" (Bonnefoy, 1977, 110).

Chapter Ten
Oneiric Reckonings

During a 1978 interview, Ionesco said he regretted that "instead of telling about things that do not exist, I began to tell about myself and to defend certain points of view and certain ideas. . . . In the name of antipolitics, I became political" (*HQ,* 9). Despite these concerns, in his last major plays, *The Man with the Luggage,* completed in 1975, and *Journeys among the Dead,* which had its previews in New York in 1980, more than ever before in his theater he tells about himself. Psychoanalytic models and his own dreams serve as the principal thematic and visual sources in these episodic explorations of his past. Polemical agendas do not disappear from these plays, but they are effectively woven into reproductions of dream language where uncanny distortions mix and mask realities.

Ionesco's interest in dream material dated back to his early attraction to surrealism, the theories of which he echoed when he wrote in 1960: "I maintain that the world is not audacious enough, and that is why we suffer. And I also maintain that it is not our monotonous everyday lives but our dreams and imagination that call for audacity, that contain and reveal essential and fundamental truths" (*NCN,* 150). Much of his theater, which evolved in tandem with an increasing fascination with first Freudian theory then Jungian archetypes, supports Freud's explanation that dreams are "often most profound when they seem most crazy" because "in every epoch of history those who have had something to say but could not say it without peril have eagerly assumed a fool's cap. The audience at whom their forbidden speech was aimed tolerated it more easily if they could at the same time laugh and flatter themselves with the reflection that the unwelcome words were clearly nonsensical."[1]

L'Homme aux valises (The Man with the Luggage)

The 19 scenes of *The Man with the Luggage* are elaborations of dreams recorded in *Fragments of a Journal* and anecdotes from various memoirs. There is no list of the dramatis personae. Only the protagonist has a sustained role, one that combines Freud's Oedipus, the Oedipus of Sophocles, and an Ionescan version of the "wandering Jew." Designated the First Man, he tries out a number of personas as he wanders in search of his identity in a country where he was apparently born but the language of which he has forgotten. His visit was meant to be brief, but inability to establish his origins has blocked his exit. He remains a bewildered foreigner.

Running into grandparents and an old uncle, the First Man is reminded that he has come to their village to find the family name of his grandmother's mother, which she had refused to reveal. A recording clerk, suggesting that she may have belonged to "a social class that's . . . undesirable . . . a persecuted ethnic minority . . . one of the doomed races," urges him to abandon his enquiry: "persecution can have its repercussions, unpleasant consequences for the descendants."[2] Rosette Lamont, noting that Ionesco "identifies himself with the Jewish historical tradition," links this scene to the Jewish origins of his mother and interprets it as a fear that haunted Ionesco during the Nazi persecution of Jews.[3] In conversation with Emmanuel Jacquart, the playwright insisted that his mother was Catholic (*TC,* 1850). Whatever the case, as Lamont and Jacquart agree, the scene calls to mind the situation of the Jews in the 1930s and 1940s and that of dissenters in postwar communist regimes. In a broader context, *The Man with the Luggage,* written as Ionesco's career as a playwright was drawing to a close, also suggests a search for the "final" purpose of his writing. The First Man carries with him two heavy suitcases. A third, containing all his papers with the names on them, has been lost. The suitcases, which represent the unconscious according to the playwright, grow increasingly cumbersome (Bonnefoy, 1977, 173).

The stage directions for the initial scene where The First Man stands clutching his two suitcases looking in the distance read simply: "a place like nowhere, shadowy gray, with the sound of water flowing" (*Plays, XI,* 9). For the Paris premiere in 1975, Jacques Mauclair (who directed the play and played the role of the First Man) and stage designer Jacques Noël created a monumental moonscape resembling a canvas by Giorgio de Chirico to accommodate the different locales of the play. They insisted that nothing about the performance should appear oneirically deformed, however. "Everything," explained Mauclair, "must seem obvious, obeying the logic of the dream which makes us accept the implausible."[4]

Political contexts are introduced during the opening dialogue, which takes place between the First Man and a painter against a militaristic background noise. "This is 1938, you know," the painter informs him. "The French Revolution's still with us. . . . The French are so full of life, so intelligent! It's a good thing it's still '38 and we haven't yet got to 1944." Almost immediately, he suggests it might be 1942 or 1950, to which The First Man replies, "1950 Paris was dead by then. Listen! What silence! But it's not silence, it's a swansong. The song of a swan on the filthy waters of the Seine" (*Plays, XI*, 10). With the scrambled effect of dream time, these historical moments are intertwined with the "revolutionary" moments in Ionesco's own existence: the year of his first return to France from Romania, the year of his permanent exile to France, and the year of his emergence as a playwright with the creation of *The Bald Soprano*. The entrance of a Charon-like figure holding an oar, who is to row the First Man to a hotel, expands the time frame to a distant mythological past. The mention of floods adds a biblical dimension to the fluid framework. As the first scene ends, the stage appears to be on fire; the image of the swan has been replaced by the suggestion of a phoenix. By the end of this very brief scene, the dramatic site is an oneiric condensation of creation, hell, revolution, and theater. It mimics dream language with its obsessive protean figures and symbols, displacements, accelerating and decelerating tempos, and odd humor.

As in a dream (or in a political situation where "rhinoceritis" is rampant), the characters alter not only from scene to scene but often from moment to moment, with role shifts and sudden chronological advances or regressions accomplished by means of onstage costume changes. The same actresses appear as mother and wife and as grandmother, daughter, and former mistresses. Father figures are equally protean: A government official suddenly becomes a doctor; a sheriff is addressed as colonel and then becomes a judge; a tour guide recalling Schafer in "At the Foot of the Wall" turns into a policeman. Schafer himself, as always a double for the playwright's father, reappears as both a king and a young bridegroom with a new bride. Gags and stage business from the music hall and early silent movies facilitate these slapstick metamorphoses. An exchange of *kepis* for sailor hats and then the addition of holster belts, for example, transform sailors into customs agents and then into menacing policemen. Recreating Ionesco's complicated filial and political situation in Romania, the First Man also tries on a vaudevillian series of names and disguises. The permutations suggest both the ruses imposed by totalitarian regimes and the isolation of the individual who either cannot or refuses to go along with the current ideological vogue.

The Man with the Luggage was described by the playwright as "my childhood, my adolescence, the quest for my own identity" (Bonnefoy, 1977, 169). The search becomes a guilt-ridden game of hide-and-seek with a ghostly cast of reproachful mothers and threatening father figures. The attempt by Ionesco's mother to take poison again becomes dramatic material, but is transformed in this play. The son is no longer a helpless onlooker as in *Victims of Duty,* but is associated with the persecuting father in a more complex rendering of filial guilt.[5] A young man's refusal in the third scene to recognize an old woman confined to one of the proliferating wheel chairs as his mother provokes a suicidal response. As he frantically gathers a flood of white pills spilling from her purse and covering the floor, she lashes out, "Hooligan! I devoted my whole life to you and your father! Now all you do is disown me! You've been harbouring this for a long time. I never thought it possible! You've been the death of me, the two of you. Your father stuck a dagger in my heart, and now *you* finish me off" (*Plays, XI,* 17).

The initial series of familial encounters builds to a nightmarish finale in the sixth scene. The First Man is confronted by a group of characters he vaguely recognizes as his family, although he mistakes his wife for his mother. The portrayal of his daughter in this scene by an Egyptian doll introduces a jarring, dreamlike effect in the strange amalgam of a wax museum image and the suggestion of ancient tombs. To the accompaniment of a siren and macabre punning with terms like "Dead End," they summon him to their land of the dead.[6] The staging recreates the tight, threatening quality of a bad dream. Advancing, either squeezed together on a platform or in a close formation on roller skates, they lead the First Man offstage. Just as they reach the wings, the characters fall over, one by one and the doll's head rolls away. The First Man jumps to freedom. Alone on stage, preoccupied with collecting his luggage, he calls out defiantly: "It's not my turn yet" (*Plays, XI,* 27).

The First Man's odyssey in the following episodes is given broader mythical and political dimensions and a blacker humor. In the seventh scene, he fails a test administered by a sphinx in a pastiche of Greek tragedy and the familiar, Freudian "examination dream," and then embarks on a guilty, matricidal course. A Jocasta figure will die as a result of his impatience to discover an identity (and to be comfortable). A stichomythic duel, ironically based on the verb "to understand," between a woman just released from a psychiatric hospital, who is desperately telephoning for help, and the First Man, who is impatient to call the consulate about his papers and also to urinate, ends with the woman's death. Thus the First Man becomes responsible for the death of another mother figure. Searching for a hotel, he finds himself in a prisonlike hospital/hotel room with four old people, where he can have a bed only if one of them dies. Reluctantly, and almost inadvertently, in the blackest scene of the play, symbolically destroying a family tree and the tree of life, the First Man helps a doctor and a nurse administer a fatal injection to an old woman who had earlier complained of a tree growing inside her. This episode is also a condemnation of euthanasia, a theme previously introduced in *A Hell of a Mess*.

The fifteenth scene shifts to a courtroom, where the First Man is tried for not eating his vegetables. During the ludicrous trial he attempts to turn the tables on the old woman who has accused him, insisting that she is the guilty one and demanding excessive retribution, hefty fines, prison, even the death penalty, as well as intercession with the authorities to obtain his exit visa. The First Man's vicious response to the old woman, recalling the dishonest court proceedings by which the playwright's father obtained custody of his children, is shocking, a measure of the difficulty in liquidating the burden of guilt vis-à-vis his mother that Ionesco had carried with him since childhood. The First Man's protests of innocence are belied when his suitcase turns out to be full of vegetables and cement.

Near the end of the play, in a scene that very closely reproduces a dream analyzed at some length in *Fragments of a Journal*, the First Man is taken in by a blond woman who is seductively costumed in shorts and a bra but is also, more like a mother, wearing matronly white gloves. Her husband, like a caricatural analyst, or perhaps Ionesco's father, offers to take charge of the suitcases.[7]

In the penultimate scene, a similar rendezvous, replicating another dream recorded in *Fragments*, culminates the oedipal quest. The Man with the Oar reappears to deliver the First Man to the dark port of Kichinev, where he is greeted by a last mother-wife-seductress, who wears a dirty skirt and is naked above the waist except for a pearl necklace. At the beginning of the scene, he wonders, "Is this it: have I arrived? (*Plays*, XI, 92). In the oedipal context of the play, even if this were his destination, the key to his origins, it is inevitable that he arrive too late. He excuses himself like a puerile Ulysses: "I've washed down dirty decks with dirty water and even the water that fell from the sky was black. I've swept pavements with a stumpy old broom. And while so many others were playing about with computers, not even a vacuum cleaner for me. I pulled up weeds with my bare hands. The others had moving-machines to do all the hard jobs for them. I've been a road-worker too" (*Plays, XI,* 94). He claims to have understood everything, but it is too late to appease the sobbing woman who had given up waiting for him. In this figure, whom the First Man finally claims to recognize and to whom he professes his love, wife and mother figures remain confused. He promises her that they will once again become professors as Ionesco and his wife once were. As she dismisses his implorations, however, because it is now dusk, her white pearls merge with the white pills from the earlier maternal suicidal scene while the First Man begs her not to swallow them.

The First Man is equally inept in tangles with the paternal side of the oedipal triangle. In contrast to the guilt that paralyzes his interactions with matriarchal figures, these scenes, many of which are charged with political messages, are characterized by a forlornly comic effrontery. Accused by a policeman in the tenth scene of identifying himself as "Netting. Profession: Mosquito catcher" on his visitor's card and using a poorly written name on his identity card, he makes an ineffectual attempt to renew language: "Perhaps the letter M is a badly written C, or perhaps the two letters M and C have been run together on purpose to make up a new one . . . with a different sound. I'm not quite sure how to pronounce it either. I gave myself that name and wrote it down to make an April fool of my boss. My passport was issued in Paris by the Government of France and my real name is on that" (*Plays, XI,* 37). At the end of the twelfth episode, in a scene that is mostly mime, the First Man responds to the threatening presence of an armed soldier, a uniformed woman, and a tourist guide–policeman by disguising himself with a false nose, a beard, a mustache, and dark glasses that he has taken from his suitcase. Pleased with himself, he observes that his bags "won't be so heavy now," and confronts them like a caricatural Rimbaud with an *I* that is another: "You don't know me. I'm someone else. It's not me, I tell you" (*Plays, XI,* 60). He is dismissed by the policeman as an idiot.

In one episode, however, his alien status elicits a sympathetic response. The authority is not a military or judicial figure reminiscent of Ionesco's father or step-family but a consul-psychiatrist, an unheeded seer in a war-torn country. Unable to name his father or his mother, or to give his age, the First Man is asked by the Consul about his profession. When he replies, I am an "existent," the Consul protests that there are so many of them and proposes registering him as a "special existent." The First Man corrects him: "Not special, specialized."[8] This Tirésias figure gives the First Man a certificate that is also a road map. At the end of the scene, the Consul responds to a deprecating observation about the First Man's ignorance of his identity: "Do we know ours? If we do have a rough idea, it's thanks to our function in society" (*Plays, XI,* 66). A policeman enters to announce that they have been stripped of their functions and thus the authorities can no longer acknowledge their existence. The Consul, freed from definitions that exclude both individuality and spirituality, expresses relief at the news.

A metaphorical ballet ends the journey. In the last scene, consisting entirely of stage directions except for a five-way exchange of "Sorry" and a brief "Quite a traffic jam," two women, two men, and two policemen repeatedly appear and disappear. They change places as riders and pushers of the ubiquitous wheelchair that will finally carry two suitcases exactly like those of the First Man. None of them appears to see the others. A whistle blows and the stage empties except for the First Man, who moves stage front with his two bags. The third bag, the one containing the manuscript, is still missing. As he stands there, the six characters return and exit in a circular pattern. Their stylized movements, regulated by the whistle, suggest the stunned state of the awakening dreamer, tantalized, perhaps frightened by the contents of the dream, but never to be in full possession of its contents or significance.

In 1953, Ionesco described his theater as a projection of an inner drama that might be "a reflection or a symbol of universal disruption. So there is no plot, no architectural construction, no puzzles to be solved, only the inscrutable enigma of the unknown; no real characters, just people without identity . . . simply a sequence of events without sequence" (*NCN,* 158–59). *The Man with the Luggage,* which has had only three major performances, two of them in the United States, is a successful creation of such an "inner drama." It is a powerful statement of loss and a fascinating visual experience in which Ionesco succeeds, perhaps as well as at any time in his career, in creating a convergence of the spoken language and the metamorphic language of the stage. It is a play that merits being better known.

Voyage chez les morts: Thèmes et variations *(Journeys among the Dead: Themes and Variations)*

Ionesco described the 27 unnumbered segments of *Journeys among the Dead,* separated only by white spaces on the pages, as "a subterranean biography," and a "dreamed autobiography."[9]

In an interview prefacing a deluxe English-language edition of this play, he explained, "I mean that the things I have seen, heard or lived through, the people I have quarreled with, or loved during the course of my existence have reappeared, and revealed themselves to me, in my dreams. After that, I put them down on paper."[10] The playwright's alter ego in *Journeys* is another restless Jean. Someone who "never liked to sleep in the same bed," he is an older version of the protagonist in *Hunger and Thirst*. There is, however, a sense, if not of closure, at least of a kind of "final" despair in *Journeys* which distinguishes it from the earlier play. In a series of tomblike rooms in a labyrinthine underworld, Jean confronts the futility of a life spent chasing oedipal phantoms and creating theater.

With occasionally disconcerting frankness, as in *La Quête intermittente*, Ionesco introduces a full sweep of his angst—from spiritual quandaries and financial worries to old literary quarrels. No longer as confident as he had been in 1958 that works of art are "live philosophies" that "do not invalidate one another," he resented Samuel Beckett's growing prestige, perceiving it as a detraction from his own (*NCN*, 36). Toward the end of the play, Jean's sister announces that Constantin (the Beckett character), who "is becoming more respected and admired every day," has just been awarded the world's most important literary prize, adding unmercifully: "No one's thinking of giving it to you any more. . . . The respect they used to have for you has practically vanished. In some countries, people haven't even heard of you. Even in France, people are forgetting you."[11] Jean admits ruefully, "I sacrificed my spiritual life and the salvation of my soul for the sake of my celebrity, and now it's all gone" (*J*, 45).

Jean's encounter with a likeness of Adamov, called Alexandre here as in a very similar episode in *Killing Game*, is both a moving reflection on the ultimate foolishness of their quarrel in the 1950s and a meditation on all the loss that life entails: "I lived passionately, in those days. It was an intense, prolific, fruitful time. . . . But for years now time has become empty, distorted. . . . I have arrived. But where? I have succeeded—in what? Everything is hollow. What we should die of is love" (*J*, 49). Alexandre appears at the end of the scene to tell Jean that he had preferred death to failure. Jean, terror-stricken at the thought of the unknown, in spite of his eternal restlessness and thirst for adventure, is not ready for death: "I'm a bourgeois at heart, which means I cling to my habits. . . . Boredom! I've got used to that. You get used to it, or rather, you don't get used to it, but you get used to not getting used to it" (*J*, 52).

Principally, however, it is the difficulty of being the son that is at the heart of this play. It takes place in a nether world that is also Romania and where the dead still age and fight old battles. Like the First Man, Jean is searching for his mother. His excuse for the long absence that caused him to lose track of her is that, like Ionesco's own impoverished mother when they lived in Paris, she "was always moving . . . and looked for ground floors or basements" (*J*, 10). Her former husband, echoing Ionesco's father's divorce court claims, pretends that she has abandoned her family, taking a train to a "place where you can't see anyone anymore" (*J*, 11). Jean accuses his father of lying. In general, however, although his violence and disloyalty remain unforgiven, the father is more parodied in *Journeys* than cruelly condemned. He has been "recycled" because he has obeyed the authorities, not into the police, as Jean immediately assumes, but "into the novel, the realist novel." It is "a branch of the Ministry for the Police," he acknowledges, "but we're not policemen. . . . I write stream-of-consciousness novels, but their stream isn't as blue as the Danube, or as the ocean you saw, or thought you saw, in Boganda" (*J*, 12). In a reverse image of a vignette in *Fragments* in which the adolescent Ionesco's enraged father pulls notebooks filled with poetry and writing exercises from his son's desk, dismissing them as trivia, the Father in *Journeys* pulls out his own enormous, worthless packet from the table drawer.

In subsequent episodes, he admits that his son has become "a tremendous success, President of the Academy, founder of a literary school, opposed by a lot of adversaries," but regrets that he did not become, "a great politician, or a general, or a chemical engineer," a situation he blames on Jean's mother (*J*, 25). Anxious to measure up, in what becomes a dreamlike condensation of themes related to paternal opportunism and infidelities, ideological "policing," and Ionesco's dissatisfaction with his career, Jean pulls his own tattered papers from a table drawer, along with bits of rusty wire, a cookbook, some "bad caricatures," and a bottle of ink that spills over the stage floor. Responding to his father's astonished "That's all," he acknowledges, "Yes, Father, that *is* all," to which his father gives the Freudian response "All that stuff is what you had in your drawers when you were a child" (*J*, 27). The jumbled contents of the table drawers, which replace the suitcases of the previous play as the symbol of both his consciously created words and his unconscious, are of little more use to him than the cement and vegetables were to the First Man. Their value must still be negotiated.

Journeys is a kind of psychological business trip, a settling of old accounts. Jean is obsessed with the issue of paternal inheritance, as are all the family members he encounters, grandparents, uncles, his despised stepmother and her brothers, his wife, and, finally, his mother. The frequent exchange of invalid bank notes corresponds to financial issues that had been frustratingly real according to Ionesco's journals, but it symbolizes primarily the burden of guilty debt which permeated Ionesco's sentiments for his mother. There are two "concluding" episodes. In the penultimate scene, Jean at last finds the specter of his mother, not a maternal figure but an unforgiving old hag, whose nails have turned into "talons, my S-hooks" and who claims to be mother, grandmother, and grandfather (*J*, 57). She hides in an attic to avoid sinking into the muck of the damp floor below, a last image of the ground-floor dwellings Ionesco had hated as a child and carried into his theater as a symbol of all the mire that ensnares human existence. The damp floor is the muddy repository of bitterness and fear of death. In spite of Jean's pleas, his mother refuses to come down: "I'm afraid, downstairs. . . . Cockroaches have been born from my tears . . . the floor's worm-eaten, the grave is under the floor" (*J*, 56). Pulled down finally by Jean and a friend, she undergoes a series of metamorphoses.

A push of a table and chair turns the scene into a courtroom where she presides like a vengeful harpy. Calling herself "the Seat of Judgment" and reminding her victims that God does not always forgive, she bids Jean stand at her right hand, a miserable Christ figure, while she delivers a last judgment, wreaking a sordid and graphically bloody vengeance on the parade of the guilty—her former husband, his second wife, and her brothers. The Captain's skull is clawed open; his eyeball ripped from its socket. The whorishly made-up Madame Simpson, as Ionesco's stepmother is called here, is clawed naked and reduced to a crippled crone.[12] Jean's father is sentenced to be hanged. As her old persecutors disappear into the wings, she strips away her rags and her false nose, uttering loud, inhuman cries. The stage is covered by mist through which sounds of laughter and sobs can be heard. When the mist disappears, the stage is empty.

The last "episode," a fitting closure to Ionesco's theater, is an antidénouement, a despairing, irrational soliloquy accompanied by the vague rustling sounds and murmurs of Jean's ghosts from the wings. The final words are "I don't know" (*J*, 65). Alone at center stage, surveying his complicated affective and literary domain from the last of the many armchairs/thrones in Ionesco's theater, Jean delivers a very long speech

composed of disjointed pronouncements and disintegrating words. From
the illogicalities emerge quintessential Ionescan messages. The observation that "They don't look as if they were going to give us the keys" is
followed by the confession that "I've lost my command of language. The
more I say the less I speak. The more I speak, the less I say" (*J*, 62).
There are echoes of political deceptions: "They've made false relations
out of the present historic" (*J*, 64). He recapitulates the theme of *The
Man with the Luggage* and the play that is now ending: "Genealogy is
where we find emanations, emanations. No, genealogy is where we no
longer find, where we have never found, emanations" (*J*, 64). Like
Lucky's dissertation in Beckett's *Waiting for Godot,* which it resembles,
the monologue is dominated by metaphysical despair: "my exposition
contains several important arguments, from which it follows that the
saved savior will save. That's all a lot of hog-wash. If there were any
hogs to wash or cows to milk, we'd do it. Have there been manisteries,
some manusferies, some matisferies, some mysteries and their acolytes
who have messed the whole thing up?" (*J*, 64).

In a parallel to his first play, Ionesco brings his entire theater to a
close with a circular ending that links *Journeys* to *The Bald Soprano. Journeys* ends where *The Bald Soprano,* the play that taught him the disturb-
ing power of circular endings, began—with a linguistic disaster. Jean is
described as "terrified" when he asks, "Have I been speaking words? Ah,
the solitudes of the sceniprosium"(*J*, 63). Ionesco defined the last speech
in *Journeys* as the culmination of his dramatic experiments, explaining
that with "the complete failure of the character who no longer understands what he says clearly, . . . language is truly tragic the way I wanted
it to be in my first play . . . where it was only amusing, or rather laughable. Now even the laughable is surpassed, as well as the derisory character, since he comes to an encounter with absolute nonsense."[13] The
closing of the circle with the final monologue in *Journeys* is a despairing
finale. What Ionesco referred to as a "half-terrifying, half-amusing"
destruction of language in *The Bald Soprano* and *The Lesson* had been carried out with a youthful verve. The confirmation of the bankruptcy of
language at the end of *Journeys* was joyless "because years and years of
life have passed, have overwhelmed me, weighing on my shoulders"
(Hubert, 1990, 247).

Journeys among the Dead was first published in installments in the *Nou-
velle Revue Française* in 1980. The original version, which is very long, has
not been staged in France, although it was well received as a radio play
in a cut version.[14] In 1983, Roger Planchon created a very successful

production entitled *Spectacle Ionesco,* interweaving scenes from *The Man with the Luggage* and episodes from *Journeys.* He staged the parade of Ionesco's phantoms as a kind of Dantesque review, emphasizing the physical and comic effect over pathos. Jean Carmet, a well-known, sardonically comic film actor who physically resembled Ionesco, returned to the stage for the first time in 30 years to play the role of Jean. He described his acting style as "charging on stage as if it were a Music Hall spectacle."[15] The staging, however, was kept simple for the most part, emphasizing the infernal barrenness of the internal and external landscapes. During the Paris performances, coffins labeled "Adamov" and "Sartre" were present onstage at the beginning of the play. A third coffin, for Ionesco, was added at the end.[16]

Chapter Eleven
Traces

"He went off toward his garden but he continued to murmur; to salvage the unsalvageable. To define the indefinable. To say the unsayable. To hear the unheard of" (*QI,* 169). In these sentences, which are nearly the final lines of *La Quête intermittente,* Ionesco shows himself to be less resigned than Pangloss at the end of Voltaire's *Candide,* and more resilient than Jean in the final monologue of *Journeys among the Dead.* His literary excursions covered considerable ground during a career that spanned more than half a century, but their themes remained remarkably consistent. "I cannot create form because I can't express what is most compelling and most horrible: life and death," he wrote in 1971 (*A,* 258). In *Exit the King,* Bérenger cries out, "I'm dying, you hear, I'm trying to tell you. I'm dying, but I can't express it, unless I talk like a book and make literature of it (*EK,* 53). In *Jack, or the Submission,* Jack capitulates while protesting, "Oh words, what crimes are committed in your name" (*FP,* 86). As early as his confrontation with Petrescu dramatized in *Nu,* Ionesco was distressed to find "nothing that worked, nothing true, nothing that did not turn into literature" (*N,* 138). The problem of language, its overworked and abused symbols having become a barrier to authenticity, never ceased to trouble Ionesco. Like his defiant Bérenger at the end of *Rhinoceros,* he struggled nevertheless to salvage what he could, because language, for all its inadequacies, might still be a path to some kind of salvation. "I am lost," he wrote in the final pages of *Present Past,* "in the thousands of words and unsuccessful acts that are 'my life,' which take my soul apart and destroy it. . . . But I have a chance to find myself again if I keep retracing my footsteps, instead of taking the first step, if I return to the explosion of the first image, there where words express nothing but light" (*PP,* 168, 170).

Because he kept "retracing," his obsessional themes were greeted by some critics as worn out, proof that he had nothing new to say. An account of his work such as this one, lining up plays and essays back to back, risks provoking a similar reaction. There is repetition in Ionesco's writing, but that is because, like jazz, it never has a definitive recording. Julio Cortázar, in an essay on jazz "takes" (successive recordings of a single theme), proposes that "the best literature is always a take; there is an implicit risk in its execution, a margin of danger that is the pleasure of the flight, of the love, carrying with it tangible loss but also a total engagement that, on another level, lends the theater its unparalleled imperfection faced with the perfection of film."[1] For Ionesco, this was true not only for productions of his plays but for his work as a whole. As he came to see his own role differently, he risked his avant-garde reputation and his popularity as an absurdist playwright. He reached out for an enhanced style and a richer context that would permit fuller expression of what he believed to be the persistent dilemma of all the "specialized existents," as the First Man defines himself, searching for meaningful answers in unacceptable circumstances. In Scene XV of *The Man with the Luggage*, the First Man, who is lying down as though on a psychiatrist's couch, refuses to pay his fee to the Young Man who appears, claiming, "you promised me the key to the mystery. You were going to reveal to me that best-kept 'secret of the world.' And where's that got me now? I don't even know what's in my own suitcase" (*Plays, XI*, 76). Besides, he is "out of foreign coins." This is a "take" on a fundamental theme in Ionesco's most effective writing: the depiction of a man wandering through existence without the necessary linguistic, existential, or spiritual currency.

Finally, it may not have been literary originality that Ionesco sought most avidly but "the expression of the origin" (*D*, 89). To imagine, to write, "is only to find again, to discover, recover what has been" (*D*, 64). Writing was his means of not losing his way on a conflicted voyage that was both a search for an identity and an attempt to become part of something universal that would help combat the finality of death. He preserved the "fragments" of his world in his plays and journals because "it is necessary to leave traces" (*PP*, 64). A description by J.-B. Pontalis of the young Rousseau captures just as aptly the paradox inherent in Ionesco's "traces." "Rousseau," says Pontalis, "travels himself; paradoxically, his comings and goings are not so much a search for other human beings whose strangeness and difference would exaggerate his otherness, as an occasion for an immediate existence through the distancing of the other who threatens to take possession of him and divide him."[2]

The anguished, contentious autobiography constituted by Ionesco's theater, essays, journals, short stories, novels, and paintings, chronicling personal but not private obsessions, reflects a conflict between the desire to be a representative of a universal experience, a modern Everyman, and the aggressive solitude of a unique individual adamantly protecting his difference. "I wanted to express a true but simple anguish," Ionesco wrote in 1987. "I wanted to tell 'my life,' but surely I have told it in such a way that my anguish or my laughter or my intimate memories have drawn in their wake other problematic elements of the epoch, of history, of society. One is never alone and whenever one speaks, one also speaks of others" (Hubert, 1987, 5). Reflecting earlier on his role in the human collective in *Present Past Past Present,* however, in a statement that keeps his "universal statements" in perspective, he maintains: "I take these collective desires, these collective obsessions, these collective anxieties and give them a system of relations, a dynamism, a dialect, a pattern, a structure that is mine alone" (*PP,* 115).

Ionesco's question "Am I a puppet, an actor, or am I real?"—never satisfactorily answered in his plays, fictions, and personal and polemical essays—was as genuine as it was permanent and insoluble (*QI,* 36). In the course of the long interrogation, he taught his contemporaries not only to ask similar questions, but, in both asking and searching for an answer, to see the world differently, more complexly, with humor and with outrage, with the eyes of the imagination open to the fantastic but also to human misery. Toward the end of *The Hermit,* the narrator puzzles, "Could it be that the unawareness was of infinite proportions?" (*H,* 126). Ionesco's "traces," marks of a deep and abiding struggle with conflicting states of wonder and anguish, have significantly lessened that dreadful possibility.

Notes and References

Preface

1. Hélène Cixous, "Difficult Joys," in Helen Wilcox, Keith McWatters, Ann Thompson, and Linda R. Williams, eds., *The Body and the Text: Hélène Cixous, Reading and Teaching* (London: Harvester-Wheatsheaf, 1990), 25.

2. Eugène Ionesco, *Antidotes* (Paris: Gallimard, 1977), 185, 325; hereafter cited in text as *A*.

3. Eugène Ionesco, "Why Do I Write?" trans. Donald Watson, in *Plays Vol. XI* (London: John Calder, 1979), 121; hereafter cited in text as *Plays, XI*.

4. Eugène Ionesco, *Découvertes* (Geneva: Skira, 1969), 64; hereafter cited in text as *D*.

5. Eugène Ionesco, *Théâtre complet*. Edition présentée, éditée et annotée par Emmanuel Jacquart (Paris: Gallimard, Bibliothèque de la Pléiade, 1991); hereafter cited in text as *TC*. Other recent studies that have been crucial to this "revisiting" include Rosette Lamont, *Ionesco's Imperatives: The Politics of Culture* (Ann Arbor: University of Michigan Press, 1993), hereafter cited in text; Marie-Claude Hubert, *Eugène Ionesco* (Paris: Seuil, 1990), hereafter cited in text; and Giovanni Lista, *Ionesco* (Paris: Henri Veyrier, 1989), hereafter cited in text.

Chapter One

1. Eugène Ionesco, Preface to *Ionesco: Situation et perspectives,* eds. Paul Vernois and Marie-France Ionesco (Paris: Pierre Belfond, 1980), 21.

2. Eugène Ionesco, *Notes and Counter Notes,* trans. Donald Watson (New York: Grove Press, 1964), 158; hereafter cited in text as *NCN*.

3. Eugène Ionesco, *La Quête intermittente* (Paris: Gallimard, 1980), 36; hereafter cited in text as *QI*.

4. Eugène Ionesco, *Un homme en question* (Paris: Gallimard, 1979), 193; hereafter cited in text as *HQ*.

5. Eugène Ionesco, *Present Past Past Present,* trans. Helen R. Lane (New York: Grove Press, 1971), 122; hereafter cited in text as *PP*.

6. For many years Ionesco gave his birth date as 1913, explained later as a bit of vanity inspired by a reference to the "new dramatists" of the 1950s as "young" playwrights (*TC*, lxviii–lxix). In *The Killer,* when the autobiographical protagonist reluctantly admits to being several years older than he had originally

claimed, an architect-police-chief-psychoanalyst replies, "We know. . . . We have files on everyone" (Eugène Ionesco, *The Killer and Other Plays*, trans. Donald Watson [New York: Grove Press, 1960], 14; hereafter cited in text as *K.*)

7. Eugène Ionesco, *Fragments of a Journal*, trans. Jean Stewart (New York: Grove Press, 1968), 108; hereafter cited in text as *F*.

8. Ionesco described the significance of this recollection in "Spring 1939," in Eugène Ionesco, *The Colonel's Photograph and Other Stories*, trans. Jean Stewart and John Russell (New York: Grove Press, 1969), 128; hereafter cited in text as *CP*.

9. The Belgian symbolist poet and playwright Maurice Maeterlinck (1862–1949) and the French Catholic poet Francis Jammes (1868–1938).

10. Gabriel Liiceanu, "An Interview with Eugène Ionesco, " *The Capilano Review* 8 (Spring 1992): 98.

11. Eugène Ionesco, "Présentation de Urmuz," *Stanford Review* III, no. 3 (1979): 301.

12. Ibid., 313.

13. The manuscript for Ionesco's adaptation, *Les Grandes chaleurs (The Heat Wave)*, is lost but is described in Lista, 1989, 32.

14. See Chapter One of Claude Bonnefoy, *Conversations with Eugène Ionesco*, trans. Jan Dawson (New York: Holt, Rinehart & Winston, 1971); hereafter cited in text as Bonnefoy, 1971.

15. Ionesco credited Flaubert with the lesson that in literature it is not the story that counts but that it be written in a way that reveals a deeper significance (*QI*, 110).

16. In a 6 April 1853 letter to Louise Colet, in Gustave Flaubert, *Correspondance II* (Paris: Gallimard, 1980), 204.

17. In 1985 Ionesco reported to Emmanuel Jacquart that he had been "born guilty, predestined to culpability" (in *TC*, XXIII). Jacquart ascribes some of Ionesco's guilt to his early religious training and his assiduous reading of the mystics.

18. Eugène Ionesco, "Lettres de France," in *Viata româneasca* (January 1939), as quoted in Gelu Ionescu, *Les Débuts littéraires roumains d'Eugène Ionesco, anatomie d'un echec*, trans. Mirella Nedelco-Patureau (Heidelberg: Carl Winter Universitätsverlag, 1989), 230; hereafter cited in text as G. Ionescu.

19. Ionesco and Adamov were friends until political differences and jealousy on Adamov's part caused a rift in 1953. Ionesco's relations with Beckett were amiable but distant.

20. Jean Anouilh, "Du Chapitre des *Chaises*," *Le Figaro* (23 April 1956), 1. As quoted in Ruby Cohn, *From Desire to Godot* (Berkeley: University of California Press, 1987), 130–131.

21. Eugène Ionesco, *Entre la vie et le rêve* (Paris: Belfond, 1977), 181; an updated version of the interview with Bonnefoy published in English translation in 1971; hereafter cited in text as Bonnefoy, 1977.

22. When *Rhinocéros* opened at the Odéon, it was perceived by some as an indication of Ionesco's forfeiture of avant-garde status. When Genet's *The*

Screens was staged there in 1966, it became a revolutionary event. Political circumstances were certainly different. Due to the legacy of the Algerian War, Genet's play so offended conservatives and the military that the theater had to be put under police protection.

23. Filmed at La Chapelle-Anthenaise in 1970 with Ionesco playing its single role. It was shown briefly at a Latin Quarter cinema in 1971, but was not a success.

24. *Maximilien Kolbe* has not been published in France. There is an English translation by Rosette Lamont in *Performing Arts Journal 17*, 6, no. 2 (1982): 32–36. Several other works by Ionesco have been made into operas, including *Le Maître,* "La Photo du colonel," *Le Tableau,* and *Le Roi se meurt.*

25. Jacques Legré, the theater director, was quoted in *Le Monde,* 30 March 1994, 19.

Chapter Two

1. Some two dozen literary magazines circulated in Bucharest during this period (G. Ionescu, 1989, 111). Among the artists and writers who became well known outside Romania were Mircea Eliade, Marcel Jones, Victor Brauner, Constantin Brancusi, and Tristan Tzara.

2. Eugène Ionesco, *Non,* trans. Marie-France Ionesco (Paris: Gallimard, 1986), 268; hereafter cited in text as *N.* Eugen Simion's preface, "Tableau d'une époque," describes the many lesser-known Romanian writers mentioned by Ionesco.

3. Ecaterina Cleynen-Serghiev notes that for Ionesco to link himself with Arghezi and his peers at the time was comparable to a young French writer's claiming to be in the company of Proust or Gide. In *La Jeunesse littéraire d'Eugène Ionesco* (Paris: Presses Universitaires de France, 1993), 51.

4. Ionesco proposes to his "cultureless" compatriots: "we must first be a little English, French, etc. For us, culture necessarily implies ' foreignization'" (*N,* 168). As a final solution, however, he suggests that the "next two centuries" be spent attempting to create a Romanian culture, an effort far less humiliating than the current "slave mentality" (*N,* 171).

5. Installments of *Hugoliad* appeared in *Ideea Româneasca* 1, nos. 2–4 (June–August 1935): 105–131; and 1–2, nos. 5–10 (September–February 1935–36: 231–256.

6. Eugène Ionesco, *Hugoliad,* trans. Dragomir Costineanu and Marie-France Ionesco, from Romanian, Yara Milos from French (New York: Grove Press, 1987), 17; hereafter cited in text as *HU.*

Chapter Three

1. Ionesco's personal journal, most of which remains unpublished, has been described as his "most vast and detailed written work" (G. Ionescu, 26).

2. Eugène Ionesco, "Spring 1939," in *CP,* 175.

3. The four children's stories were subsequently edited separately with engagingly fantastical illustrations by Étienne Delessert. In 1979 they were adapted as a play which had a successful run in Europe and North America.

4. Julia Kristeva summarizes this position when she says that to claim that thought exists in a form other than language "would amount to an idealism whose metaphysical roots are only too visible . . . an instrumentalist conception of language, whose basis presupposes the existence of thought or symbolic activity without language, by its philosophical implications leads to theology." In Julia Kristeva, *Language the Unknown: An Initiation into Linguistics*, trans. Anne M. Menke (New York: Columbia University Press, 1989), 7.

5. Eugène Ionesco, *Discours de reception d'Eugène Ionesco à l'Académie Française et réponse de Jean Delay* (Paris: Gallimard, 1971), 11.

Chapter Four

1. Rosette C. Lamont and Melvin J. Friedman, eds., *The Two Faces of Ionesco* (Troy, N.Y.: Whitson Publishing Company, 1978).

2. Beckett generally refused to interpret his plays. Ionesco proposes that "Beckett's work is a permanent appeal to God, it's exactly an S.O.S.," citing *Waiting for Godot* as an example (*A,* 243). Beckett had insisted, however, that if he meant Godot to be God he would have said so.

3. Job asks "why should human beings see light of day if God prevents them from discerning their 'way'?" (As cited in Norman C. Habel, *The Book of Job: A Commentary* [Philadelphia: Westminster Press, 1985], 63).

4. It is striking that here Ionesco writes of the use of words and not words themselves as being at the heart of the betrayal, a reversal of his approach to language early in his career. Remarking on the "extravagant beauty of words," he notes the irony of the fact that he and many other playwrights made fun of them in their theater (*HQ,* 109).

5. Eugène Ionesco, *Le Blanc et le noir* (Paris: Gallimard, 1985), 19; hereafter cited in text as *BN.*

6. Eugène Ionesco, "Saul Steinberg, Richard Lindner," in *Derrière le miroir* 241 (October 1980): 11, 14.

7. As quoted in Michel Vais, "Interview d'Eugène Ionesco," in *L'Ecrivain scénique* (Montreal: Les Presses de l'Université du Québec, 1978), 72.

Chapter Five

1. Other French-speaking dramatists writing in an absurdist vein include Boris Vian, Roland Dubillard, René de Obaldia, Robert Pinget, Romain Weingarten, Francis Billetdoux, Jean Vauthier, Georges Schéhadé, and, early in their dramatic careers, Marguerite Duras and Fernando Arrabal. Absurdist theater became an international phenomenon with works by Harold Pinter and Tom Stoppard (British); Edward Albee, Sam Shepard, Jack Gelber, and Arthur

Kopit (American); Gunter Grass (German); Max Frisch (Swiss-German); and Vaclav Havel (Czech).

2. Albert Camus, "The Myth of Sisyphus," in *The Myth of Sisyphus and other Essays,* trans. Justin O'Brien (New York: Random House, 1955), 37; hereafter cited in text. The term "absurd" first gained wide currency in French literature in the late 1920s and 1930s through the works of the novelist and essayist André Malraux (1901–1976).

3. "The Theater of Cruelty" is the title of one of Antonin Artaud's manifestos, later published in *The Theater and Its Double* (see note 18 below). Emmanuel Jacquart created the title *Le Théâtre de dérision* (Paris: Gallimard, 1974). The term "metaphysical farce," invented by Rosette C. Lamont, was first published in her "The Metaphysical Farce, Beckett and Ionesco," *French Review* 34, no. 4 (February 1959): 319–28.

4. Eugène Ionesco, *Improvisations, or the Shepherd's Chameleon,* in *The Killer and Other Plays,* trans. Donald Watson (New York: Grove Press, 1960), 114.

5. See George E. Wellwarth, *The Theater of Protest and Paradox* (New York: New York University Press, 1964; rev. ed. 1971).

6. Jean-Paul Sartre, "Myth and Reality in Theater," trans. Frank Jellinek, in *Sartre on Theater,* Michel Contat and Michel Rybalka, eds. (New York: Random House, 1976), 135–136; hereafter cited in text as Contat and Rybalka. Sartre offers a very positive assessment here of works by Adamov, Genet, Ionesco, and Beckett. He saw the purpose of these works very differently from Ionesco, however, concluding that "the new theater is in no way absurd, but is returning to the great fundamental theme . . . man as event and man as History within the event" (157).

7. Eugène Ionesco, *Notes et contre-notes* (Paris: Gallimard, 1966), 332. The English translation does not include the additions made to a 1967 edition of this work.

8. Jean-Paul Sartre, *Nausea,* trans. Lloyd Alexander (New York: New Directions, 1964), 127.

9. Arthur Adamov, *Je . . . ils* (Paris: Gallimard, 1969), 115.

10. Eugène Ionesco, in his Preface to Marie-Claude Hubert, *Langage et corps fantasmé dans le théâtre des années cinquante* (Paris: Jose Corti, 1987), 5; hereafter cited in text as Hubert.

11. This was also true for Genet who, because of his background as an orphan and a prisoner, came to literary French as an outsider.

12. Roger Shattuck and Simon Watson Taylor, eds., *Selected Works of Alfred Jarry* (New York: Grove Press, 1965), 80.

13. The College of Pataphysics, founded after World War II to perpetuate Jarry's anarchistic spirit, counted Ionesco among its "Transcendent Satraps."

14. Echoes of Apollinaire are found particularly in *Le Vicomte (The Viscount),* which was written in 1950 but not performed; in *Jacques, ou la soumission (Jack, or the Submission);* and in *Victimes du devoir (Victims of Duty).*

15.   George E. Wellwarth and Michael Benedikt, eds., *Modern French Theatre: An Anthology of Plays* (New York: Dutton, 1966), 56.

16.   The reasons for the expulsion were complex, a mixture of incompatible temperaments, politics, and Breton's rejection of the theater as too commercial.

17.   The notion of "speaking surrealist" is borrowed from Henri Béhar, *Étude sur le théâtre dada et surréaliste* (Paris: Gallimard, 1967), 162, an outstanding resource on dada and surrealist theater.

18.   Antonin Artaud, *The Theater and Its Double*, trans. Mary Caroline Richards (New York: Grove Press, 1958); hereafter cited in text as Artaud, 1958.

19.   Artaud's call for the replacement of the author by directors creating spontaneous productions obviously did not find favor with the highly literary absurdist playwrights.

20.   See Eric Sellin, "Surrealist Aesthetics and the Theatrical Event," *Books Abroad* 2 (1969).

21.   As quoted in Claude Abastado, *Eugène Ionesco* (Paris: Bordas, 1971), 28.

Chapter Six

1.   Jacques Lemarchand, Preface to Eugène Ionesco, *Théâtre I* (Paris: Gallimard, 1954), 9.

2.   Jean-Baptiste Jeener in *Le Figaro* (13 May 1950). As quoted in *Petites scènes, grand théâtre*, ed. Genevieve Latour (Paris: Délégation à l'Action Artistique de la Ville de Paris, 1986), 58.

3.   Eugène Ionesco, *Four Plays: The Bald Soprano; The Lesson; Jack, or the Submission; The Chairs*, trans. Donald M. Allen (New York: Grove Press, 1958), 9; hereafter cited in text as *FP*. The adjective "English" is used 17 times in the initial stage directions of *The Bald Soprano*, which are sometimes read aloud at the beginning of the play.

4.   André Breton, *L'Anthologie de l'humour noire* (Paris: Jean-Jacques Pauvert, 1966), 176.

5.   *La Cantatrice chauve*: "Anti-piece d'Eugène Ionesco, suivi d'une scène inédite. Interprétations typographiques de Massin et photo-graphiques d'Henry Cohen d'après la mise-en-scène de Nicolas Bataille au théâtre de la Huchette" (Paris: Gallimard, 1964). Reprinted with an introduction by Massin in *TC*, 1891–1929.

6.   Both Massin's interpretation and Ionesco's image recall Antonin Artaud's stage directions for a critical moment in *Le Jet du sang (The Jet of Blood)*, which call for live pieces of human bodies to shower down on stage along with masks, architectural debris, and alembics.

7.   Tristan Tzara, *Seven Dada Manifestos and Lampisteries*, trans. Barbara Wright (London: John Calder; New York: Riverrun Press, 1981), 35.

8. Jacques Lemarchand, *Le Figaro littéraire,* October 1952, as quoted in *NCN,* 175.

9. After a 1951 performance of *The Lesson* in Brussels, the actor playing the professor had to flee the theater through a back door to escape outraged patrons demanding their money back.

10. According to Emmanuel Jacquart, Cuvelier staged the final scene of *The Lesson* as a "kind of erotic, languorous tango," with the professor moving toward and then away from the pupil to underline her conflicted rejection/acceptance of his sexual overtures (*TC,* 1496–1497).

11. A male actor played Marie in the first productions because of the physical force with which she disarms the professor, but the practice of casting a male was later dropped.

12. Cuvelier was able to persuade Ionesco that the armband gesture shrank the dimensions of the play. It remains, however, in Ionesco's written stage directions.

13. Eugène Ionesco, *Rhinoceros and Other Plays,* rrans. Derek Prouse (New York: Grove Press, 1960), 140.

14. Proliferating eggs come up again in Ionesco's *L'Oeuf dur (The Hard-Boiled Egg),* a film scenario, and in a sketch, *Pour préparer un oeuf dur,* an absurd parody of a cookbook that becomes a linguistic free-for-all.

15. It was a later "avant-garde," one with which Ionesco's theater did not generally find favor, that first presented these plays together in 1977. Lucian Pintille's production at the Theatre de la Ville emphasized eroticism: Jack was naked to the waist, Roberta entirely so during the seduction scene. As described by Emmanuel Jacquart (*TC,* 1521).

16. For English-speaking audiences, translation did not serve these plays well, because much of the humor depends on homophonic distortions of French.

Chapter Seven

1. Ionesco uses the term "ontological void" in his description of *The Chairs* (Bonnefoy, 1971, 83).

2. In a 1972 "metaphysical interpretation" of *The Chairs,* a Swiss director replaced the arrival of the Orator with an image of Christ on the cross, claiming, "This is what the couple was waiting for without really knowing it" (Lista, 1989, 38). An unlikely interpretation in 1951, in the 1970s it fit with the growing importance of Ionesco's spiritual quest.

3. Marie's explanation for the anguish of the passing years is that "they've changed time. Or maybe the longer you go on, the deeper in you get" (*CP,* 31–32).

4. Eugène Ionesco, *Three Plays: Amédée; The New Tenant; Victims of Duty,* trans. Donald Watson (New York: Grove Press, 1959), 118; hereafter cited in text as *TP.*

5. Choubert's fall matches the dissipation of Ionesco's mystical euphoric experience: "Suddenly, the world became itself again. . . . The world has fallen back into a hole" (Bonnefoy, 1971, 32).

6. It has been suggested that the strange lady in *Victims* is Choubert's mother, an interpretation supported by the appearance of a similar mother-wife figure in Ionesco's *L'Homme aux valises*. See Nancy Lane, *Understanding Eugène Ionesco* (Columbia: University of South Carolina Press, 1994), 70.

7. When Ionesco created his own mise-en-scène for *Victims*, he emphasized the spiritual dimension of the ascension by having Choubert climb a silver ladder while the stage was bathed in an intense blue light (Lista, 1989, 42).

8. *The Colonel's Photograph* contains six short stories, five of which became plays. The title story became *The Killer*; "Oriflamme" was the point of departure for *Amédée*; "A Victim of Duty" was expanded into *Victims of Duty*; "The Stroller in the Air" became *A Stroll in the Air*; "Rhinocéros" was transformed into Ionesco's most famous play. The sixth story, "The Slough," was made into a film scenario, *La Vase*, in 1966.

9. Tzvetan Todorov, *The Fantastic: A Structural Approach to a Literary Genre* (Ithaca, N.Y.: Cornell University Press, 1975), 167.

10. In the third act, Ionesco mocks his critics by having Amédée explain that he is writing a "play in which I'm on the side of the living against the dead. . . . I'm all for taking sides, Monsieur, I believe in progress. It's a problem play attacking nihilism and announcing a new form of humanism, more enlightened than the old" (*TP*, 69).

11. *Amédée* is autobiographical. Cramped households, financial and marital difficulties, and living in fear were familiar problems (see Lamont, 1993, 106, and *TC*, 1575). Some of Amédée's lines expressing self-doubt and depressed lethargy come from *Present Past* and *Fragments*. Amédée's suggestion that the corpse was a child left in their care has been related to the Ionescos' loss of their second child in 1947 (Lista, 1989, 43).

12. Eugène Ionesco, as quoted in Simone Benmussa, *Ionesco* (Paris: Seghers, 1966), 99; hereafter cited in text as Benmussa.

13. See Gilbert Tarrab, *Ionesco à coeur ouvert* (Montreal: Le Cercle du Livre de France, 1970), 43–44; hereafter cited in text.

14. For a detailed analysis of the circle in Ionesco's theater, see the chapter entitled "Les Variantes du cercle" in Paul Vernois, *La Dynamique théâtrale d'Eugène Ionesco* (Paris: Editions Klincksieck, 1991), 86–99.

15. Amédée's improbable escape is involuntary and accompanied by regrets.

16. Other short plays from the early 1950s include *Le Vicomte (The Viscount)*, a "gallery" of antitheater techniques influenced by Apollinaire's *The Breasts of Tirésias*; two sketches adapted from *The Viscount*, *La Nièce-épouse (The Niece-Wife)* and *Les Salutations (Greetings)*; *La Jeune Fille à marier (Maid to Marry)*, in which the daughter turns out to be a mustached, 30-year-old man; and *Le Salon de l'automobile (The Motor Show)*, a dadaist farce consisting entirely of incongruous sounds and word associations.

17. *Scene for Four* is not dated. Based on similarities to other early sketches, Emmanuel Jacquart places its composition in the very early 1950s (*TC,* 1600).

18. Jorge Lavelli, "Mon travail sur Ionesco" in *TC,* 1445–1446. Lavelli staged Ionesco's *The Killing Game* in 1970 and *Exit the King* at the Comédie Française in 1979.

19. Eugène Ionesco, *The Leader,* in *Rhinoceros and Other Plays,* trans. Derek Prouse (New York: Grove Press, 1960), 116; hereafter cited in text as *R.*

20. Eugène Ionesco, *The Picture,* in *Hunger and Thirst and Other Plays,* trans. Donald Watson (New York: Grove Press, 1969), 110; hereafter cited in text as *HT.*

21. This annotation is not included in the English translation of *The Picture.*

22. The English translation of *The Picture* ends with the return of the Painter, who witnesses the Large Gentleman about to turn the gun on himself.

23. Eugène Ionesco, *Improvisation, or the Shepherd's Chameleon,* in *K,* 120.

24. Roland Barthes was the author of a treatise on the "diseases" of costumes.

Chapter Eight

1. Pierre Marcabru in "Ionesco a-t-il fini de nous étonner: Table ronde entre Alain Bosquet, Pierre Marcabru, Gilles Sandier, et P.-A. Touchard," in *Arts* (22–26 February 1963): 5.

2. Ionesco acknowledged identifying most closely with the dying Bérenger of *Exit the King.* In Ahmad Kamayabi Mask, *Ionesco et son théâtre* (Paris: Editions Caractères, 1987), 164; hereafter cited in text.

3. Jean Delay, in *Discours de réception d'Eugène Ionesco à l'Académie Française et Réponse de Jean Delay* (Paris: Gallimard, 1971), 52.

4. A *"tueur à gages"* is a hired killer. The deletion of *"sans gages"* from the title of the English translation diminishes Ionesco's emphasis on the gratuitous quality of the murder.

5. Although Ionesco insisted that *The Killer* turned the leftists against him, Elsa Triolet, a communist writer, enthusiastically compared Bérenger to Don Quixote, Molière's Monsieur Jourdain, Dicken's Pickwick, and Pagnol's Marius, "above all a man of our time . . . resembling many of our acquaintances whom we have perhaps been wrong to mock and treat with impatience" (Elsa Triolet, "Un M. Bérenger," *Les Lettres Françaises* 763 [5–11 March 1959]: 1, 7).

6. As described in Genevieve Latour, ed., *Petites scènes, grand théâtre* (Paris: Délégation de l'Action Artistique de la Ville de Paris, 1986), 160.

7. In a conversation reported by Rosette Lamont, Ionesco said that Dudard was Sartre (Lamont, 1993, 145).

8. An allusion perhaps to a description by Denis de Rougemont of Hitler's being introduced by a projection of lights, which was one of Ionesco's sources for the play.

9. See, for example, Étienne Frois, *Rhinocéros* (Paris: Hatier, 1970), 28.

10. Denis de Rougemont, *Journal d'une époque* (Paris: Gallimard, 1968), 318–320. As quoted in *TC*, 1408–1409.

11. Jean Vigneron, writing in *La Croix* (February 1960), as quoted in Bonnefoy (1977, 205).

12. The world premiere of *A Stroll*, like that of *Rhinocéros*, took place in Düsseldorf.

13. Eugène Ionesco, *A Stroll in the Air; Frenzy for Two or More*, trans. Donald Watson (London: Calder and Boyers, 1965, 20–21; hereafter cited in text as *S*.

14. Eugène Ionesco, in an interview with Alain Célérier in *Libération* (26 May 1962).

15. Speaking for his author without being thoroughly convincing, Bérenger contends that "the truth is to be found in a kind of neurosis. . . . It's not there in a healthy mind, in neurosis lies the truth, tomorrow's truth, which contradicts the apparent truth of today" (*S*, 21).

16. Eugène Ionesco, "Critiques, vous vivez de moi!" reprinted in *Antidotes* (*A*, 259–262).

17. Jean-Jacques Gautier, *Le Figaro littéraire* (7 December 1966), quoted by Emmanuel Jacquart (*TC*, 1725).

18. Eugène Ionesco, *Exit the King*, trans. Donald Watson (New York: Grove Press, 1963), 73–74; hereafter cited in text as *EK*.

19. Gilbert Guilleminault, "*Le Roi se meurt* de Ionesco," in *L'Aurore* (12 December 1966).

20. Colette Godard, "*Le Roi se meurt*," *Le Monde* (24 November 1976).

Chapter Nine

1. Lamont notes that the name identifies Jean with the playwright because Ionesco is the Romanian equivalent of Johnson (1993, 207).

2. Dr. Faustroll is the title character in a novel by Alfred Jarry.

3. This mother figure appears in a dream recorded in Ionesco's journal (*F*, 52).

4. Emmanuel Jacquart cites, among other examples of religious motifs, the link to the mystical itinerary toward God in the writings of St. John of the Cross (*TC*, 1749–1753).

5. Eugène Ionesco, quoted in "Interview Ionesco/Serreau," in *Le Nouvel observateur* 66 (February 1966):28–29; cited by Emmanuel Jacquart (*TC*, 1747).

6. French students must pass the baccalauréat examination to qualify for university admission.

7. Eugène Ionesco, *La Lacune*, in *TC*, 911.

8. Michel Benamou and Eugène Ionesco, *Mise en train, première année de français* (New York and London: Macmillan, 1969), 117.

9. Eugène Ionesco, *L'Avant-scène théâtrale* 673/674 (July–September 1980): 31.

10. Other titles that Ionesco considered were *The Catastrophe, Endemic Disease, The Plague,* and *The Epidemic.* At the time of its world premiere in Düsseldorf, the play was called *Le Triomphe de la mort, ou La Grande comédie du massacre (The Triumph of Death, or the Great Comedy of the Massacre).* As described in Lista, 1989, 100.

11. A *jeu de massacre* is a carnival game in which the object is to knock down figures with tossed balls. Jorge Lavelli conceived of the first episode as a bowling game in which all the players had made strikes. See Lavelli, "Mon travail sur Ionesco," in *TC*, 1450.

12. Eugène Ionesco, *Killing Game.* trans. Helene Gary Bishop (New York: Grove Press, 1974), 76; hereafter cited in text as *KG.*

13. In the Grove Press English translation, these scenes are designated "New Scenes A and B."

14. Albert Camus, *The Plague,* trans. Stuart Gilbert (New York: Alfred A. Knopf, 1974), 278.

15. Jorge Lavelli was awarded the Prix de la Critique Dramatique for the best play of the year and the Prix Dominique for staging.

16. Ionesco's preparation for writing *Macbett* was reported in Lista, 1989, 101.

17. Eugène Ionesco, quoted by Vera Russell and John Russell in "Ionesco on Death," *Chicago Sun Times,* 15 September 1963; and cited by Hugh Dickenson in "Eugène Ionesco: The Existential Oedipus," in Rosette Lamont, ed., *Ionesco: A Collection of Critical Essays* (Englewood Cliffs, N.J.: Prentice-Hall, 1973), 117–118.

18. Jan Kott, *Shakespeare Our Contemporary,* trans. Boleslaw Taborksi (Garden City, N.Y.: Doubleday, 1966), 85.

19. Eugène Ionesco, quoted in "Ionesco: Les Paranoïaques de la politique," an interview by Claude Cézan, *Les Nouvelles littéraires* 2313 (24–30 January 1972): 23.

20. Eugène Ionesco, quoted in "Ionesco fait du cinéma," an interview by Lucien Attoun, *Les Nouvelles littéraires* 2315 (7–13 February): 26.

21. Eugène Ionesco, *Macbett,* trans. Charles Marowitz (New York: Grove Press, 1973), 10); hereafter cited in text as *M.*

22. Eugène Ionesco, *The Hermit,* trans. Richard Seaver (New York: Viking Press, 1974), 85; hereafter cited in text as *H.*

23. Eugène Ionesco, *A Hell of a Mess,* trans. Helen Gary Bishop (New York: Grove Press, 1975), 51–52; hereafter cited in text as *HM.*

24. Philippe Tesson, "Ce formidable bordel," *L'Avant-Scène* 542 (1 June 1974): 33–35; quoted by Emmanuel Jacquart in *TC*, 1813.

25. Ionesco explained this conception of *A Hell of a Mess* to Marie-Claude Hubert (Hubert, 1990, 257).

Chapter Ten

1. Sigmund Freud, *The Standard Edition of the Complete Works of Sigmund Freud*, Vol. V (London: Hogarth Press and Institute of Psychoanalysis, 1953), 444.

2. Eugène Ionesco, *The Man with the Luggage*, trans. Donald Watson and Clifford Williams, in *Plays*, XI. I have chosen to quote from this translation, rather than from the much livelier adaptation by Israel Horovitz based on an English translation by Marie-France Ionesco (*Man with Bags* [New York: Grove Press, 1977]), because it is a more exact translation. Horovitz's version is generally closer to the spirit of Ionesco's writing, however.

3. Lamont indicates that Ionesco's mother was probably the daughter either of converted Jews or of the descendants of *conversos*, which meant that Ionesco could have been labeled a Jew according to the definitions promulgated by Nazi Germany (Lamont, 1993, 228–230).

4. Jacques Mauclair, "Mon travail sur Ionesco" in *TC*, 1444.

5. The anecdote, reported in *Present Past Past Present*, was also incorporated into *Victims of Duty*.

6. The Egyptian doll is also an allusion to the *Egyptian Book of the Dead*. See Emmanuel Jacquart's notes in *TC*, 1836.

7. Ionesco interpreted this "erotic dream" as representing a state of "moral impotence. . . . I want to go, but it's my luggage that prevents me. I want to take my luggage with me." His analyst countered: "Actually you don't want to be released. The luggage is an excuse, a pretext. It's the first thing you would give up if you really wanted emancipation" (*F*, 65–66).

8. "Je suis un existant . . . existant spécial" (*TC*, 1256). Watson and Williams have unfortunately translated this as "I am a lifesaver" which does not capture the fundamental difficulty of being or of retaining one's individuality.

9. Eugène Ionesco, interviewed along with Philippe Sollers by Arnelle Héliot, in *Le Quotidien de Paris* (28 March 1984).

10. Eugène Ionesco, in a 1987 interview with Verena Heyden-Rynsch, in Eugène Ionesco, *Journeys among the Dead: A Play with Lithographs*, trans. Barbara Wright (New York: Limited Editions Club, 1987), ix.

11. Eugène Ionesco, *Journeys among the Dead*, trans. Barbara Wright (London: John Calder; New York: Riverrun Press, 1985), 45; hereafter cited in text as *J*. Samuel Beckett was awarded the Nobel prize in 1969.

12. This scene from *Journeys among the Dead* invites comparison to a trial scene leading to cannibalism in Fernando Arrabal's *L'Architecte et l'empereur d'Assyrie (The Architect and the Emperor of Assyria)*, in *Théâtre V* (Paris: Christian Bourgois, 1967); trans. Fernando Arrabal, *Plays*, vol. 3 (London: Calder & Boyars, 1970).

13. Eugène Ionesco, in an interview with Arnelle Héliot in *Le Quotidien de Paris*, 28 March 1984.

14. The 1980 world premiere of *Journeys among the Dead* in an English translation at the Guggenheim Museum in New York was cut short by Ionesco's quarrel with the stage designer, according to Rosette Lamont (1993, 278). The play was performed in English at the Riverside Studios in London in 1986.

15. Jean Carmet, as quoted in *Le Journal quotidien Rhones Alpes*, 15 February 1984.

16. In 1975 Roger Planchon had created a similar spectacle entitled *AA: Théâtres d'Arthur Adamov*, using Adamov's plays and autobiographical writings. Ionesco may well have registered the irony of being "resurrected" in a manner similar to that of his deceased former friend.

Chapter Eleven

1. Julio Cortázar, *Around the Day in Eighty Worlds*, trans. Thomas Christensen (San Francisco: North Point Press, 1985), 136.

2. J.-B. Pontalis, *Entre le rêve et la douleur* (Paris: Gallimard, 1977), 151.

Selected Bibliography

PRIMARY SOURCES

Plays in French

Théâtre I. Paris: Gallimard, 1954. Contains *La Cantatrice chauve; La Leçon; Jacques, ou la soumission; Les Chaises; Victimes du devoir; Amédée, ou comment s'en débarasser.*

Théâtre II. Paris: Gallimard, 1958. Contains *L'Impromptu d'Alma, ou le caméléon du berger; Le Tueur sans gages; Le Nouveau locataire; L'Avenir est dans les oeufs; Le Maître; La Jeune Fille à marier.*

Théâtre III. Paris: Gallimard, 1963. Contains *Rhinocéros; Le Piéton de l'air; Délire à deux; Le Tableau; Scène à quatre; Les Salutations; La Colère.*

Théâtre IV. Paris: Gallimard, 1966. Contains *Le Roi se meurt; La Soif et la faim; La Lacune; Le Salon de l'automobile; L'Oeuf dur; Pour préparer un oeuf dur; Le Jeune homme à marier; Apprendre à marcher.*

Théâtre V. Paris: Gallimard, 1974. Contains *Jeux de massacre; Macbett; La Vase; Exercices de conversation et de diction française pour étudiants américains.*

Théâtre VI. Paris: Gallimard, 1975. Contains *L'Homme aux valises; Ce formidable bordel.*

Théâtre VII. Paris: Gallimard, 1981. Contains *Voyages chez les morts, thèmes et variations.*

Théâtre complet. Edition présentée, établie et annotée par Emmanuel Jacquart. Paris: Gallimard, Bibliothèque de la Pléiade, 1991.

Special Editions

La Cantatrice chauve: Interprétations typographiques de Massin et photographique d'Henry Cohen d'après la mise-en-scène de Nicolas Bataille au Théâtre de la Huchette. Paris: Gallimard, 1964.

Délire à deux: Essai de calligraphie sonore par Massin d'après l'interpretation de Tsilla Chelton et de Jean-Louis Barrault à l'Odéon-Théâtre de France. Version scénique. Paris: Gallimard, 1966.

Plays in English Translation

Exit the King. Translated by Donald Watson. New York: Grove Press, 1967.

Four Plays: The Bald Soprano; The Lesson; The Chairs; Jack, or the Submission. Translated by Donald M. Allen. New York: Grove Press, 1958.

The Gap. Translated by Rosette Lamont. *Massachusetts Review* 10, no. 1 (Winter 1969): 119–27.

A Hell of a Mess. Translated by Helen Gary Bishop. New York: Grove Press, 1975.

Hunger and Thirst and Other Plays: The Picture; Anger; Salutations. Translated by Jean Stewart and John Russell. New York: Grove Press, 1969.

Journeys among the Dead. Translated by Barbara Wright. London: Riverrun Press, 1984.

The Killer and Other Plays: Improvisation, or the Shepherd's Chameleon; Maid to Marry. Translated by Donald Watson. New York: Grove Press, 1960.

Killing Game. Translated by Helen Gary Bishop. New York: Grove Press, 1974.

Macbett. Translated by Charles Marowitz. New York: Grove Press, 1973.

Man with Bags. Adapted by Israel Horowitz, based on a translation by Marie-France Ionesco. New York: Grove Press, 1977.

Rhinoceros and Other Plays: The Leader; The Future Is in Eggs, or It Takes All Sorts to Make a World. Translated by Derek Prouse. New York: Grove Press, 1960.

Scene. Translated by Rosette Lamont. *Performing Arts Journal* 24 (1984): 105–112.

A Stroll in the Air; Frenzy for Two or More. Translated by Donald Watson. New York: Grove Press, 1968.

Three Plays: Amédée; The New Tenant; Victims of Duty. Translated by Donald Watson. New York: Grove Press, 1958.

Ionesco's plays have been published in 12 volumes by John Calder in London. Translations and titles vary somewhat from American versions.

Special Editions in English Translation

The Bald Soprano. Translated by Donald M. Allen. New York: Grove Press, 1965. Photographic interpretations by Massin and Henri Cohen, followed by a previously unpublished scene.

Journeys among the Dead, with lithographs by Eugène Ionesco. Translated by Barbara Wright. New York: Limited Editions Club, 1987. Preceded by "Conversation with Ionesco and Verena Heyden-Rynsch."

Other Works in French

Antidotes. Paris: Gallimard, 1977. Essays.

Le Blanc et le noir. Saint Gall, Switzerland: Erker Verlag, 1981; reprint, Paris: Gallimard, 1985. Essay and lithographs by the author.

Contes no. 1–4. Illustrated by Etienne Delessert. Paris: Harlin Quist and François Ruy-Vidal, 1969–1970; reprint, Paris: Gallimard, 1983–1985. Stories.

Découvertes. Geneva: Skira, 1969. Journal.

Discours de réception d'Eugène Ionesco à l'Académie Française et réponse de Jean Delay. Paris: Gallimard, 1971. Speech.

Entretiens avec Claude Bonnefoy. Paris: Belfond, 1966. Revised and expanded as *Entre la vie et le rêve.* Paris: Belfond, 1977. Interviews.

Un homme en question. Paris: Gallimard, 1979. Essays.

Hugoliade. Translated from the Romanian by D. Costineanu and Marie-France Ionesco. Paris: Gallimard, 1982. Criticism.

Journal en miettes. Paris: Mercure de France, 1967. Journal.

Non. Translated from the Romanian by Marie-France Ionesco. Paris: Gallimard, 1986. Originally published as *Nu*. Bucharest: Vremea, 1934. Essays.

Notes et contre-notes. Paris: Gallimard, 1962; rev. ed., 1966. Essays.

La Photo du colonel. Paris: Gallimard, 1962. Short stories.

Présent passé passé présent. Paris: Mercure de France, 1968. Journal.

La Quête intermittente. Paris: Gallimard, 1987. Journal.

Le Solitaire. Paris: Mercure de France, 1973. Novel.

Other Works in English Translation

The Colonel's Photograph and Other Stories. Translated by Jean Stewart and John Russell. New York: Grove Press, 1969.

Conversations with Eugène Ionesco. Translated by Jan Dawson. New York: Holt, Rinehart and Winston, 1971.

Fragments of a Journal. Translated by Jean Stewart. New York: Grove Press, 1968.

The Hermit. Translated by Richard Seaver. New York: Viking Press, 1974.

Maximilian Kolbe. Translated by Rosette Lamont. *Performing Arts Journal* 17 (1982): 29–36. Opera libretto.

Mise en train, première année de français. With Michel Benamou. French-language textbook with dialogues by Eugène Ionesco. New York: Macmillan, 1969.

Notes and Counter Notes: Writings on the Theater. Translated by Donald Watson. New York: Grove Press, 1964.

Present Past Past Present. Translated by Helen R. Lane. New York: Grove Press, 1971.

SECONDARY SOURCES

Bibliographies

Hughes, Griffith R., and Ruth Bury. *Eugène Ionesco: A Bibliography*. Cardiff: University of Wales Press, 1974.

Kyle, Linda Davis. "Eugène Ionesco: A Selective Bibliography, 1974–1978." *Bulletin of Bibliography* 37, no. 4 (1980): 167–184.

Leiner, Wolfgang. *Bibliographie et Index thématique des études sur Eugène Ionesco*. Fribourg: Editions Universitaires Fribourg Suisse, 1980.

Criticism

Because space here is limited, only books are listed. For articles on Ionesco, consult the Notes and References section. See also the extensive bibliography in Giovanni Lista, *Ionesco* (see entry below), and the annual bibliography of criticism in *Modern Drama*.

Abastado, Claude. *Ionesco*. Paris: Bordas, 1971. An outstanding critical survey. Includes play reviews and an interview with Ionesco.

Benmussa, Simone. *Ionesco*. Paris: Seghers, 1966. An in-depth analysis of early plays emphasizing stage language.

Blocker, H. Gene. *The Metaphysics of Absurdity*. Washington, D.C.: University Press of America, 1979. Examines philosophical themes linking Camus, Sartre, Ionesco, and Beckett.

Bradby, David. *Modern French Drama, 1940–1990*. Cambridge: Cambridge University Press, 1991. A detailed discussion of contemporary French drama. Includes substantial production data.

Bradesco, Faust. *Le Monde étrange de Ionesco*. Paris: Promotion et Edition, 1967. A somewhat dated defense capturing "human" qualities of Ionesco's early plays.

Brater, Enoch, and Ruby Cohn, eds. *Around the Absurd: Essays on Modern and Postmodern Drama*. Ann Arbor: University of Michigan Press, 1990. Important historical perspectives. Includes essay on Ionesco.

Brito, Ferreira de. *Le Réel et l'iréel dans la dramaturgie de Beckett, Ionesco et Tardieu*. Porto: Associação de jornalistas e homens de letras do Porto, 1983. A thematic study focused primarily on Ionesco.

Cleynen-Serghiev, Ecaterina. *La Jeunesse littéraire d'Eugène Ionesco*. Paris: Presses Universitaires de France, 1993. Extensive documentation on Ionesco's early career in Romania.

Coe, Richard N. *Ionesco: A Study of His Plays*. Edinburgh: Oliver and Boyd, 1971; rev. ed., London: Methuen, 1971. An excellent, broad-ranging analytic survey. Includes photographs, an extensive bibliography, and a translation of *The Niece-Wife*.

Cohn, Ruby. *From Desire to Godot: Pocket Theatre of Postwar Paris*. Berkeley: University of California Press, 1987. Lively accounts of absurdist theater. Discusses *The Bald Soprano* and *The Chairs*.

Corwin, Michel. *Le Théâtre nouveau en France*. Paris: Presses Universitaires de France, 1963; rev. ed., 1987. A brief but comprehensive study of revolutionary French playwrights and theater trends during the 1950s and 1960s.

Dobrez, L. A. C. *The Existential and its Exits: Literary and Philosophical Perspectives on the Works of Beckett, Ionesco, Genet and Pinter*. London: Athlone Press; New York: St. Martin's Press, 1986. Analyzes absurdist theater in a philosophical context.

Donnard, Jean-Hervé. *Ionesco dramaturge ou l'artisan et le démon*. Paris: M. J. Minard, 1966. Discusses themes and dramatic devices through the Bérenger plays.

Duckworth, Colin. *Angels of Darkness: Dramatic Effect in Samuel Beckett with Special Reference to Eugene Ionesco*. London: Allen and Unwin, 1972. A helpful comparative study.

Duvignaud, Jean, and Jean Lagoutte. *Le Théâtre contemporain: Culture et contre-culture*. Paris: Larousse, 1974. A sociological analysis of the French theater during the 1950s and the 1960s.

Esslin, Martin. *The Theatre of the Absurd*. New York: Doubleday, 1961; rev. ed., London: Penguin, 1970, 1980; New York: Pelican, 1983. The essential work that introduced the notion of theater of the absurd.

Favre, Yves-Alain. *Le Théâtre de Ionesco, ou le rire dans le labythrinthe*. Paris: Editions Jose Feijoo, 1991. Examines labyrinthian structures in *The Bald Soprano, The Lesson*, and *Rhinoceros*.

Féal, Gisèle. *La Mythologie matriarcale chez Claudel, Montherlant, Crommelynck, Ionesco et Genet*. New York: Peter Lang, 1993. Includes a psychoanalytic study of *Amédée*.

Frickx, Robert. *Ionesco*. Paris: Nathan-Labor, 1974. An in-depth analysis of works through *Macbett* and *The Hermit*. Preface by Ionesco.

Frois, F. *Rhinocéros*. Paris: Hatier, 1970. A critical study of political and literary sources.

Gaensbauer, Deborah B. *The French Theater of the Absurd*. Twayne's World Authors Series 822. New York: Twayne Publishers, 1991. Analytical survey of dramatic innovations in the theater of Adamov, Beckett, Ionesco, Genet, and Arrabal.

Grossvogel, David I. *The Blasphemers: The Theater of Brecht, Ionesco, Beckett, Genet*. Ithaca, N.Y.: Cornell University Press, 1965. An early comparative examination of the "new theater."

Hamdan, Alexandra. *Ionescu avant Ionesco: Portrait de l'artiste en jeune homme*. Berne: Peter Lang, 1993. A critical study of Ionesco's early writing. Includes a bibliography and texts in French and Romanian.

Hayman, Ronald. *Eugène Ionesco*. New York: Frederick Ungar, 1976. A thorough critical study, including an interview with Ionesco.

Hinchcliffe, Arnold P. *The Absurd*. London: Methuen, 1969. Analyzes the "absurd" in philosophical and literary contexts.

Hubert, Marie-Claude. *Langage et corps fantasmé dans le théâtre des années cinquante*. Paris: Librairie Jose Corti, 1987. A stimulating theoretical assessment of Ionesco, Beckett, and Adamov, emphasizing the physicality of their theater. Includes a preface by Ionesco and an interview with him.

———. *Eugène Ionesco*. Paris: Seuil, 1990. A major work covering Ionesco's writing and painting. Includes illustrations and an important interview with Ionesco.

Ionescu, Gelu. *Les Débuts littéraires roumains d'Eugène Ionesco, anatomie d'un échec*, translated by Mirella Nedelco-Patureau. Heidelberg: Carl Winter Universitätsverlag, 1989. An extensive analysis of Ionesco's Romanian publications from 1926 to 1940. Includes excerpts from early journals.

Jacobsen, Josephine, and William R. Mueller. *Ionesco and Genet: Playwrights of Silence*. New York: Hill and Wang, 1968. An early comparative study in absurdist context.

Jacquart, Emmanuel. *Le Théâtre de dérision*. Paris: Gallimard, 1974. One of the best studies of Beckett, Ionesco, and Adamov.

Jomaron, Jacqueline de, ed. *Le Théâtre en France*, Vol. 2, *De la révolution à nos jours*. Paris: Armand Colin, 1992. Outstanding reference work on the theater.

Kamyabi Mask, Ahmad. *Ionesco et son théâtre*. Paris: Editions Caractères, 1987. Reedited in 1992. A deferential approach. Includes an interview with Ionesco.

Lamont, Rosette C., ed. *Ionesco: A Collection of Critical Essays*. Englewood Cliffs, N.J.: Prentice-Hall, 1973. Helpful introductions to Ionesco's early writing.

———. *Ionesco's Imperatives: The Politics of Culture*. Ann Arbor: University of Michigan Press, 1993. A primary resource for Ionesco studies, emphasizing the historico-political background and based on extensive research and discussions with the playwright. Includes chronologies and production notes.

——— and Melvin J. Friedman, eds. *The Two Faces of Ionesco*. Troy, N.Y.: Whitson, 1978. Essays examining literary, political, biographical, and metaphysical themes. Includes an essay by Mircea Eliade.

Lane, Nancy. *Understanding Ionesco*. Columbia: University of South Carolina Press, 1994. A well-documented, comprehensive survey.

Latour, Genevieve, ed. *Petites scènes, grand théâtre*. Paris: La Délégation à l'Action Artistique de la Ville de Paris, 1986. An invaluable collection of excerpts from reviews and interviews with playwrights from 1944 to 1960.

Laubreaux, Raymond, ed. *Les Critiques de notre temps et Ionesco*. Paris: Garnier, 1973. Excerpts from press and critical studies.

Lazar, Moshe, ed. *The Dream and the Play: Ionesco's Theatrical Quest*. Malibu, Calif.: Undena, 1982. Published proceedings of 1980 symposium at the University of Southern California. Includes an essay by Ionesco.

Lewis, Allan. *Ionesco*. Twayne's World Authors Series 239. New York: Twayne Publishers, 1972. An early survey of Ionesco's writing.

Lista, Giovanni. *Ionesco*. Paris: Henri Veyrier, 1989. A descriptive analysis of all Ionesco's plays, with extensive photographic documentation and exhaustive bibliographies. An exceptional resource.

Mignon, Paul-Louis, ed. *Les Entretiens d'Helsinki ou les tendances du théâtre d'avant-garde dans le monde*. Paris: Michel Brient, 1961. Proceedings of the Eighth Congress of the International Theater Institute. Includes an address by Ionesco and critical responses.

Norrish, Peter. *New Tragedy and Comedy in France, 1945–70*. Totowa, N.J.: Barnes & Noble, 1988. Informative chapters on Sartre, Camus, Beckett, Ionesco, Adamov, Genet, and Arrabal.

Saint, Tobi. *Eugène Ionesco, ou à la recherche du paradis perdu.* Paris: Gallimard, 1973. Subjective essay on Ionesco's dramatic themes. Helpful background on Romanian influences.

Satjin, Nico. *Le Labyrinthe de la cité radieuse: Les Pérégrinations de Bérenger chez Ionesco.* Amsterdam: Rodopi, 1982. An analysis of time, space, and death in *Tueur sans gages.*

Serreau, Genevieve. *Histoire du nouveau théâtre.* Paris: Gallimard, 1966. A valuable early study of "new theater," enhanced by the author's personal acquaintance with avant-garde directors and playwrights.

Tarrab, Gilbert. *Ionesco à coeur ouvert.* Montreal: Le Cercle du Livre de France, 1970. Four interviews preceded by a sociological analysis.

Vais, Michel. *L'Ecrivain scénique.* Montreal: Les Presses de l'Université du Quebec, 1978. Examines stage language in works by Beckett, Weingarten, Genet, and Ionesco. Includes an interview with Ionesco.

Valency, Maurice. *The End of the World: An Introduction to Contemporary Drama.* New York: Oxford University Press, 1980. A somewhat unsympathetic approach to Ionesco.

Vernois, Paul. *La Dynamique théâtrale d'Eugène Ionesco.* Paris: Editions Klincksieck, 1972; rev. and expanded ed., 1991. A very substantial and highly original, scholarly thematic study.

_____, ed. *L'Onirisme et l'insolite dans le théâtre français contemporain.* Paris: Editions Klincksieck, 1974. Includes a discussion of proliferation in Ionesco's theater and of *Hunger and Thirst.*

_____, and Marie-France Ionesco, eds. *Situation et perspectives.* Paris: Pierre Belfond, 1980. Proceedings from the 1978 Cérisy colloquium on Ionesco. Preface by Ionesco.

Vos, Nelvin. *Eugène Ionesco and Edward Albee.* Grand Rapids, Mich.: William B. Eerdmans, 1968. A brief comparison of spiritual themes in Ionesco's early works.

Wellwarth, George E. *The Theater of Protest and Paradox.* New York: New York University Press, 1964; rev. ed., 1971. Analyzes French, German, English, and American avant-garde playwrights.

Wulbern, Julian H. *Brecht and Ionesco.* Urbana: University of Illinois Press, 1971. A comparative study "correcting" Ionesco's perspective on Brecht.

Special Journal Issues

L'Avant-scène théâtre 373/74 (February 1967).

Cahier des saisons 15 (Winter 1959).

Cahiers Renaud-Barrault 29 (February 1960); 42 (February 1963); 53 (February 1966); 97 (January 1978).

Tulane Drama Review 7, no. 3 (Spring 1963).

Index

The Author

Deborah Gaensbauer is a professor in the Modern Language Department at Regis University, Denver, Colorado. She is the author of *The French Theater of the Absurd* in Twayne's World Authors Series. Her articles on Eugène Ionesco, Marguerite Duras, Virginia Woolf, and Leonora Carrington have appeared in *Modern Drama,* the *French Review, Comparative Literature Studies,* and *Women's Studies: An Interdisciplinary Journal.*

The Editor

David O'Connell is professor of foreign languages and chair of the Department of Foreign Languages at Georgia State University. He received his Ph.D. in 1966 from Princeton University, where he was a National Woodrow Wilson Fellow, the Bergen Fellow in Romance Languages, and a National Woodrow Wilson Dissertation Fellow. He is the author of *The Teachings of Saint Louis: A Critical Text* (1972), *Les Propos de Saint Louis* (1974), *Louis-Ferdinand Céline* (1976), *The Instructions of Saint Louis: A Critical Text* (1979), and *Michel de Saint Pierre: A Catholic Novelist at the Crossroads* (1990). He is the editor of *Catholic Writers in France since 1945* (1983) and has served as review editor (1977–1979) and managing editor (1987–1990) of the *French Review*.